How To Build A
Harley-Davidson Torque Monster

How To Build A
Harley-Davidson
Torque Monster

Bill Rook

MOTORBOOKS

First published in 2007 by MBI Publishing Company LLC
and Motorbooks, an imprint of MBI Publishing Company,
Galtier Plaza, Suite 200, 380 Jackson Street, St. Paul, MN
55101-3885 USA

The information in this book is true and complete to the best
of our knowledge. All recommendations are made without
any guarantee on the part of the author or Publisher, who also
disclaim any liability incurred in connection with the use of
this data or specific details.

We recognize, further, that some words, model names, and
designations mentioned herein are the property of the
trademark holder. We use them for identification purposes
only. This is not an official publication.

Motorbooks titles are also available at discounts in bulk
quantity for industrial or sales-promotional use. For details
write to Special Sales Manager at MBI Publishing Company,
Galtier Plaza, Suite 200, 380 Jackson Street, St. Paul, MN
55101-3885 USA.

To find out more about our books, join us online at
www.motorbooks.com.

ISBN-13: 978-0-7603-2911-5
ISBN-10: 0-7603- 2911-7

Library of Congress Cataloging-in-Publication Data

Rook, Bill, 1955-
    How to build a Harley-Davidson torque monster / by Bill Rook.
        p. cm.
    ISBN-13: 978-0-7603-2911-5 (softbound)
    ISBN-10: 0-7603-2911-7 (softbound)
    1. Harley-Davidson motorcycle--Motors--Modification. 2.
Harley-Davidson motorcycle--Performance. 3. Harley-Davidson
motorcycle--Customizing. 4. Torque. I. Title.
TL448.H3R66 2007
629.28'775--dc22
                                    2006034493

Editor: James Michels
Designer: Michael Cawcutt

Printed in China

Author bio: A sea captain by trade, Bill Rook has been hot
rodding Harley-Davidson motorcycles since 1972. Along the way,
he's picked up an incomparable base of knowledge from which to
build the ultimate high-performance, yet streetable, V-twin
engine. He resides in Seward, Alaska.

On the cover: Acceleration requires torque. This biker appears
to have plenty. *Photo by Matt Polito*

On the back cover: The author and his '59 Sporty.
Author photo

CONTENTS

INTRODUCTION

Building a high-performance street motor takes hours of planning, none of which should involve guesswork. Every part of the combination has to be analyzed. To build a happy motor, every part must complement the other parts. And if the motor is happy, you will be, too. Your only limits are your knowledge and your budget!

Example: If you install a huge carburetor, straight drag pipes, or a maximum-effort cam on an otherwise stock motor, your results and performance gains will most likely be disappointing. You must first take the time to understand how the parts will complement the package.

To do this, you'll need to learn how the different components function together and how to modify existing parts to make them perform better.

You can go out and spend $500 on a fancy exhaust system. Or you can spend nothing, fix the system you have, and end up with better results. The choice is yours.

Consider the dreaded drag pipes. If you want to run these things, do you know what diameter to run, how long they should be, and how to calculate the rpm they will deliver their top performance at? When you're done reading this book, you will.

As the old adage goes, if someone tries to sell you something that sounds too good—or too chrome—to be true, chances are it is. The most important thing you need to do before you open up your wallet is open up your mind and absorb the knowledge that will make your performance goals reality. To help you avoid pitfalls while accomplishing your performance goals, I've assembled this information onto the following pages based on lessons I've learned over the years.

Armed with this information, I hope you'll be able to make the right choices the first time around. Remember, I've only scratched the surface of what the big dogs know, and, as a rule, they don't buy power from a dealership or a chrome catalog. They build power from knowledge and proper planning.

I first started trying to make Harleys run better and faster over 30 years ago. Back then, some performance parts were available; the key word here is "some." Today, an awesome array of performance parts are available, from crankcase vents to completely built and ready-to-run 120-plus-inch monster motors. If you were to list all the performance parts available from all the different manufacturers in one book, you would end up with thousands and thousands of pages. New parts hit the market every day, changing the world of high-performance V-twins at an incredible pace. Because of this, it's impossible for me to say that one part, or a combination of parts, is best, because tomorrow I may find something that's even better.

Example: On a recent Twin Cam camshaft change, Andrews Products had the best cam grind to produce the torque band I wanted, but the cam used all the stock gears and chains. Given a choice for that particular motor (due to the cam's lift and the installed valve spring's pressure), I would have preferred to use a set of all-gear drive (S&S Cycle style) cams. But gear drive cams were not available from Andrews at the time. Shortly after completing the work on the motor, I received the new Andrews catalog, and found the same cam grind I had just installed, but with the all-gear option available! As I said, things are changing at a very fast pace.

Performance books often present information, then expect you to assume the information is correct just because it's in print. I am going to try a slightly different approach. In this book I'll not only present you with some essential information, but also, whenever possible, provide you with a brief explanation of the basic concepts that support the information. If you understand the theories behind performance modifications, your knowledge will be more complete and you'll be more successful when you apply it.

As a matter of fact, my main goal is not to tell you what to do, but to help you better understand the concepts required to make successful performance modification decisions. I'll try to focus on the basic theories behind making power modifications—the ones that remain constant and never change regarding making power.

When you purchase a Harley, the two most important publications you should acquire are its Harley-Davidson service manual and its parts manual. I'll assume you have these and won't waste a lot of space covering disassembly and assembly techniques that are adequately covered by those books. In the case of aftermarket parts, they usually come with supplemental instructions when their installation techniques differ from those of stock parts.

With the vast array of performance parts available today, it's easy for some manufacturers to slip in a few that don't quite live up to their claims or your expectations. Some things work and some things just cost money! To help you save money, I'll try to present enough performance theory for you to be able to make logical decisions. Armed with this information, you'll be able to make the right choices when it comes time to open your wallet, and your performance modifications goals will become a successful reality.

Good luck!
–Bill

ACKNOWLEDGMENTS

WHERE DID THIS STUFF COME FROM?

Over the years, I've kept notes on all the information I learned (mostly through trial and error) in pursuit of my favorite pastime—making Harley-Davidson motorcycles run better and go faster.

Also, smart people ask questions. I must know a lot of smart people, because they're always asking me things. I'll often respond in writing, partly so they don't forget my answers, but mostly because I learn a lot more myself that way.

So, this book is based on a compilation of notes and answers. I tried to present the information in a way you might find enjoyable, so it's (hopefully) like talking about bikes over a beer with a buddy. Although a gallant attempt was made to organize things, given the compilation aspect, I still jump around a bit. If you come across something you don't fully understand, don't dwell on it, as I'll probably explain it later. And, you'll get more out of the book if you read the whole thing, as I may have inexplicably put some key information about, say, combustion chambers in the magneto chapter.

Now it's time to express my gratitude to everyone who, directly or indirectly, helped me with this project.

First and foremost, I want to thank my daughter. Thanks, Kaitlin, you're my world. Without you, all the bikes on the planet wouldn't make a bit of difference to me.

Thanks to everyone who made an effort at staving off the wrath of any English teachers who suffered the misfortune of having me in their class and are still alive to talk about it.

Thanks to all the people I've encountered in Harleydom over the last thirty-plus years who shared their experiences, information, and lies with me. This includes writers, customers at my shop, folk I met along the road, and, of course, the pros at Branch Flowmetrics, S&S Cycle, Andrews Products, Zipper's Performance, Yost Performance and everyone else.

Last, I'd like to thank my parents for giving me their genes. Genes that compel me to take everything apart so I can see how it works, and genes that allow me to learn from my mistakes so I can put it all back together again.

Should you have any complaints about the statements, opinions or information contained in this book, please feel free to blame any of the people noted above.

Just kidding. Don't blame anyone but me.

Bill Rook
Seward, AK

CHAPTER 1 POWER THEORY 101

THE INTERNAL COMBUSTION ENGINE

Your motor is basically a heat pump; it utilizes heat energy produced from burning a mixture of air and fuel. This expanding heat energy is then used to force a piston down a cylinder. The piston is attached to a connecting rod, which is attached to a crank. As the piston is pushed down the cylinder, the connecting rod turns the crank. In the simplest of terms, to make more power all we have to do is generate more heat and then maximize its utilization.

There are four main ways to accomplish this:

1. Modify the intake components to maximize the amount of air and fuel we can get into the cylinders.

2. Modify the ignition system and/or the shape of the combustion chamber to maximize the burn efficiency of the air/fuel mixture.

3. Modify the motor to maximize heat energy transfer through thermal efficiency and/or the reduction of friction.

4. Increase the displacement of the cylinders.

Before we can begin to discuss power modifications, you should understand the important differences between torque and horsepower.

TORQUE AND HORSEPOWER

If you ask someone how much power their bike turned on a rear-wheel dynamometer (dyno), they'll tell you how much horsepower their bike has made. Horsepower numbers sound good, but they don't give you a clue about how a bike will perform and accelerate through its total operating range. Only the shape, placement, and peak location of the torque curve will let you know about the bike's true ability to accelerate.

TORQUE

Torque is the actual twisting force that makes you accelerate from a stop to highway speed. Without the twisting force of torque to produce rpm, a motor will have zero horsepower. Torque is a force that can be physically measured.

HORSEPOWER

Horsepower is the engine's ability to sustain a workload. By definition, it is the ability to continuously lift a weight of 33,000 pounds to a height of 1 foot in 1 minute of time. There is no simple way physically to measure horsepower on our motorcycle. But we can measure the bike's torque and then we can determine our horsepower with this formula: (torque x rpm) ÷ 5252 = horsepower.

As you can see, without the twisting force of torque to produce rpm, you would have zero horsepower. And the higher up the rpm band you can move your torque band, the more horsepower you will make. This is the reason why high-rpm

imported sportbikes produce impressive horsepower numbers without equally impressive torque numbers.

So let's look at the differences between torque and horsepower. We'll use two very basic rules of physics to help understand these two types of power.

Rule 1: A body at rest will remain at rest unless we apply a force to the object to start it moving. For our purposes, this force is the torque, or twisting force, used to cause a motorcycle to accelerate. The more torque we apply, the faster we accelerate.

Rule 2: A body in motion will tend to stay in motion unless we apply an opposite force to the object to slow it down. On a motorcycle, friction, mainly in the form of wind drag, is the primary force that slows the bike down. So to maintain a constant speed, we only need to apply enough power to overcome friction. This ability to maintain a given workload is a simple example of horsepower.

Let's look at torque and horsepower as they relate to our motorcycle in the real world. Say you are following a big-rig down the highway and you decide to pass. You open the throttle to allow more air and fuel into your engine to produce more power. The twisting power of torque forces your motorcycle to accelerate. Your rate of acceleration will be dictated by the amount of torque your motor can produce and the gear ratio between the motor and your rear wheel. The more torque you can apply to the rear wheel, the faster you will accelerate.

After you pass the truck, you close the throttle, reducing the amount of air and fuel entering your engine until you are flowing only enough to produce the required amount of power to maintain your given speed—or, in other words, to maintain your engine's workload. This is an example of horsepower. The amount of horsepower you must produce is always proportional to the workload you want your engine to sustain.

Let's look more closely at horsepower. Say we have two motorcycles with identical gearing, wind drag, and weight. Bike A's motor can produce 25 horsepower, while Bike B's can produce 100 horsepower. The gearing dictates the motors must turn 2,500 rpm at 50 miles per hour. The weight and wind drag dictate 10 horsepower is needed to sustain it. We now accelerate both bikes to 50 miles per hour, then maintain that speed.

Question: Now that both motorcycles are doing 50 miles per hour, how much horsepower is Bike A's motor producing at 2,500 rpm versus Bike B's?

Answer: Both motors are producing the same, only 10 horsepower! That's because only 10 horsepower is required to sustain each motor's workload at 50 miles per hour.

The point is that extremely high horsepower is not required to maintain normal speeds.

If we want to maintain a speed of 150 miles per hour, that would require a substantial amount of horsepower, due to the increased workload.

Note: The same bike that only required 10 horsepower to do 50 miles per hour may require over 100 horsepower to maintain the workload at a speed of 150 miles per hour. Only a small amount of horsepower is required to sustain the workload at speeds less than 50. As speeds increase over 50, the required horsepower to maintain the workload will increase substantially. Most V-twin motorcycles only require about 50 horsepower to maintain the workload at a speed of 100 miles per hour. But first, you must have enough torque to accelerate to 100 miles per hour!

Now let's look at torque. Bike A has only 25 lb-ft of torque at 2,500 rpm, while at the same rpm, Bike B has 100 lb-ft of torque. Both weigh the same and have the same gear ratios and wind drag. If both bikes accelerated from a stop to 50 miles per hour, which bike would reach 50 first? Bike B has four times the ability to twist the rear tire as Bike A, so it can accelerate much faster.

Reduced to their simplest definitions: Torque makes you accelerate and horsepower keeps you going at a given speed. Most people want to modify their bikes so they can accelerate faster. If acceleration is your ultimate performance goal, torque is the ticket.

When it comes to making power, size does matter.

MORE TORQUE

Up to this point, I've pounded you with torque, torque, and more torque! And I'm not done with you yet.

I've been deliberately playing down the importance of horsepower, but I will go on record here—hold your breath—horsepower is also important. Sorry, that's as far as I'll go on the subject.

My goal here has been to change your whole perspective about what power means. When someone asks you about power, I want you to think torque first, then horsepower. To design and build a performance street motor, first think about these items: the width of the torque band, the shape of the torque curve, and the location of maximum torque on the torque curve.

If you want a bike that's not much fun but produces lots of horsepower, just move the location of your peak torque to the top end of your power band. Now you have lots of horsepower, but not much twisting power (torque) where you need it—low in the rev range where you do most of your starting and cruising. Is this what you really want?

CONSIDER THIS
EXTREME EXAMPLE OF TORQUE

When I'm not home playing with one of my bikes, I'm at sea making my living as the captain of a government oceanographic research ship. This ship is a great analogy to demonstrate the raw power of torque truly.

The ship displaces 600-long tons, which means the ship actually weighs a little over 1.3 million pounds. It is powered by a 4,539-ci electro-motive-diesel (EMD) eight-cylinder marine diesel engine. Here's your test question: How much horsepower do you think this 4,539-ci monster motor produces?

If you guessed only 820 horsepower, you'd be correct. So how does a lowly 820-horsepower motor propel a 600-ton ship? Easily. The ship does it with raw power, because this 820-horsepower motor also produces a little over 5,300 lb-ft of torque!

So what is most important thing that propels my ship through the water? Is it the horsepower or the torque? The same thing that works for the bike, works for the boat!

A motor that produces an astounding 5,300 lb-ft of torque and only 820 horsepower may not sound logical, and you probably won't have to look far to find self-proclaimed V-twin performance experts who will say that it just isn't possible. Please tell them where to obtain a copy of this book.

Let's check the math to see if it adds up. Our horsepower formula is (torque x rpm) ÷ 5252 = horsepower. My ship's engine is a slow-turning powerplant; full power is at a little over 800 rpm. 5,300 lb-ft x 800 rpm = 4,240,000. 4,240,000 ÷ 5252 = 807 horsepower. That's pretty close to the motor's rated 820 horsepower. The math proves that this is true and indeed logical. Torque always rules!

HORSEPOWER AND THE FACTS OF LIFE

To produce high horsepower you need two things:

1. A motor that will be able to rotate at very high rpm

2. A motor that will produce its peak torque at high rpm

The best way to accomplish this is by using a short stroke-to-bore combination; the reason has to do with piston speed. You can only push a piston so fast (4,500 feet per minute is considered near maximum) before piston damage occurs. By using a shorter stroke, rpm can be raised while keeping piston speeds at a safe level to avoid damage. Here you must come face to face with the facts of life: Harley-style V-twin engines have a large stroke-to-bore ratio. Because of this, they will not be able to turn high rpm numbers before piston damage occurs. Fact: If you can't plug that high rpm number into the formula, you're not going to produce high horsepower!

Example: A modified 95-inch stock-stroke Twin Cam motor, with proper planning and the right parts, can produce around 100 horsepower, 100 lb-ft of torque, and it displaces 1546 cc. Let's compare it to a short-stroke four-cylinder sportbike motor with a displacement of only 750 cc, which is less than half the displacement of the 95-inch Twin Cam.

The 750-cc sportbike will only be able to produce 50 lb-ft of torque, only half the torque of the modified 95-inch Twin Cam. Most importantly, this four-cylinder sportbike will produce its lowly 50 lb-ft of torque at 12,000 rpm.

Question: How much horsepower could this small four-cylinder sportbike produce? Remember, it only has less than half the displacement of our modified 95-inch Twin Cam and can only produce half the torque.

Answer: This little 750-cc four-cylinder sportbike has the potential of producing a whopping 114 horsepower: (50 lb-ft x 12,000 rpm) ÷ 5252 = 114 horsepower. This is over twice the horsepower of a stock 80-inch Evo and almost twice the horsepower of a stock Twin Cam.

The lesson to be learned here is this: Because of our V-twin's long stroke, thus its limited ability to turn high rpm (because of piston speed limitations), horsepower is one form of power not easily obtainable to us. If you want high horsepower, buy a multicylinder Japanese sportbike. Japanese manufacturers have plenty of high-horsepower bikes for sale.

We may not be able to produce high horsepower on our V-twins, but there is one important type of power we can produce in spades—torque! So when we modify our motors, we have to concentrate on what we do best and utilize and maximize our torque band.

THE V-ROD AND TORQUE

Unless you have been hiding in a cave, you know that Harley-Davidson, or the Motor Company, has come out with a new motor. It was plastered on the covers of most bike magazines. "The impressive new 115 hp, 9,000 rpm beast." I was just finishing this book when the news came

out, so I'm compelled to say something about it. Being a long-stroke Harley performance guy, I think of power differently and wasn't overly impressed with the numbers, even if they were correct.

When I saw 115 horsepower and 9,000 rpm, the first thing I thought was that the motor would not produce impressive torque (its importance should be obvious by now). What torque it did have must peak up in the rpm stratosphere, although still below the Japanese sportbike's ionosphere range. Let's look at the numbers and see if I was right.

On closer inspection, we find the 115 horsepower is shaft output, not rear wheel. So right from the start, the horsepower numbers are slightly misleading. Looking further, we find that rear-wheel power is only somewhere around 103 horsepower at 8,250 rpm, and the maximum produced torque is only 70 lb-ft way up at 7,000 rpm. This is about what I expected.

Don't get me wrong, this bike will be quick, and I'm not going to dump any of my HDI stock over it. I'll admit it is a bold move for the Motor Company and, considering ever-tougher EPA regulations, it may become its future. But to go really fast, you're going to have to wind this motor up until it sounds like a hive full of angry hornets.

Personally, I'm spoiled. I'm used to having this bike's maximum 70 lb-ft of torque on tap at just above an idle, with 100 lb-ft or more of torque available a few thousand rpm later! How about you?

BEFORE WE GET STARTED, THERE ARE TWO IMPORTANT THINGS TO CONSIDER

Most V-twin owners don't have the skills or equipment to perform their own major engine modifications, thus they rely on others to perform them.

If you fall into this category, make sure the person who is going to carry out the work is skilled in performance modifications, because you will get better results from someone who does them on a daily basis. Just because someone is trained to repair stock motorcycles does not mean he knows how to modify a motorcycle precisely to perform the way you want.

Make a list of what you expect from the end results of the modifications. What type of torque band do you want to produce? Where do want your peak torque to occur?

The biggest mistake you can make is just to say you want to make more power, because the word "power" is typically thought to mean horsepower. If someone just increases your horsepower at the top end, your bike may end up less fun to ride than it is right now.

Countless times, I've heard people complain that they just installed a big cam or whatever, and now their bike won't get out of its own way unless they go down a couple of gears. Don't let this happen to you! When you talk to your mechanic, say what kind of torque band you want and at what rpm you want to achieve peak torque.

Example: If you have a heavy touring bike, you don't want

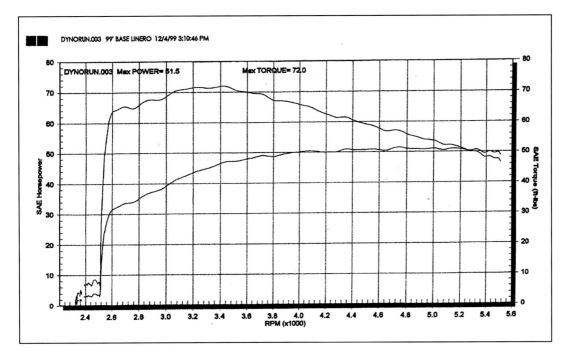

DYNORUN.003 99' BASE LINERO 12/4/99 3:10:46 PM

DYNORUN.003 Max POWER= 51.5   Max TORQUE= 72.0

I was able to test ride one of the early production Victory motorcycles extensively in 1998. The bike's power felt quite adequate, and, for a heavyweight cruiser, it had no acceleration problems. At a later date, my friend Alex put his Vic on a rear-wheel dyno to see where the acceleration and power came from. Obviously, this bike's acceleration rate came from its broad torque band low in the rev range and not from the 51.5 maximum horsepower.

a narrow torque band that peaks at 5,000 rpm. On this type of bike, it's better to have a flat, broad torque band that peaks around 3,500 rpm.

PEAK VOLUMETRIC EFFICIENCY

Peak torque generally happens at the location of peak volumetric efficiency, or in other words at the location of your induction system's peak flow. Torque will increase until you reach the location of your induction system's peak flow, or peak volumetric efficiency, and then torque will start to diminish as rpm increases.

Peak horsepower is reached at the point where torque starts falling faster than rpm is increasing. At this point, the game is over. Shut her down!

TC-88 COMPRESSION AND CYLINDER HEAD INFORMATION

The true mechanical compression on a stock TC-88 (88-inch Twin Cam) is 8.8:1. The true corrected stock TC-88 compression is only 8.1:1. (We'll get into defining the six different kinds of compression measurements in Chapter 6.) An 8.1:1 corrected compression is too low for performance work! Branch Flowmetrics says the heads on the TC-88's combustion chambers max out at 83 cc.

The stock TC-88 head gaskets range from 0.055 inch to as much as 0.070 inch. This is entirely too big for performance work and will not create useful squish band turbulence!

SQUISH BANDS OR QUENCH AREA

A squish band, or quench area, is the area between the cylinder head and the top of the piston. By setting this area up correctly, when the piston reaches top dead center (TDC), the air and fuel in the squish band will be violently squeezed into the center of the combustion chamber.

This causes extreme turbulence that homogenizes the air/fuel mixture. The end result of this induced turbulence is a more-efficient mixture burn, which means increased power and improved gas mileage. Setting up a squish band properly will yield free power, so always take advantage of it!

ALUMINUM HEAD SQUISH BANDS

The squish band on V-twins with aluminum cylinders and heads must not exceed 0.040 inch, or it will be of little use. For true performance work, this motor should have a squish band set at a tight 0.025 to 0.030 inch cold. Note: Always slowly warm an engine up when running this tight of a squish band and before flogging the motor. If you don't do this, the pistons may impact the cylinder head—a very bad thing!

Aluminum cylinders and heads can grow as much as 0.050 inch when the engine reaches operational temperatures. So if your squish band is at 0.030 inch cold, it will grow to around 0.080 inch when it gets hot.

I'm presently running a very tight 0.025 inch cold on my modified 95-inch Dyna, and it works great for me. Of course, I have to let my engine idle for five minutes before I can ride, and then I have to keep the rpm down for the first 10 minutes of riding. Oh yeah, I also have to pull my heads off and clean off carbon buildup every 10,000 miles or so. I know, it sounds like a lot of work.

But guess what? My brake-specific fuel consumption (BSFC) is so low, because of the extreme turbulence this tight squish band creates, that I'm getting over 45 highway miles from 1 gallon of gas on a 100-horsepower motor! This gas mileage is almost 10 miles per gallon better than some stock 60-horsepower Twin Cams.

As you go through this book, you'll realize that when you're making a high-performance street bike, almost every decision will revolve around compromises. "Compromise" is the central theme when you build a high-performance street motor, so you'll see the word throughout this book.

SQUISH BANDS
FOR IRON CYLINDERS AND HEADS

Cylinders and heads made of iron do not expand as much as aluminum, so you can't use the same tight squish band. Note: Some motor builders are now machining hemi-heads so they have a usable angled (usually at 30 degrees) squish band. If you have one of these modified heads, set the squish band at 0.035 to 0.040 inch cold.

Note: Exceeding the above-referenced squish band heights on either of these types of heads will diminish the usefulness of a squish band and will not create good combustion chamber turbulence. Poor combustion chamber turbulence will reduce power and gas mileage.

COMPRESSION RATIOS

For performance work (with a good combustion chamber design), to make good power and low-end torque you should run a corrected compression ratio on pump gas of no less than 8.8:1 and no more than 9.2:1 if using 92-octane (high-test) pump gas. Here in Alaska, where 90-octane pump gas is often the highest level available, a 9:1 maximum corrected compression is a good compromise. Corrected compression for motorcycles is always computed by using the intake valve-closing event at 0.053-inch lift after bottom dead center (ABDC).

Cranking compression on a new stock TC-88 is approximately 140 to 145 psi. For maintenance purposes on stock motors, Harley says anything over 90 psi is okay.

However, unless you're running a turbo, a motor won't produce much low-end torque (and will have diminished top-end power) with only 90 psi of cranking pressure. For performance work, I like the cranking compression to be at least 175 psi for an engine with a good combustion chamber design and a good squish band. On my TC-95 with a TW-55 cam, I'm presently running 185 psi. With a TW-37B cam I was running 205 psi, and the motor really pulled hard at low rpm! Silver, the modified 1200 XL my ex-wife took with her, is also running 185 psi. Again, stock on the Twin Cams is around 140 to 145 psi. High cranking compression is a good indication that strong low-end torque is possible.

CHECKING COMPRESSION
WITH A LEAKDOWN TESTER

Your motor should always be warm during this test. On some stock motors, cylinder leakdown can be as high as 7 to 8 percent! Anything above 8 percent is tired and needs serious work to make any power. A 3 to 5 percent leakdown is a good percentage; racers try for 2 percent (or less) whenever possible! Anything we can do to increase our engine's sealing ability (rings and valve seats) will increase power.

On the surface, a leakdown of 8 percent doesn't sound too bad. In reality, it is devastating to your ability to make power. Why? Depending on your motor's efficiency, only about one-third of the heat energy (or pressure) developed in the cylinder ends up being used to push the piston down the cylinder. The rest of the heat energy is absorbed by the motor, lost to friction, or vented out of your exhaust system.

So if only one-third of the combustion pressure is used to push the piston down the cylinder and you're losing 8 percent of that pressure, you are theoretically losing 24 percent of your possible recoverable power! If you only have three-quarters of your engine working for you, you're not going to be very competitive.

IGNITION ADVANCE

The ignition advance curve has to be set to the rpm the motor is turning, so peak combustion pressure will occur at 12 to 17 degrees after top dead center (ATDC). Different engine combinations burn fuel at different rates, so ignition events and advance curves must be tailored to each individual engine combination. The best way to determine the advance curve is with dyno testing.

IGNITION TRIVIA

Dyno testing has shown there is almost no performance advantage in running single-fire ignition systems over the old dual-fire (wasted spark) systems. About the only thing the single-fire systems do better is provide a much smoother idle.

MAXIMUM TWISTING FORCE

The maximum pressure, or twisting force (torque), is exerted on the flywheel when the connecting rod is positioned at a 90-degree relative angle to the flywheel on the power stroke. Ideally, you want the maximum burn pressure in your cylinders to occur at this location. To have a 90-degree relative angle, the flywheel crank pin should be located at an approximate 45-degree angle from vertical. A 45-degree angle for the rod, plus a 45 degree angle for the crank pin, equals 90-degree relative angle.

AVERAGE PISTON SPEED

Average piston speed should be kept below 4,500 feet per minute for long piston life. Average piston speed bursts of up to 5,000 feet per minute may be acceptable for very short durations. Keep in mind that, at this speed, you're pushing your equipment and risking excessive piston-skirt

Here you can see the Twin Cam's crankcase gases being vented into the intake tract. Although not ideal for performance, this method is often used on street motors.

wear and possible piston seizing. This is one reason why abused strokers often live short lives. You should never rev cast pistons above the 4,500-foot-per-minute average piston speed.

PISTONS

With the release of the Twin Cam, Harley started using hypereutectic cast pistons. They are also sold under the Screamin' Eagle performance product line. These pistons are more durable than the standard cast pistons and have a higher silicone content (approximately 12 percent). They are stronger than the early stock cast pistons, but still have limitations. Never run these pistons above 6,200 rpm with stock 4-inch stroke, and less on motors with a stroke over 4 inches. For high rpm (above 6,200) use, always run high-quality forged pistons!

STOCK ROD-TO-STROKE RATIOS
Stock Sportsters (all): 1.816:1
Stock Evo Big Twin: 1.751:1
Stock Twin Cams: 1.917:1

The connecting rod-to-stroke ratio is best when its ratio is closer to 2:1.

The ideal 2:1-rod-to-stroke ratio is another V-twin compromise. We only have so much room in the crankcase, so the closer we can get to the 2:1 ratio, the better. In reality, automotive racers continue to increase power output with rod-to-stoke ratios as high as 3:1.

CRANKCASE BREATHERS

Unlike the old Harleys, modern Harley engines vent their lower-end crankcase gas pressure through and out their cylinder heads, so they are often referred to as top-end breathers. For true high-performance work, this vapor pressure should be vented externally to the outside atmosphere. As high-performance street motors are often a combination of compromises—

for aesthetics, simplicity, or both—the breathers are often vented back into the intake tract. This can dilute the fresh incoming air/fuel mixture and cost you power, although it does make the EPA folk happy. Personally, although not ideal for a maximum effort engine, I feel this option is an acceptable compromise for a street bike.

Note: This venting compromise is especially true of the new Twin Cam motors. Their redesigned breathers do an excellent job of removing oil from the mixture in comparison to the older Evo-style breathers.

HEAD PORTING

One of the biggest obstacles to making power with a modern Harley is the fact that its cylinder heads are flow restricted. To begin this discussion, it's important to understand that no cam will change the flow restriction limitations of a cylinder head.

For example, let's consider the intake port of Harley's new Twin Cam engine. For its displacement, it is very flow restricted. At a valve lift of 0.400 inch, the intake port on a Twin Cam flows approximately 120 cfm. Guess what happens if you completely remove the valve from the head? The intake port will still flow only 120 cfm. On an 88-inch motor, 120 cfm is not going to get you very far up in the rpm range before you run out of airflow. Only professionally ported heads or aftermarket performance heads will overcome this problem.

Although it's tempting to run for your Dremel tool and start grinding away at the aluminum, please refrain from doing so. Unless you know what you're doing, you have a good chance of making things worse.

The most critical flow area in the cylinder head is the bowl area, which is directly above the valve seat, to the short side radius. I will cover cylinder heads later in this book in Chapter 8, where I will explain how you can make your heads flow better without ruining them in the process.

Question: Is bigger really better?

Answer: No! You can carve out a port that's big enough for an elephant to crawl though and you'll just make less power.

This giant port could flow cubic yards of air, but without velocity, it's useless. A professional head porter will balance the port so it flows not only volume, but also maximum mixture velocity for its intended use or power band. This skill really earns money for a pro.

APPROXIMATE MAXIMUM INTAKE FLOW VALUES WITH STOCK UNMODIFIED HEADS

Ironhead XL:	100 cfm
883 Evo XL:	101 cfm
1200 Evo XL:	113 cfm
Evo Big Twin:	127 cfm
Twin Cam:	120 cfm

Formula to convert known flow cfm values to desired cfm flow values:

(new flow cfm ÷ current flow cfm) x current known flow cfm = desired cfm flow

Example: convert 125 cfm at 12 inches H_2O to flow at 10 inches H_2O

10 inches divided by 12 inches = 0.8333
0.8333 x 125 cfm at 12 inches H_2O = 104 cfm at 10 inches of H_2O.

Note: The value of 10 inches of H_2O is the standard for Harleys, and 28 inches of H_2O is becoming the standard for automotive use. The higher the test pressure, the easier it is to see small changes in flow.

STOCK HEAD FLOW NUMBERS

It's important to understand that not all flow numbers are equal. It's hard (as in almost impossible) to compare flow data numbers from different sources and know what you're getting, or how one set of numbers compare to another set. As we saw above, flow rates can be expressed by different flow test pressure values. As the test pressure is increased, the flow numbers go up.

Example: A port that flows 100 cfm at a test pressure of 10 inches will flow 280 cfm at a test pressure of 28 inches. So the first thing you need to do is convert the test pressure to a standard, say 10 inches of H_2O.

If you know the test pressure used to measure the port, you can easily convert it by using the above-referenced formula.

But now you have a new problem, and that is the test equipment. Not all flow benches are the same. You have cheap entry-level benches that simply measure air through a washer, and then you have super-high-end benches. If you had your head's flow measured by Branch Flowmetrics, for example, you will not be able to compare their flow numbers to the numbers you would get from a cheaper (flow through a washer) flow bench.

I once asked Branch Flowmetrics why their flow numbers were so low compared with other companies' flow numbers. I was told it's because nobody else uses a flow bench like the "one-of-a-kind" bench they built, and what's more, you can't compare its flow numbers to those of any other company's bench!

In addition to the differences in testing equipment, there is a more sinister problem: the way the bench operator tests the ports. Consider the intake port. Honest porters will flow the head using an intake manifold and carburetor to get realistic intake tract flow numbers. Unscrupulous testers may shove a velocity stack on the port and then test it. In a letter I received from Jerry Branch, he calls testing like this "as phony as hell!"

But guess what, it happens all the time. Let the buyer beware. When in doubt, call and talk with the head porter before you send them your heads and money!

WHAT OIL SHOULD I RUN IN MY HARLEY?

Which oil, 100 percent pure petroleum-based Harley brand oil or 100 percent synthetic oil?

It's hard to open up a motorcycle magazine today without seeing something about synthetic oils, which is a good thing! The general public is finally getting a clue about something that professional racers and high-performance enthusiasts have known and practiced for years.

There may be dealers who say that if you put anything other than 100 percent pure Harley oil in your bike, you will void your warranty when your Harley blows up. The fact of the matter is this: if a product manufacturer states that you can only use its brand of oil in its product, it has broken the law, because the government forbids manufacturers to require you to use a specific brand of oil in their products.

Harley stock (360) oil is really good stuff, as far as petroleum-based oils go, and it will work fine for the average rider. The only real exception to this rule may be for those who operate their bikes in extremely hot climates. They should look long and hard at synthetic oils.

On the other hand, the performance guy is not your average rider. Remember, your motor is just a heat pump. To make more power, you must modify your motor so it generates more heat to push the piston down the cylinder. And if you're generating more heat, you need to work harder to protect your motor from the increased heat. More heat equals more power; overheating equals engine damage!

Compared to petroleum-based oils, synthetic oils do an excellent job of reducing engine and drivetrain friction. As we have already covered, friction is a major cause of power loss. Anything we can do to reduce engine friction increases the amount of power we can get to the rear wheel.

Less friction equals more power!

For many years now, my favorite oil has been Mobil 1 100 percent synthetic oils. For a Harley-type air-cooled V-twin engine, the fully synthetic Mobil 1 V-Twin 20W-50 motorcycle oil is hard to beat and is one of the best air-cooled V-twin oils out there!

On the downside, this oil is often hard to find and also rather costly, at approximately $8.50 per quart in 2001. So to save yourself a few bucks, you can do as I do and run Mobil 1 Tri-Synthetic Motor Oil 15W-50. Like the 20W-50, it's also a CF-rated oil and it's 100 percent synthetic.

Over the years, I've had great results with Mobil 1 oils when used in high-performance Harleys. The best part is that Mobil 1 15W-50 is not hard to find (you can even find it at Kmart or Wal-Mart), and it costs about half as much as the Mobil 1 V-Twin 20W-50.

Note that other brands of 100 percent synthetic motorcycle oils can work as well as, or maybe even better than, Mobil 1. Whatever you decide, the use of synthetic oil in an air-cooled motor is always a wise choice.

I like synthetic oil so much that I run it in all of my vehicles, two- and four-wheeled. I even run synthetic oil in my lawnmower and snow blower. You pay a little more upfront, but you save in the long run with extended engine longevity due to reduced friction and engine wear. Also, by reducing parasitic power loss to friction, you increase the amount of power you can deliver to the rear wheel.

SYNTHETIC OIL RECOMMENDATIONS

1. You should always allow piston rings to break-in and seat fully (minimum of 1,000 to 1,500 miles) before switching to 100 percent synthetic oils. Synthetics oils work so well at reducing engine wear caused by friction, your rings may take many thousands of miles to seat properly otherwise.

Preferably, we'd like our engine's rings to be seated as soon as possible. It is true that new motor tolerances are better than they were in the past and motor break-in periods are not as traumatic. Even with that said, I still recommend using non-synthetic oil for the break-in period.

2. If you are going to run synthetic oils, only use oils that are 100 percent synthetic. Tests have shown that

petroleum/synthetic blends do not perform anywhere near as well as 100 percent synthetic oils and show little advantage over plain petroleum-based oils.

3. If this synthetic motor oil stuff works so much better than petroleum-based oils, should you use synthetic oils in the rest of your motorcycle's driveline? Yes!

For the Big Twin's primary chain/clutch case, the fully synthetic Mobil 1 MX4T 10W-40 motor oil is best. Again this oil is costly, so I use Mobil 1 Tri-Synthetic 15W-50 instead.

In the Big Twin's transmission gear case, I run the fully synthetic Mobil 1 75W-90 gear lubricant. Harley recommends its new 20W-50 synthetic for its transmissions, but I would go with the extra protection of the 75W-90.

For the insanely fast Sportster enthusiast, until I get better information, I recommend running either the fully synthetic Mobil 1 20W-50 or Tri-Synthetic 15W-50 as a replacement for Harley's stock XL Sport-Trans fluid.

The problem with the Sportster is the clutch and transmission gears share the same case, so you need to run on oil that is light enough for the clutch to work, but also strong enough to resist oil sheer and protect the transmission gears. If you live someplace really hot and if your clutch will work with the 75W-90 gear lube, by all means use it, as it will provide the best gear protection. If not, the 20W-50 or 15W-50 should still protect parts better than the stock H-D Sport-Trans lube.

I predicted the Motor Company would eventually catch on to this performance trend and offer its own line of 100 percent synthetic Harley motor oils, and it has.

I have seen people (some of whom claim to be officially certified Harley mechanics) writing to magazines and posting stuff on the internet claiming you should never use synthetic oil in your Harley because it is too slippery. Saying that oil is too slippery is the equivalent of telling your employer that you are being paid too much and would be much happier working for half your salary. I think not! We know that one way to increase power to our rear wheel is to increase our motor and drivetrain efficiency. One way to increase efficiency is to reduce power-robbing friction. If I could purchase oil that would totally eliminate friction, I would buy gallons of it. My bottom line: Oil can't be too slippery.

SYNTHETIC OIL AND GASKETS

There is one possible downside to using synthetic oil that you should be aware of: how it interacts with gaskets. Most gaskets are designed to wick or absorb oil as part of their sealing process. Petroleum-based oils are absorbed into the gasket material. The petroleum oil will, in time, break down and form a sludge, or tar-like substance, and seal the gasket.

Synthetic oil is superior to petroleum-based oil because it will not break down and change into the gunk that seals the

Oil temperature gauges are an inexpensive insurance policy. I highly recommend their use on performance street motors.

gasket. However, a small amount of oil may continually wick through some gaskets, which can be annoying, but it is a small price to pay for the added performance of synthetic oil.

GOT COLD OIL?

I consistently see articles about hot oil and oil coolers. But what about the other side of the oil temperature problem, oil that is too cold?

For oil to lubricate your motor properly, the oil temperature should be a minimum of 180 degrees Fahrenheit. Ideally, the temperature should remain at a constant 210 to 220 degrees Fahrenheit and should never exceed 250 degrees Fahrenheit. Coping with excessive oil temperatures is another way synthetic oils win hands down, as they can withstand temperatures that will turn petroleum-based oils into tar!

One of the annoying byproducts of the combustion process is water vapor. When this vapor enters your crankcase it can, and will, condense into water. Water is not only a poor lubricant, but it will also turn your oil into an emulsified foam, which will not go through your oil pump easily or lubricate parts efficiently. The longer the engine is allowed to operate with below-optimum oil temperatures, the more water will accumulate in your oil.

Water boils at 212 degrees Fahrenheit, so if we regularly get our oil temperature to reach or exceed 212 degrees Fahrenheit, the water turns to vapor and is vented out of the motor via the crankcase breathers. If the oil is not regularly heated to this temperature, the water content in the oil will accumulate—a bad thing if you're looking for long engine life.

Is this a common problem with Harleys? Yes! And it's especially true of bikes that are operated in colder environments, like the northeast, northwest, and Alaska. For example, with an outside air temperature of 60 degrees Fahrenheit, I can ride my XR-1000 for an hour. and its oil temperature in the oil tank will rarely go above 150 degrees Fahrenheit. With the same outside air temperature on my wife's modified 1200-XL and under normal riding conditions, her oil tank's temperature rarely climbs much above 180 degrees Fahrenheit.

So what should we do? Install an oil heater? No. The only simple solution is to change your oil more frequently than its regularly scheduled change rate.

This is a good reason why you should always use an oil tank thermometer. Without one, you won't know your oil temperature. The oil temperature in your oil tank will always be slightly lower than the temperature of the oil that's circulating inside your motor.

WARM-UP PROCEDURES

We have discussed cylinder expansion, squish bands, synthetic oils, and the problem of cold oil, so this is good time for me to go on record about my recommended procedures for warming up your motor.

The Motor Company's owner's manual basically describes the technique for proper starting of a cold V-twin motor as the following:

1. Twist the throttle to inject a small amount of fuel into intake manifold.

2. Pull the enrichener (for some reason, Harley has mislabeled this as a "choke" for years) knob all the way out and engage the starter.

3. When the motor starts, push the enrichener in to the least amount required to keep the motor running.

4. Drive away and have a nice day.

5. After a short period of riding, completely shut the enrichener off.

Dealerships make a lot of money with billable labor hours and parts to do engine rebuilds and repairs, so I guess this practice makes financial sense from their perspective. One thing that really confuses me is why the people who write articles for magazines spew the same dubious advice. I recently read an article written by someone whom I considered to be a very knowledgeable fellow. He wrote, "By the way, the best way to warm up a cold V-twin engine is by riding it." I couldn't believe it. If you did this on any of my modified bikes, it would be last time I ever let you ride one! Now that I got that out, let's discuss the subject.

Several things happen after your motor has sat unused for a period of time. Among others, the oil drains to the bottom of your motor and cools, and the metal parts contract.

Your motor is designed to operate with warm oil (210 to 220 degrees Fahrenheit) lubricating its surfaces, and with all of its parts expanded to their normal operating dimensions. When you first start your engine, it needs to supply oil quickly to the operating surfaces. If the bike hasn't been ridden in a while, though, the oil will be cold and thick. For oil to perform properly, we know it should be at normal operating temperature. Here in Alaska, that can take some time. New multigrade oils help with the thick oil problem, but if you're running an old bike with straight 50-weight oil in it, that stuff is like molasses below 50 degrees Fahrenheit. Even in Florida, if you ride your bike cold, more engine wear can accrue during the time it takes your motor to get to its normal operating temperature than in several hundred miles of riding!

Another issue to consider is the expansion problem. As the engine warms, its tolerances change. The motor is designed to work best when the internal parts have reached their normal expanded tolerances.

This is especially true for modified motors. For example, we know that the aluminum from which our cylinders are made will grow by as much as 0.050 inch when the motor reaches normal operating temperature. If you have a performance motor with a very tight squish band setup and you don't allow your cylinders a chance to expand, your pistons can impact the cylinder heads. This causes very ugly and expensive things to happen that will ruin your day.

So . . . I recommend that you always allow your motor some time to warm up before you ride it. I use the "hand on the rocker box" test. When the rocker boxes on the top of the cylinders start to get warm, I'm good to go.

Finally, you should always allow your motor and oil to reach its normal temperature before you try to impress yourself or others!

This is a guess on my part, but I think the main reason for the factory's "no warm-up time required" recommendation is because it is afraid riders will use an excessive amount of enrichening during the warm-up period (and most do), causing their motors to load up with carbon and soot, which makes them perform poorly. Riders would then blame the motorcycle instead of themselves for the error.

I recommend that you use the least amount of enrichener/choke you can to keep the motor running and always shut it off completely as soon as you can. I further recommend you get used to using the throttle, along with the throttle friction knob, to keep the motor running during the warm-up process. This will prevent the motor from loading up with carbon and/or fouling your spark plugs.

EXAMPLE OF PROPER WARM-UP PROCEDURES IN THE REAL WORLD

Let's take another look at my ship. Professionally licensed engineers man the engineering department. The main engine is heated by the ship's boiler, and its engine block is always kept at a temperature between 100 and 120 degrees Fahrenheit.

When started, the engineers require that the engine be allowed to warm up for a minimum of 30 minutes if it will be used for light service. If the engine will be required to start under hard service, it requires a one-hour warm-up period. There is no "push the starter button and go" mentality on the ship.

Now, consider the following example. Several years ago I read a story about a fellow who logged an unbelievable amount of miles (I think it was in the 200,000-mile range) on a stock Big Twin without requiring any major work on the engine. This feat amazed a lot of people, including folk at the Motor Company.

At the time, if you had 50,000 miles on a stock top-end, that was considered good. If memory serves me right, the Motor Company traded this fellow a brand new Big Twin for his old bike, in order to dissect his powertrain to see how, and why, it lasted so long without requiring any major work.

The fellow was asked the secret behind his motor's longevity. His answers were right on the mark and very important for anyone wishing for long engine life.

He religiously changed his oils at or before their required change intervals, which, back then, was 3,000 miles. He always did hot oil changes, never cold oil changes.

I totally agree with this practice; it's the only one I follow.

Here's what's going on: As a byproduct of the combustion process, your oil gets contaminated over time. When your oil is hot and circulating, it picks up contaminants and emulsifies them. The oil filter removes large particles, but the small particles stay suspended in the oil and are circulated throughout your oil system. When you shut your bike down, the oil cools. As it cools, some of these small particles fall out of suspension and settle to the bottom of your oil tank and motor. If you change your oil when the oil is cold, there's a good chance these contaminants will stay inside your oil system. Then, any particles left inside your oiling system will contaminate the new oil.

This is the reason why I recommend this practice. Actually, I take the process one step further. After I drain the oil and remove the filter, I also remove the spark plugs and spin the motor a few times until oil stops coming out of the oil filter mounting plate and the tank drain plughole.

I then replace the filter and oil tank drain plug and almost fill the oil tank. With the spark plugs still removed, I spin the motor so the oil pump is primed with new oil. I then reinstall the spark plugs and start the bike. When the oil is up to normal temperature after a brief ride, I top off the oil tank. This is very easy to do and can add years to your engine's life.

The fellow also said he never rode his bike with a cold motor! He always allowed the engine and oil to warm up first, before going riding. By doing this, his motor had a chance to expand to near-normal operating tolerances and his oil had a chance to warm up some so it could properly protect the motor.

These two simple techniques—allowing your motor to warm up before riding the bike, and conducting proper and regular oil changes—will increase the life of your motor.

OIL CHANGES

In the near past, the oil and filter change interval recommended by auto and bike manufacturers was every 3,000 miles. The EPA wants us to save ourselves and thus mandated oil change intervals be increased to 5,000 miles. So if you look in your new owner's book, it will say change your oil and filter at the new mandated 5,000-mile interval.

To give you an example of how much Harley oil change intervals have changed, consider this. Over 20 years ago, in the early 1980s, Harley recommended that you change your oil and filter every 1,250 miles on some of its bikes. The oil change interval of 5,000 mile is four times longer now than it was then!

Here's the problem with the whole concept. The oil we use today contains additives that help remove contaminates and keep our motors clean and happy. These additives can consist of up to 25 percent or more of the volume of oil you pour into your oil tank, and the problem is, they break down or are consumed before the oil itself loses its lubricating properties. Today's synthetic oils extend the lubricating properties of the oil even further.

So when we change our oil, it's mainly because the additives have been used up, not because of the loss of lubricating properties. Personally, I feel that 5,000 miles is stretching things too far. On a stock motor running synthetic oil, it should be okay, but if you're running petroleum-based oil, I would not recommend it. When your performance motor wears out from the 5,000-mile oil-change intervals and needs to be repaired, don't expect the EPA to fork over any money toward the repair bill. It's never going to happen. You can, however, keep the world a cleaner place by always returning your used oil to an oil-recycling center.

So . . . what should you do? I recommend you go back to the old 3,000-mile oil-change interval, and change it even more frequently if you live somewhere that gets extremely cold or hot.

Oil changes will extend your engine life and help you make more power for a longer period of time. So in my modified street performance motors, I change oil about every 2,500 miles. These motors occasionally get run hard and, compared to the cost of a motor, oil and filters are cheap insurance!

SNAKE OIL

There are hundreds of products on the market designed to be added to your fuel and oil systems. Some of these products work, some work a little, while others can reduce performance and engine life. Your job as a consumer, and performance enthusiast, is to do your homework and research these products before you buy them. The internet is a useful tool for doing this.

A few things to consider: The companies that make these products will only have positive things to say about them. They will tell you what their product is supposed to do. Your job is to find out if the product lives up to their claims. Also, if you're getting your information from internet chat rooms, keep in mind that these people may know less about what their talking about than you. Remember, the internet is where you'll find statements like "synthetic oil is too slippery."

From experience, I avoid many of these products. My feeling is, if they really made the oil or gas perform better, chances are the refiners would be putting it in their products themselves.

Gasoline octane boosters are a good example. Some of these additives will boost the octane rating of gasoline by a small amount, while others don't work as well. You'd be much better served by designing and building a motor that will run on available fuel than by relying on expensive additives to boost your motor's gasoline octane rating.

There are several products that I do use and recommend. For example, two that work well are Techron Concentrate, made by Chevron, and BG-44K, made by Ryno Performance Products.

Both are designed to clean and remove contaminants from your fuel system, valves, pistons, and combustion chambers. An easy way to increase power output is by exploiting squish bands. When you run tight squish bands, you need to be concerned about carbon and other substances that can and will build up on your pistons and in your combustion chambers. If the carbon buildup gets excessive, your piston could impact your cylinder head. If this happens, catastrophic engine damage can occur.

Another problem is that carbon deposits can cause hot spots, a common cause of pre-ignition. Pre-ignition can destroy even the most expensive motor. Occasionally adding a healthy dose of Techron Concentrate or BK-44G to your gasoline will keep your motor clean and running to its full potential. These two products are as beneficial for older hemi-head Harleys as they are for newer Evos and Twin Cams.

Gasoline stabilizers are another product worth using. Gasoline will, in time, break down; this is commonly called stale gas. If you are going to store your bike for more than a couple of months, you should use a good gas stabilizer. One product that I use is STA-BIL, made by the Gold Eagle Company. Mixing in the proper amount of a product like STA-BIL can keep your gas fresh for over a year. Remember, if you're running an oxygen sensor, always check to see if it's compatible with the product.

WHAT KIND OF HARLEY TO MODIFY?

I am often asked which V-twin I prefer to modify for power. My typical answer is this: Any bike that is not modified is a perfect bike to be modified.

A light 883 Sportster will respond to performance modifications just as well as a 900-pound bagger. The only difference will be the type of power band you want the modification to yield. With any model V-twin, you can build a low-end torque monster or top-end horsepower machine. Modify it from mild to wild, or just about anything in between. People do build baggers to be top-end horsepower machines and run them on the drag strip. Some people like to be different!

The only limitations for power modifications on a stock motor are your budget and the power and rpm that the lower-end can withstand before things break.

Personally, I lean toward Sportsters and Twin Cams because, in stock form, they provide a more rigid platform and their pushrod geometry and oiling systems are better.

THINGS TO CONSIDER ABOUT MODIFICATIONS

Due to their disproportionate size-to-displacement difference, a large heavy bike like a bagger will always require more work to accelerate at the same rate as a smaller and lighter bike like the Sportster.

Due to their weight difference, common sense and physics dictates that it requires a lot less work and money to make a 500-pound Sportster go fast than an 800-pound Electra Glide.

It is always easier to build a high-output small-displacement motor than it is to build a high-output large-displacement one. Also, highly modified Sportster and Twin Cam motors do not suffer from the same engine/transmission flexing problems as the older Big Twins do, and their pushrod angle is better.

CONSIDERING A USED MODIFIED BIKE?

The type of bike you choose to modify is obviously influenced by your individual taste in bikes and your budget. Any bike that's stock can be improved. The key word in that statement is "stock"! For several reasons, I recommend you always start with a motor that is as stock as possible. This statement will be unsettling to people wishing to sell bikes with modified motors, but I have several reasons for recommending this. Note that minor external changes to a motor, like carburetors, exhaust pipes, and ignition systems should not be of major concern.

If the motor is in near-stock condition, there is a greater chance that the previous owner was more interested in cruising, putting around town, or just posing with the bike. So the motor may not have been beaten to death by a power-crazy lunatic. This is not always the case! I have seen several fools in my small town that beat the living heck out of a stock bike trying to impress themselves.

With a stock motor, you also know essentially what parts are inside and that the Motor Company put them there.

If the motor has already been modified, chances are it was not modified just for looks and it has probably gone a few or more rounds with the above-mentioned power-crazy lunatic.

Unless the deal is too good to pass up, I personally try to avoid used bikes that have been extensively modified. When purchasing a bike with a modified motor, you may be relieving its owner of a giant headache. Which means it will now be your headache! When I see a used bike for sale with a highly modified motor, I always ask myself (and you should, too) these questions:

1. If the owner has spent considerable time and money building the perfect, modified street motor, why does he want to sell it?

2. Who modified the motor? Was the person(s) who did the work experienced in building performance motors?

3. How much use—or should I say abuse—has the motor undergone since it was modified?

This does not mean you can't get a good deal on a bike with a modified motor, but you never know what you're going to end up with. I've known people who have invested a considerable amount of time and money on major power modifications. After the novelty of having a hot rod motor wore off, they sold the bike. The next time I saw them, they were riding a different bike, powered by a stock motor.

This seems to occur when a modified motor is overbuilt. If you do this, you can and will end up with a bike that is a lot less fun to ride than the one you started with.

When buying a used modified bike, you should be aware that a few of these self-proclaimed backyard motor experts assembling motors may not be qualified to change your spark plugs, let alone perform complicated engine modifications.

Another problem you can encounter is that this type of "expert" often doesn't know what actually works and what will just cost you money and will put together an illogical motor combination for use on the street or maybe even worse. If you get stuck with a motor like that, first you have to figure out where the expert went wrong; then you have to determine what to do to correct it. Rest assured that this is going to cost you money!

If you run into a bike that has a modified motor and the deal is too good to pass up, do these things before you buy it:

1. Have the owner make a list every part that's in the motor, right down to the brand of gaskets used in assembly.

2. Ask for parts documentation—that is, receipts for all the parts used to build the modified motor and anything else that was changed on the bike.

3. Find out who assembled the motor, and ask around about what kind of reputation the person(s) or shop has for building modified street motors.

4. Find out when the motor was modified and how many miles have been put on it since the modifications were done.

5. Find out what you can about the current owner. Is the owner the kind of person who takes care of equipment or who has a reputation for beating stuff to death?

6. This one is the most important thing to do before you buy a used modified bike, because it will tell you if you're getting a deal or a dog! Have the owner run the bike on a dyno before you hand over your money. If you have to, offer to pay for this yourself. Be there to witness the test, and do not accept dyno results that were allegedly conducted earlier.

Unlike some people, the dyno doesn't lie. By analyzing the dyno information, you will know if the builder knew what he was doing and assembled a collection of parts that work together as a total engine package. For example, by analyzing the torque curve, you can tell if this bike will be fun to ride on the street or will be a miserable beast.

7. And, finally, take your time! Think about what you're about to take on, and don't rush into a deal you may regret later. A seller that is on the level should work with you to gather the required information.

If other parts of the bike have been modified, don't forget to get the same type of information about those parts. Be aware that motorcycles are stolen and stripped for parts. Good luck!

In closing, if I have given you the impression that I'm down on people buying used bikes and/or motors other people have modified, you're correct. I'm the poor fool who's been stuck

trying to correct the mistakes of others, and it's no fun! It's a classic case of "been there, done that, don't want to do it again, but I know I will."

Consider this when you do performance modifications to your motor. It doesn't always guarantee the resale value of your bike will increase. In fact, often the exact opposite happens. This is a good reason always to hang on to your old stock parts.

PERFORMANCE MOTOR KITS—GO FAST IN A BOX

One of the goals of this book is to help you realize that creating a performance street motor involves a lot more than just slapping a couple of performance parts on your stock motor. Each part you choose must work in harmony with the other parts, and they all must work together as a total package. It's the classic case of the whole needing to be greater than the sum of its parts. The goal is to assemble what is called a happy motor; this will also make you happy.

Many of us are constrained by a budget. As the old speed shop saying goes, "We sell horsepower. How much can you afford?"

Luckily, performance kits have a wide price range. Assembling performance street motors will often involve compromises, so be prepared to deal with them.

Your motor will only perform as well as the parts you choose to assemble it with. Cutting corners to save a few bucks can cause a loss in both power and engine longevity. Also, if you get just one part of the combination wrong, it could severely affect your performance results. If you have a firm understanding of performance modifications, the results you end up with should come close to your expectations. But the fact remains that you will not know for sure what you've created until you dyno test it. If you're lucky, you'll get the results you expected. But unfortunately, all too often people are disappointed when they read the numbers. After making a serious investment in both time and money, power results that fall short of your expectations are the last thing you want.

Okay, are there any surefire ways of knowing what your end results will be before you buy a single part? Yes, there are, and they're called motor kits, or performance packages.

There are literally hundreds of kits to choose from. Some kits are simple bolt-on affairs you can assemble yourself, while others may involve engine case disassembly and modification before reassembly. With so many kits out there to choose from, you should be able to find one that meets your power requirements and, hopefully, your budget.

KIT SUGGESTIONS

When considering a performance kit, I would highly recommend you first look at kits from one of the major performance manufacturers. Respected names in high performance like S&S, Zipper's, Branch Flowmetrics, Carl's

Speed Shop, and Edelbrock (just to name a few) are safe choices. These companies have the expertise and capital to invest in dyno testing many different part combinations, so they can come up with a winning package. Not only that, but most of the manufacturers I just listed also make their own performance parts. If you can't find what you want, make it yourself. If you hold up your end of the bargain by correctly installing and tuning their kit, your performance results should measure up to your expectations.

Your first move is to contact the vendors and get information on their kits. The more vendors you contact, the more choices you will have. You'll want to know what comes with their kits and what—if anything—you must provide. For instance, some kits may not come with gaskets. You will want to see honest rear-wheel dyno charts so you'll know what kind of power the kit produces and, most importantly, where they produce it. You'll also want to know if the kits are bolt-on or if the cases have to be split and machined. Understand that if the cases need to be split and machined, it will involve a potentially substantial additional cost.

After you've seen what's available, your next consideration is your budget. It always comes down to how much power you can afford. Kit prices range from several hundred to several thousand dollars. With such a large variation in cost, you should be able to find something that fits your budget. If you're looking at kits from the top

end of the price range (we're talking over $4,000), you may want to consider purchasing a complete performance motor. S&S, for example, has a wide selection of performance motors to choose from. For under $8,000, S&S will sell you a 124-inch Twin Cam beast of a motor that will bolt right into your stock frame. Use the same advice when selecting a complete motor as you would when purchasing a kit.

PICKING A KIT

As I stress throughout this book, don't be suckered in by big horsepower numbers. Horsepower does not make you accelerate, torque does. All the kits' manufacturers should be able to provide you with a dyno chart containing accurate torque and horsepower information. You will want to pay close attention to that essential torque curve, because it will tell you how and where the kit makes its power. As always, you'll want a strong and broad torque band, not a small peaky band.

The location of a particular kit's peak torque is also important for application choices. A bagger that spends most of its time on the highway packing two up plus camping gear and towing a trailer will require a different torque band than a stripped-down Dyna that you use to blast around town on solo. For the bagger, you'll be looking for a kit with big torque numbers, between 2,000 to 4,000 rpm. Producing a peak torque of 100-plus lb-ft at around 3,500 rpm will keep this heavyweight cruiser happy. The easiest way to increase torque is by adding cubic inches and

People often ask how long I have been into scooters. The truth is, since age one, although I'll admit my first ones were considerably underpowered.

Keeping with the family tradition, we're starting our daughter, Kaitlin, off at an early age, too. Thanks to Daddy, her scooters aren't lacking in power!

compression. Unlike adding cubic inches, we are limited in getting substantial torque increases from compression alone with the gasoline that's available today.

For the Dyna Pilot, on the other hand, you may be looking for a much different type of torque band. Torque-wise, you will be interested in what's going on between 2,500 to 5,500 rpm. The lighter-weight blaster may be better served with a kit that has its peak torque hitting at around 4,000 to 4,500 rpm. To help collect lots of speeding tickets, a kit that's still building horsepower at 6,000-plus rpm will be a good choice, but note that a Big Twin kit that does this will require the ability to flow massive amounts of air and will probably cost you more than the bagger's tow-truck kit. The Dyna Pilot will want to add inches, too. Increasing bore size from stock would be a good route to use for top-end power.

IT'S ALL IN THE TUNING

I stated that reliable kit manufactures would provide you with accurate dyno charts so you would know exactly what each kit should produce. Let's say the kit you purchased should develop 100 horsepower and 100 lb-ft at a given rpm. You properly installed the kit, wheeled it on the dyno, and got only 84 horsepower and 88 lb-ft. Could this happen? You bet it can—it's called not being tuned! I can guarantee you the kit makers will have the motor tuned to perform at its best before they put it on the dyno. The air/fuel ratio will be as flat as they could make it from idle to redline, hovering somewhere around 12.6:1 to 13:1. Timing will be set to produce the best power; if an offset is needed, the timing will be offset. The pushrods and everything else on the motor will be adjusted and tuned to produce the best power.

The most overlooked part that will kill the kit's ability to perform is the exhaust system. People will spend $3,000-plus on a performance kit, then hang a set of offensive Big Suckers 2 1/2-inch straight drag pipes on it and wonder why their motor is performing so badly. This is my last and most important piece of advice for motor kits; always find out what exhaust system was used on the manufacturer's kit when it was tested. If it's a tunable system, find out what baffle or how many discs were used to produce the best power.

The White Brothers E-series 2-into-1 pipe is one of several tunable 2-into-1 systems used to milk out maximum power from engine combinations. This may be the very system used to test your kit. Unfortunately, some traditionalists (me included) don't care for the 2-into-1 look or the sound they produce. If your motor combination was tuned using a 2-into-1 system and you want to run a 2–into-2 system, please do yourself a favor and call the kit maker. Ask for advice on an alternate system that will not drastically reduce the kit's performance.

KIT SUMMARY
- Performance kits do work, and I recommend them.

- Kits take all the guesswork out of matching the correct combination of parts.

- You can pick a kit that delivers exactly the power band you want (within reason, of course).

- With the wide variety of kits available, you'll probably find one that's in your budget.

- You'll save time and money by getting the correct set of matched performance parts the first time around.

NOTES:

_____

_____

_____

_____

_____

_____

_____

_____

_____

_____

_____

_____

_____

_____

CHAPTER 2 TUNING INTAKE AND EXHAUST TUNING

TUNING THE LENGTH OF YOUR INTAKE SYSTEM TO THE INDUCTION TRACT PULSE

The best way to increase cylinder fill and exhaust scavenging is to tune your intake tract and exhaust tracts length to a specific rpm.

For the intake tract, the most tuners try to tune it to is the third or fourth pulse. The second pulse is the strongest, but because its length is so long, it is often impractical to use. Drag racers often make good use of the next strongest pulse, the third pulse. But again, it's often impractical to use it for street use because of its length.

So for the street bike, the weaker but still useful fourth pulse is often used. The formula used to calculate this is based on the speed of sound (1,120 feet per second at 60 degrees Fahrenheit). The length is measured from the face of the intake valve to the end, or opening, of the intake system. This could be the mouth of the carburetor, air cleaner, velocity stack, or whatever is at the open end.

The use of 1,120 feet per second for the speed of sound is another tuning compromise, because this figure does not take into consideration the temperature of the intake or exhaust gasses. The speed of sound increases approximately 1 foot per second for each degree of temperature rise. This is why dyno tuning is so important when making final tuning adjustments.

INDUCTION TRACT PULSE FORMULA

Second pulse: (1,120 x 1/2 intake cam duration x 0.96) divided by rpm = length in inches

Third pulse: (1,120 x 1/2 intake cam duration x 0.705) divided by rpm = length in inches

Fourth pulse: (1,120 x 1/2 intake cam duration x 0.538) divided by rpm = length in inches

Here is an example of tuned lengths for a Twin Cam running the Andrews TW-55 cam:

Rpm	Second pulse	Third pulse	Fourth pulse
4,000	33.33 inch	24.48 inch	18.68 inch
5,000	26.66 inch	19.58 inch	14.94 inch
6,000	21.22 inch	16.32 inch	12.94 inch

I used the above example because I'm testing this cam at the moment in my Twin Cam project bike. Its intake duration is 248 degrees. Presently, for street use, my intake tract is 9.975 inches long. At this length, it would be tuned to the fourth pulse at a little over 7,000 rpm. Too bad the rev limiter shuts her down at 6,200 rpm! Now if I were so moved as to put a few dollars down on a friendly drag race, I would remove my S&S air cleaner and install my 4-inch S&S velocity stack. The intake tract would then be 13.35 inches, and this would tune my intake track to the fourth pulse at approximately 5,600 rpm, which is right at the middle of my shift point. Remember: The guy that wins is the guy that does his homework.

EXHAUST TRACT TUNING

Over the years I have wasted a lifetime's worth of money on exhaust systems! At one time I had so many damn Ironhead Sportster exhaust systems around my house that when someone came over and said he had an ironhead Sportster, I wouldn't let him leave without taking a free set. The wife was always happy to see another set go out the door.

You could say that I am exhausted from the subject of exhaust systems. If I never spend another dollar on a set I'll be happy, but I know that's not going to happen. So don't expect me to tell you what type of exhaust system to buy, because I'm not. You're on your own. But be warned: Bring lots of money, as exhaust systems are rather expensive nowadays.

Don't get me wrong. I'd love to tell you what exhaust system to buy, but I can't and neither can anyone else. There is no such beast as one exhaust system that will perform better than any other exhaust system for every bike in every power band. But if you're lucky and do lots of testing, you may come close.

Today, there are an inexhaustible variety of systems to choose from. Twenty years ago, if someone had told me people would be shelling out $1,000 for a set of drag pipes, I would have told him he was nuts. But, today, people are doing just that! It seems people buy exhaust systems now mainly for looks and/or the sound, while performance often seems to be a secondary thought. I'll discuss some of the basics on exhaust systems and you can go from there.

Understand that a true performance exhaust system, matched and tuned to your motor combination, will yield substantial improvements in both torque and horsepower. For this reason you should always attempt to find that system. Now for the bad news: Exhaust systems have gotten very spendy and, unless you know something I don't, the testing method is "buy and try."

For instance, I'm a traditionalist and prefer the looks of 2-into-2 exhaust systems on V-twins. Recently, BUB Enterprises got together with Gerald Rinehart, of NASCAR exhaust fame, and designed the Rinehart by BUB stepped-header systems for Harleys and other brands. I was itching to try them out on the dyno to see what they'd do for my Twin Cam project bike. What held me back was the same thing that holds most of us back from finding that perfect exhaust system. That's money, as they retail for around $750! Luckily, the taxman returned a few of the hard-earned dollars I sent him last year, so now there's a new set of Rineharts strapped on the Twin Cam project bike waiting to see the dyno. I added my own little twist and installed an oxygen sensor on the front pipe. (More about that later.)

RULES ON EXHAUST SYSTEMS

Almost any aftermarket exhaust system will outperform the restrictive EPA-mandated mufflers that come stock on the bikes.

The only real way to find out what exhaust system will work best for you is to do comparison tests using your own bike with different exhaust systems on a rear-wheel dyno.

Advertisements for exhaust systems that include dyno

This is an anti-reversion (AR) exhaust pipe. Notice the bulge in the pipe where it connects to the cylinder head; this is where the AR cone is located. The purpose of the cone is to prevent reversion. It also directs the hot exhaust gases to the center of the pipe, which can help even out the temperature of the pipe. As you can see in this case, doing this has prevented bluing.

printouts are seductive, yet also very misleading. Even if the tests were conducted properly, they will not provide the same results for your bike unless the test bike is identical in all ways to yours. Even small differences in components or tuning can make a big difference in exhaust system performance.

Like cams, no exhaust system will provide you with the best low-end torque and the best high-end horsepower. You must pick one or the other, or compromise between the two.

There are basically two types of exhaust systems: the 2-into-2 and the 2-into-1. Of these, the latter will often provide the best all-around street performance. Generally, when compared to 2-into-2 systems, the 2-into-1 systems will often improve midrange torque, but not necessarily your top-end horsepower simultaneously.

Free flowing 2-into-2 exhaust systems can often be tuned to make good top-end power, although low-end power with this setup may be soft. Adding some back pressure can improve low-to-midrange power, but it will

do so by sacrificing top-end power.

Long header pipes make better power at low rpm, and conversely, shorter header pipes make better power at high rpm. This is the reason short header pipes are found on drag bikes.

Exhaust systems that provide some back pressure or restriction will often provide good low-end torque at the sacrifice of top-end horsepower.

Free flowing exhaust systems that provide almost no back pressure often produce good high-rpm horsepower at the expense of low-end torque. Also, these systems, like drag pipes or systems with excessively large diameter pipes, can cause bad low-end performance and make slow speed carburetor tuning extremely difficult. Performance engine and carburetor builders, like S&S Cycle, are very clear on this point.

Any exhaust system designed to limit reversion, called anti-reversion (AR) systems, are better than a system not designed to do so. Reversion, as used here, refers to exhaust gasses flowing back into the combustion chamber at the end of the exhaust stroke. This can limit power by interfering with cylinder refill, as well as by contaminating the fresh air/fuel charge with leftover exhaust gases. The AR step or cone should be located as close to the exhaust port as possible.

EXHAUST PIPE BLUING
AND ANTI-REVERSION (AR) PIPES

If there is one thing that almost all V-twin owners agree on, it's that blued exhaust pipes are ugly. You shell out hard earned money for a shiny new set of chrome-plated beauties, and within short order, they're blued and ugly as sin.

In the past, exhaust pipes did not command the price they do today. Routinely, I would just slap on a new set every year, except for the years I had slapped on two or three. (Now you know how I ended up with all those ironhead Sportster exhaust pipes!) In the past, I tried most of the standard methods to keep bluing at bay, and here's what I learned:

One of the common excuses for blued pipes is a poor state of tuning. It's true that an improperly tuned motor will produce excessive exhaust temperatures, but even with the best tune, chances are your pipes will sooner or later blue.

Another anti-bluing method was to coat your pipes with several coats of 1,500 degree Fahrenheit flameproof paint. I tried that numerous times. It may slow the bluing down, but sooner or later they will blue.

Next they came out with water-based ceramic paint coatings that cured like pottery under the high exhaust temperatures. This actually will works for a while, but as you can guess, sooner or later the pipes will blue. The problem with the coating is that it doesn't expand and contract at the same rate as the pipes, so the coating cracks and falls off. When that happens, the pipes turn blue where the coating is missing.

It seems like the only surefire way to deal with exhaust-pipe bluing is to cover the pipes with a chrome-plated shield and ignore the blued pipes under it. This is the best and only guaranteed way to deal with bluing. Some pipes are now constructed using double wall tubing. Although expensive, it accomplishes the same thing as the shields.

About five years ago, I purchased and installed a set of tapered dual anti-reversion exhaust pipes, made by Khrome Werks, on my old 1959 XLCH hot rod. This style of pipe has a tapered AR cone mounted inside the inlet end of the header pipe. It's similar to the device sold as an exhaust torque valve to people who like to run pipes that are entirely too big for their motors. Several brands of AR pipes are constructed this way. The Khrome Werks pipes have been on the old 1959 for almost five years now, and the chrome is still free of any bluing. It's true that this old warhorse rarely sees more than 500 miles a year, and the motor is always kept in a very high state of tune, but five years and no bluing is a great feat.

Other than a miracle worthy of the Pope's attention, why is there no bluing on my 1959 hot rod's pipes? My best response is that, as the exhaust gasses flow through the AR cone, they are forced to the center of the pipe, so instead of direct flame contact, the contact is indirect. Therefore the heat can be distributed more evenly along the surface of the pipe, instead of just at the very beginning. Will this also work on your bike? Because of all the variables involved, I can't say. What I can say is that heat shields always work.

TUNING HEADERS

Exhaust header pipes can be tuned for flow velocity and to the pulse wave. We'll start with the one that requires the most math.

EXHAUST-GAS PORT VELOCITY

Optimum exhaust-gas velocity is between 280 and 300 feet per second. Too much velocity causes wall friction and increases back pressure. Too little velocity reduces power and throttle response. What we want is a header that flows approximately 290 feet per second in the middle of the shift point for drag racing, or the middle of the power band for a street bike. The formula we use is this: (pistons speed ÷ 60) x (bore squared ÷ the diameter of the inside of the header pipe squared) = exhaust gas velocity. See? Some real math is involved.

Let's first take a look at piston speed. To calculate piston speed, double your stroke, divide it by 12, and then multiply that by your desired rpm: [(stroke x 2) ÷ 12] x rpm = piston speed. You now have piston speed in feet per minute. This value is then divided by 60, and you now have piston speed at feet per second. Next, we square the bore's diameter, or bore x bore.

Then we take the inside diameter (i.d.) of the header pipe and square it: i.d. x i.d. Next we divide the bore squared by the header i.d. squared. Here is what it would look like:

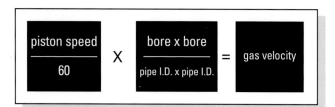

Remember what you learned in school about fractions: First you multiply across the top; then you multiply across the bottom; then you divide the top figure by the bottom figure to get your answer. I know you remembered that!

Let's see what the math looks like for the velocity of 1 3/4-inch (1.75-inch) header pipes at 3,000 rpm on a 95-inch Twin Cam motor.

Here's a breakdown of the information: bore = 3.875 inches; stroke = 4 inches; the header pipe's outside diameter (o.d.) = 1.75 inches; and the i.d. of a 1.75-inch pipe = 1.625 inches. Let's look at the math.

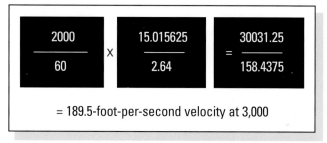

= 189.5-foot-per-second velocity at 3,000

Here are examples of exhaust-gas header velocities for my Twin Cam 95 with 1.75-inch-o.d. headers. This example will work for any 95-inch Twin Cam running 1.75-inch pipes.

Remember, the ideal exhaust-gas velocity is between 280 and 300 feet per second with an average of 290.

Rpm		Feet per second
3,000	=	190
4,000	=	253
4,500	=	284
5,000	=	316
5,500	=	348
6,000	=	379
6,200	=	392

In the example above, the ideal header velocity would occur at 4,600 rpm with a header velocity of 290 feet per second. This is an ideal rpm for my Twin Cam, because it falls close to the location of my peak torque and right in the middle of my cam's power band of 3,000 to 6,200 rpm.

For drag racing, this motor might benefit from 2-inch-o.d. pipes, which will reduce lost power from pipe wall friction and mean flow velocity.

It's important to note that even on a motor displacing 95 inches, the 2-inch-o.d. drag pipes will only be tuned to the very top of the power band at 6,000 rpm. Now you can see why even a large 95-inch motor won't perform very well on the street with 2-inch-o.d. drag pipes. Just think what they'd do to the performance of a smaller-displacement bike like an 883 or 1200 Sportster. But guess what? You'll run into people out there running 2-inch drag pipes on 883 Sportsters, and they'll tell you how bad those big pipes sound. Now that you can do the math, you will know the sound is not the only thing that's bad about the combination!

EXHAUST PIPE INSULATING

Exhaust gasses cool as they travel down the inside of an exhaust pipe, and the cooler they get, the slower they'll flow. Drag racers often use insulating wrap around their headers in an attempt to keep exhaust temperatures and exhaust-gas velocities high to take advantage of inertia scavenging.

PULSE WAVES

In addition to tuning for header flow velocity, you can also tune the pipe length to the energy pulse wave to take advantage of wave scavenging. Here is a common formula to use: [(180 degrees + the exhaust valves opening event at before bottom dead center [BBDC]) x 950] ÷ the middle rpm of your shift point = header pipe length in inches.

Example:
The Andrews TW-55 cam opens the exhaust valve at 52 degrees BBDC.
180 + 52 = 232
232 x 950 = 220,400
220,400 ÷ 5,500 (rpm at the middle of my shift point) = 40.07
We end up with a pipe length of 40.07 inches.

In this example, adjusting the header pipe length to 40 inches is a good approximation until we can dyno tune the pipes.

Here's an example of calculated exhaust header lengths for straight pipes for my Twin Cam 95-inch project bike with the Andrews TW-55 cam to take advantage of wave scavenging:

Rpm		Length
2,000	=	110.2 inches
3,000	=	73.4 inches
4,000	=	55.1 inches
5,000	=	44.1 inches
6,000	=	36.7 inches

On my 95-inch Twin Cam, the middle of the shift point is at 5,500 rpm. Calculations show us that a header length of approximately 40 inches would be a good starting point, but it's just an approximate length.

For tuning, you would dial the pipe length in by cutting the pipe an inch at a time and testing it on a dyno. In this case, you may want to start off with a 42-inch or longer header pipe and tune back from there.

Remember that straight pipes only work over a narrow power band of about 1,500 rpm; go above or below it and their performance will suffer. The only thing that will remain constant when running drag pipes is the noise level! For a street performance bike, the noise does not equal power.

I have a sign in my shop that reads: "The difference between making noise and making power is simple. Anybody can make noise!"

LET'S REVIEW WHAT WE'VE LEARNED

We know that homework and fine-tuning will both pay you back with extra power.

But do you see the main problem with performance tuning? It only works over a narrow power band of about 1,500 rpm.

What's the most important lesson that we should have learned from this? Because street motors have to operate from idle to redline, they can only be tuned to a limited degree, so they can't be fine-tuned for the entire operating range. As always, street motors have to get by with a bunch of tuning compromises.

But let's get back to the friendly drag race with my trusty 95-inch Twin Cam. If we used our knowledge, we could try the following:

1. Remove the air cleaner and install the 4-inch velocity stack; this tunes the intake tract to 5,600 rpm.

2. Lose the street pipes and install 2-inch-o.d. headers pipes with the ends cut at 40 inches; remember, always use a strait cut at the end of the pipe.

With luck, these two simple changes will put more torque to the street, cut your elapsed time (ET), and make the guy in your rearview mirror look just a little bit smaller.

Now you know how to calculate the tuned diameter for flow velocity and the tuned length for the pulse wave on your exhaust system. Remember, these figures are approximates and every motor is a little different. The final numbers must be refined and tuned through dyno or track testing.

CHAPTER 3 **ABOUT CAMSHAFTS ...**

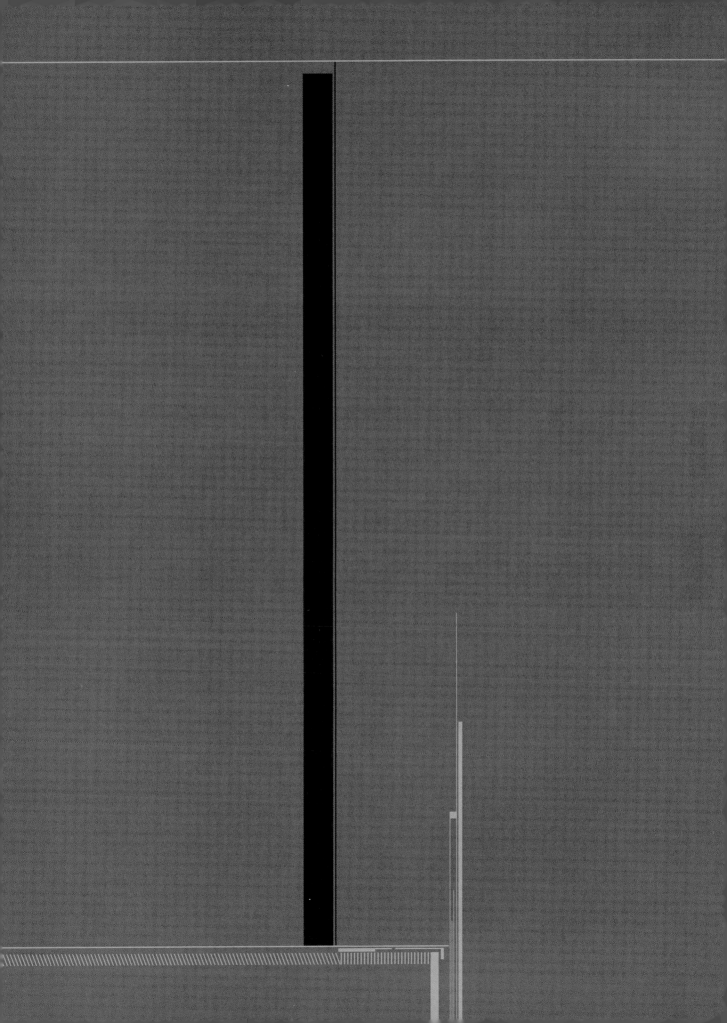

THE MOST IMPORTANT QUESTION TO ASK YOURSELF ABOUT CAMS IS . . .

Before choosing a cam, the first question you should ask is how much power are you willing to give up to make a little more power elsewhere? That's right, I said give up power! The old adage "you can't have your cake and eat it, too" comes into play when selecting a cam. No cam will increase your low-end torque and increase your top-end horsepower at the same time. You must give up one to get the other.

If you're going for strong low-end torque for two-up riding or passing that big rig on your bagger, you must give up high-rpm horsepower. If you want high top-end horsepower, you must give up your low-end torque and your ability to accelerate quickly on a throttle roll-on.

If you want to accelerate quickly with a bike that is set up for top-end horsepower, you will need to look for a lower gear. If you want both increased torque and top-end horsepower, think more cubic inches!

The number-one device that restricts cylinder filling—thus your ability to make power—on a V-twin engine is the cylin-

As the old saying goes, there's no replacement for displacement! If you want more torque and horsepower, adding cubic inches is a sure way to get there. Pictured on top is a stock Twin Cam 88, and bottom is a stock 883XL.

der head and intake tract. No cam can change the restrictive flow quality of your stock cylinder heads.

The only thing you can do with a cam is lift the valves a little higher and hold the valves open a little longer to try to increase cylinder fill. Of course, doing this will hurt your low-end performance.

When you make a cam change, you're moving the location of your peak torque (and peak volumetric efficiency) and changing the shape of the torque curve. On a street bike, a broad flat torque band is always preferable over a short peaky torque band. On the other hand, drag racers are well served with a narrow torque band that produces maximum horsepower at the top-end.

HERE ARE MY 26 GENERAL CAM RULES TO HELP YOU AVOID SCREWING UP

Cam rule 1: Remember, without torque you can't make horsepower. When you look for a cam, always look at the torque band the cam will produce. Don't be suckered in by the peak horsepower number. Horsepower doesn't make you accelerate, torque does!

Cam rule 2: Due to EPA regulations, the first priority of modern stock cams is to meet strict pollution requirements; only secondarily are they designed to make as much power as possible while meeting those requirements. As EPA requirements go up, power goes down.

Cam rule 3: The real reason you change your cam(s) is to increase your motor's volumetric efficiency at a predictable location. Because this can only happen in a narrow power band, you must first decide where you want your peak volumetric efficiency (VE) to happen.

Cam rule 4: When choosing a cam for street use, always choose a cam that will produce the broadest/flattest torque band in the middle of the rpm range, where your motor spends most of its time. Failing to do this will cause you to end up with disappointing performance results.

Cam rule 5: Choose the right cam for your specific application. Cam choice must be balanced with the total engine combination for you to achieve the desired results. Unfortunately, improper cam choice is a common mistake.

Cam rule 6: When the cam's intake valve closing event changes, your corrected compression ratio will also change.

Cam rule 7: Therefore, when installing a cam with more duration and later closing intake valve timing, always adjust the corrected compression ratio back to the required ratio. If you don't, your new cam may make less power across the board than the one it's replacing.

Cam rule 8: Generally, increasing lift without increasing duration will make more low-end power.

Cam rule 9: Generally, increasing duration without increasing lift will move the point of peak torque higher up the rpm band, thus sacrificing low-end power.

Cam rule 10: Generally, increasing both lift and duration will also increase your top-end power by moving peak torque to a higher rpm, while often sacrificing low-end power.

Cam rule 11: When increasing both lift and duration, adjusting your corrected compression ratio can makeup for some of that lost low-end power.

Cam rule 12: Generally, closing the intake valve sooner increases the corrected compression ratio and the low-end power (torque).

Cam rule 13: Closing the intake valve too soon, without adjusting the corrected compression ratio, can cause excessive cylinder pressures that lead to detonation problems.

Cam rule 14: Increasing the cam's duration and closing the intake valve later can decrease detonation in a detonation-prone motor with poor combustion chamber shape and/or poor turbulence. This is because you are lowering the corrected compression ratio and decreasing pressure in the cylinder.

Cam rule 15: Opening the exhaust valve too early can waste power by bleeding off cylinder pressure too soon. It can also cause extreme and damaging exhaust-tract temperatures.

Cam rule 16: Opening the exhaust valve too late can cause inefficient cylinder scavenging and possible air/fuel mix dilution caused by exhaust gas contamination.

Cam rule 17: The exhaust port should flow approximately 80 percent of what the intake port flows. If it flows less than 80 percent, you may want to consider a dual-pattern cam. In this case, it would be a cam with more exhaust duration than intake duration. A low exhaust-to-intake flow ratio is a common problem with Harley's stock heads.

Cam rule 18: Generally, a large-displacement motor can handle, and often requires, more cam than a small-displacement motor to perform to its full potential.

Cam rule 19: Generally, a motor with increased stroke can handle more cam (lift and duration) than a motor with a shorter stroke.

Cam rule 20: A light bike can usually handle more cam than a heavy bike, because it takes less torque to accelerate a light bike than a heavy bike at the same rate. Because of this, a light bike can sacrifice a few lb-ft of

low-end torque to gain more power on the top end.

Cam rule 21: When in doubt about which cam to use, always be conservative. Too much cam or the wrong cam can make a bike hard to tune, not street-worthy, and very disappointing to ride.

Cam rule 22: Choosing the wrong cam for a particular application will not only cost you power, but will also cost you money!

Cam rule 23: Cams come two ways, modified or bolt-in. Modified cams require spring spacing and/or modification to the stock heads before installation. Failing to adjust spring spacing when installing a cam for modified use will lead to catastrophic engine damage. Bolt-in cams can be installed in stock heads without adjusting valve spring spacing.

Approximate lift limitations for bolt-in cam applications:

Ironhead Sportster	0.425 inch
Evo Sportster	0.500 inch
Shovelhead Big Twin	0.450 inch
Evo Big Twin	0.500 inch
Twin Cam	0.510 inch

Cam rule 24: When installing a power adder or booster (like a turbocharger), you'll want a cam that has less intake duration, one with more exhaust duration, or one with both. Talk to the people that make turbo kits for more information.

Cam rule 25: If running a nitrous oxide (N2O) system, you should always check with the system's manufacturer about what cam it recommends for use with its system.

Note: Nitrous oxide works by adding extra oxygen molecules to the combustion chamber, which will be covered in Chapter 4.

Cam rule 26: This is the most important rule! If you're not exactly sure which cam to use, always consult a cam maker or someone who does know before spending or, worse, wasting your money. A self-proclaimed expert will be of little help here, so make sure you really trust the person with whom you consult. Remember, it's your money! Using computer software programs can also be useful in comparing different cams.

CAM LOBE HEIGHT

To determine valve lift, multiply the cam's net lobe height by the rocker arm ratio to get total valve lift.

CAM VALVE LIFT

Generally, the amount you lift a valve is proportional to the intake valve's diameter. The bigger the valve, the higher the recommended valve lift.

This is why valve lifts on four-valve heads are much lower

Early Sifton SL Sportster cam set.

Early Sportster cams installed in a cam case cover. Remember: The cams are always installed first before the cover; this picture is for illustration only.

than that on two valve heads. Valves in the four-valve heads are smaller so they don't have to be lifted as far to accomplish the same valve lift percentage.

For a performance street motor, we'll want a cam that lifts the valve over 25 percent of the valve's diameter. With modified or aftermarket heads, valve lifts of 28 to 30 percent are normal for street performance use, but recent trends in valve lifting are moving higher.

VALVE LIFT LIMITATIONS

It's important to understand that the height you need to lift a valve is regulated by the head's ability to flow air.

Eventually you will reach a point where lifting the valve higher no longer increases cylinder filling.

Let's look at an example of the stock Twin Cam head. Harley designed these heads with very small ports and valves, so they will have good mixture flow velocity but not much volume. They'll produce good power (torque) in the low to midrange of the power band where these motors spend most of their time.

Let's look at some numbers: Branch Flowmetrics tested a stock Twin Cam head on its unique flow bench. The volume, or cfm (cubic feet per minute), of air flowed continued to increase up to a valve lift of 0.400 inch, at which the port was flowing 118.6 cfm. Branch Flowmetrics continued lifting the valve and then removed the valve completely; 118.6 cfm was still all the port flowed.

So what is the lesson from this information? That lifting the valve higher than the port's maximum flow point, which in this case was only 0.400 inch, will not gain much in the way of airflow. So to get more power from stock Twin Cam heads, we'll need to address valve timing, not valve lift.

To get more cylinder refill, we can open and close the valves faster with a more aggressive ramp profile, open the intake valve sooner, close the intake valve later, and make use of more valve overlap. Of course, every one of these timing changes can hurt low-end power. Remember, it's all about compromises.

In summary, peak torque happens at the location of peak volumetric efficiency, and torque continues to increase until you reach the location of peak volumetric efficiency. After that, torque will start to diminish as rpm continues to increase. When your torque starts decreasing faster than rpm is rising, horsepower also stops rising and the game is over.

INTAKE VALVE OPENINGS

To make good power, cams need to lift the intake valve by 75 percent or more of its total lift at maximum piston velocity. On a V-twin, maximum piston velocity occurs at roughly 70 to 73 degrees ATDC, depending on stroke and rod length.

ADVANCED OR RETARDED CAM TIMING

Let's start with definitions. Cam advance will increase low-to-midrange torque, but reduce top-end power.

Cam retard will increase top-end power, but reduce low-to-midrange torque.

Here are two examples: The Andrews TW-37B and TW-55 Twin-Cam cams are both advanced by 2 degrees.

TW-37B
Lobe separation angle = 104
Lobe center = 102 (2 degrees advanced)

TW-55
Lobe separation angle = 106
Lobe center = 104 (2 degrees advanced)

CAM OVERLAP

Cam overlap happens when the intake and exhaust valves are

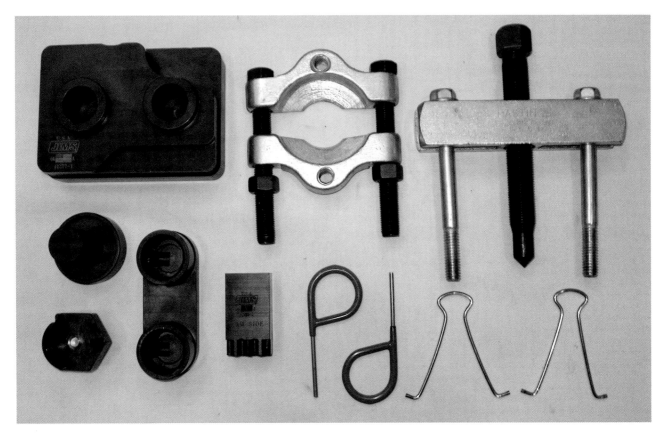

These are a few specialty tools I use to change cams in the new Twin Cam motors. Unless you plan to do several cam changes, it will be more cost effective to take your cam support plate to someone who already has the tools and pay them to change your cams.

both open at the same time and the piston is at or near TDC. Overlap is handy because it uses mixture inertia—the low-pressure energy caused by fast-exiting exhaust gasses—to start the intake gasses moving into the cylinder before the piston reaches TDC.

The real benefits of cam overlap become beneficial at high rpm. At low rpm, excessive cam overlap can be detrimental to a smooth idle and to low-speed performance.

Too much cam overlap can also make an engine hard or almost impossible to tune at low rpm, and either it or a late intake-valve closing event will cause excessive reversion. I'll cover reversion in Chapter 7, Compression 101.

Intake tract reversion is caused by the exhaust gasses and intake mixture, or just the latter, being pushed out of the cylinder backwards, past the intake valve, and back into the intake tract.

Other causes of reversion are restrictive exhaust systems or systems with no back pressure at all, like straight drag pipes. Running an exhaust system designed with an anti-reversion steep or cone at its beginning, or a system designed to reduce reversion by other means, like the Thunder Header, is always a wise choice for a street bike.

Remember that for straight drag pipes to be beneficial, they must be tuned to the exhaust wave pulse and will only work efficiently in a narrow power band width of approximately 1,500 rpm. When outside of that narrow power band width,

you're just making noise with straight drag pipes.

Almost all engines cause some degree of intake tract reversion. Too much reversion causes a rough idle, makes it hard to tune a motor at idle and low rpm, and also causes a loss of power at low speeds.

To use cam overlap to help prevent reversion, try to stay with a cam that has the smallest amount of overlap required to meet your performance needs. It's impossible to provide hard numbers on overlap, because everything depends on the motor combination you're running, and the motor's designed and intended use. Personally, I've had good results on performance motors running cams with 40 degrees of overlap and a lobe separation angle of 106 degrees or less.

LOBE SEPARATION ANGLE (LSA)

Lobe separation angle (LSA) is grounded into a cam and cannot be altered. To calculate LSA, add the intake lobe centerline to the exhaust lobe centerline (LC) and divide by 2.

(Intake LC + exhaust LC) ÷ 2 = LSA

CHANGING CAMS

Until the release of the Twin Cam, changing Harley cams just required a feeler gauge, a micrometer, and basic shop tools. The Twin Cam, on the other hand, requires several expensive

specialty tools to change the cams and bearings. These tools cost about same as a whole cam kit.

With the specialty tools in hand and access to a hydraulic or large arbor press, changing the cams is not too hard. You just need to be extra careful when you press the old cams and bearings out and the new ones in, because one slip could destroy your outer cam support plate and cost $$$!

Note: If you're changing cams on a 1999 Twin Cam, you need to replace the defective early rear cam drive gear (this gear has a weak cast-in set key) and install the later style version. You'll find even stronger drive gears available from aftermarket manufactures, like Andrews.

S&S and Andrews both carry a line of camshafts that use all-gear drive to replace the entire chain drive setup the stock Twin Cam system uses. The gear drive cam setup will make a little more noise than the chain drive setup, but it'll provide more accurate valve timing. And because the gear drive cams rotate in a different direction, higher lift cams can be run without lobe-to-lobe interference.

Note: S&S Cycle holds the patent rights to the gear drive cam setup for Twin Cam motors.

GEAR DRIVE TWIN CAM CAMS

Do you need to run gear drive cams in your Twin Cam? Maybe.

The Motor Company switched to chain drive cams to meet ever-increasing EPA noise regulations. By doing so, it reduced noise and improved the pushrod angle. Improving the pushrod angle on Big Twins was long overdue.

The chains used in Twin Cam motors are driven by two automotive-style timing chains referred to as silent chains. To help keep them at the proper tension, plastic fiber shoes and springs are used as chain tensioners.

Chains and tensioner shoes, however, have two weak points that should be addressed.

First, the chains are not installed tight. They have a small amount of slack in them and spring-loaded plastic shoes are used to help control this slack. Because a small amount of slack exists in the chains, it is reported that cam timing can fluctuate up to about 4 degrees.

The second weak point is the plastic shoe itself, as there is a chance the shoes will wear out, and people worry that pieces of plastic could interfere with the motor's oiling system. Again, high-quality synthetic oil will help prevent shoe wear.

So, do you need to install gear drive cams? It depends on your motor and your budget. Here's my opinion on the subject: If you're running stock valve springs and bolt-in cams, you would be better off worrying about a giant meteor from outer space destroying the Earth than worrying about the cam chain setup in your motor.

If you're a running a high-lift cam with an aggressive ramp profile, or modified heads with extra-strong valve springs, or both, gear drive cams make sense and may warrant the extra cost.

Consider this, though: The chains and shoes in your motor are paid for, so changing to gear drive cams will double the cost of the parts required for the cam change parts.

A rear-wheel dyno test may show the change in power from

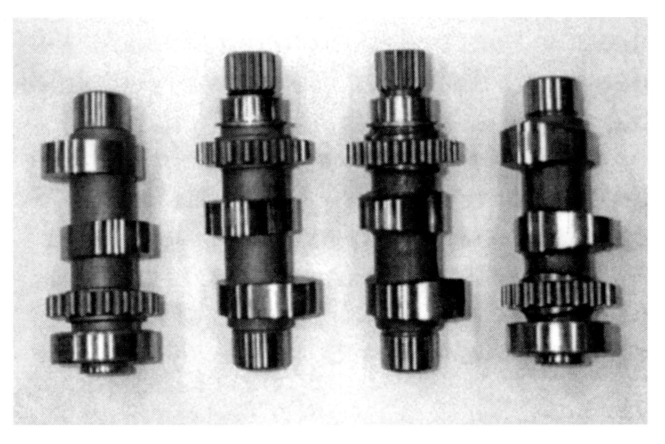

Twin-Cam cams: An Andrew's TW-37B (left) and a stock A cam for carbureted Twin Cams (right). The stock cams are rather rough looking when compared with aftermarket cams. There are two reasons for this. Production costs can be kept down, and you aren't ever supposed to see the stock cams anyway.

the stock chains, but you probably won't be able to feel the difference when you're riding the bike.

The plastic tensioner shoes will wear out over time, as most things do. How much damage they'll do in the long term is unknown to me, for I haven't had the chance to examine any high-mileage motors exhibiting excessive shoe wear.

I recently had a motor open that was running strong valve springs (185-psi seat pressure) and a bolt in 0.510-inch cam. This motor just had a little over 5,000 miles on it, 4,000 of which were with synthetic oil, and the shoes had zero wear on them. I only saw a slight mark on the shoes at the point where they engage the chains. You guessed it; running synthetic oil reduces shoe wear.

One advantage of gear drive cams is the fact they rotate in the opposite direction of chain drive cams, so you can run much larger lift gear drive cams without lobe-to-lobe interference. This is very attractive to people dealing with maximum effort motors for which high lifts are desired.

With the Andrews TW-55 cam, shown on p. 38, you can see the problem of lobe-to-lobe clearance when running the stock chain drive setup. The TW-55 has a 0.550-inch lift, and as you can see, there is not much clearance between the lobes. With the stock chain setup, 0.570 inch is about the maximum lift you can run with the stock rocker arm ratio, so if

you want to run a higher lift than that, you will have to use the gear drive setup.

Whenever you run high-lift cams in the Twin Cam motor, or any motor, always check for cam-lobe-to-cam-case clearance. Some high-lift cams will require that the cam chest be relieved for a proper fit.

The Motor Company switched to chain drive cams to reduce internal engine noise. It goes without saying that gear drive cams make more noise than the stock chain drive cams do. But with the loud exhaust systems most people run, you'd never know it.

LIFTER NOISE TIP

A local fellow just made the move up to a Harley Big Twin after years of riding foreign bikes and was annoyed by the sound his valvetrain made. I told him to fire up the bike and let me listen.

Valvetrain noise often comes from the lifters, and to me, his bike sounded perfectly normal for a stock Twin Cam.

It's a good thing he hasn't heard a Harley's valvetrain noise at its worst, like in an old production XR-1000 engine! With the valve lash properly set to factory specs for the solid-roller lifters, the upper end of those motors sounded like a rock crusher going full tilt. To remove some of the racket, I used to set the valve lash on the XR to half of the stock

39

This is a picture of me in New Jersey in 1980. The bike is an 80-ci Shovelhead Low Rider and the white stuff is snow. Does a little snow stop me from going for a ride? Of course not, and, yes, that's a pony bottle of Miller I'm holding! Snow, beer, bike: Sometimes I wonder how I've survived to have more gray hair than brown.

recommendation, which helped but it was still annoyingly loud.

The new Twin Cams and Sportsters run automotive Chrysler-style hydraulic-roller lifters, which are better than earlier Harley lifters.

If you want to improve your lifters and reduce tappet noise, try running a set of JIMS Big Axle Powerglide lifters (or their equivalents) and lightweight 7/16-inch aluminum pushrods. These lifters will help quiet even the nastiest beast if you're running performance cams, and will benefit street performance motors, too.

Be aware that if you do the work yourself, the lifters, pushrods, and gaskets will set you back about $400 in parts. If you change to shorter pushrod tubes to aid in adjusting the lifters, the cost will increase. But it's a nice upgrade for a stock or modified bike to quiet things down in the valvetrain.

You will also want to change the rear cam bearing in the cam support plate from the old-style ball bearing type to the later and stronger roller bearing type.

Using roller rocker arms on cams with lifts of 0.550-inch or more is always a good idea, as they will reduce side-thrust friction and increase valve guide and valve stem life.

Street performance motors with performance cams will also benefit from performance lifters like JIMS big-axle "Powerglide" lifters. The lifters also help to quiet down valve-train noise when running performance cams.

If you upgrade your lifters on an Evo or older V-twin, don't forget to upgrade your lifter blocks to matched performance units.

OTHER TWIN CAM CONSIDERATIONS
If you are planning to build an all-out maximum-effort Twin Cam motor, you may also want to consider upgrading

four other engine components:

1. The cast cam support plate: If you have an early cam support plate, you may want to trade it for a newer support plate, part number 25267-99B. The aftermarket also has a machined billet unit that is stronger than the stock cast support plate and is designed to be used with high-lift radical cams.

2. The rocker arm support plate: Again, the aftermarket has a stronger support plate that should be used when you're using valve springs with extreme seat pressures.

3. Cylinder-to-case studs: These are the four long studs that hold the heads and cylinders to the engine case. Harley's Screamin' Eagle line has stronger-than-stock heavy-duty case studs. If you decide to replace your studs, this would be an ideal time to upgrade to the stronger Screamin' Eagle studs.

4. Adjustable pushrods: If you run modified heads, you will need to use adjustable pushrods. Aluminum pushrods are lighter and make less noise than moly pushrods. Large-diameter aluminum pushrods work fine in most street applications. If you're building a maximum effort engine, though, by all means use the stronger and heavier moly steel pushrods. If you're rich, run the new titanium ones; they have the strength of the steel with the light weight of aluminum.

TWIN CAM SHORT PUSHROD TUBES

The stock Twin Cam lower pushrods tubes are rather long and make the task of adjusting the pushrods rather difficult. If you are planning to run stiffer moly-steel-style pushrods on your Twin Cam, you may want to consider purchasing the quick-install moly-steel pushrod set from H-D's Screamin' Eagle line, which comes with the shorter pushrod tube assemblies. The H-D part number for the Twin Cam quick-install moly steel pushrod kit is 17997-99.

If you choose to run a different brand of pushrods, you can piece together these shorter tubes by buying individual parts from Harley, but it is rather expensive. The last time I did this, the cost was about $60 for the four shorter lower tubes and the four retainer clips.

Here are the required parts you'll need to piece together the shorter pushrod tubes. These tubes will make the job of adjusting your adjustable pushrods easier:

Four pushrod covers, lower H-D 17938-83
Four keepers, pushrod covers H-D 17634-99

NOTES:

_____

_____

_____

_____

_____

_____

_____

_____

_____

_____

_____

_____

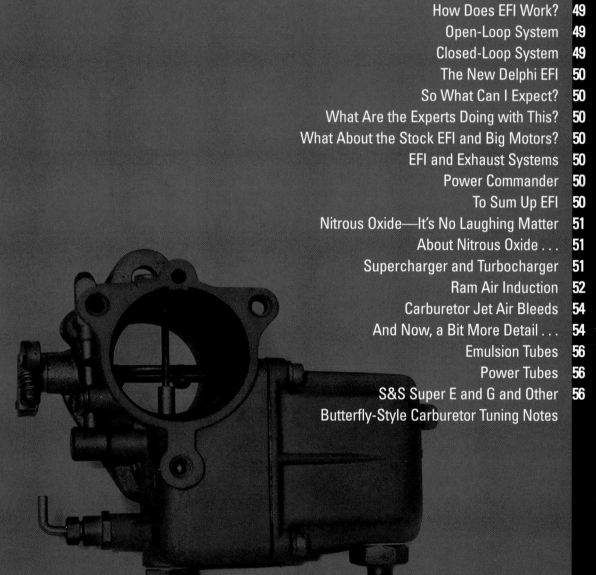

CHAPTER 4 **MIXING AIR AND FUEL**

OVERVIEW

Over the years, I have wrenched on just about every type and brand of carburetor popular for V-twins. I still remember the first time, many years ago, when I disassembled my first SU constant-vacuum carb. I was amazed at how complicated SU had made the job of mixing air and fuel together and naively thought the constant-velocity (CV) carb fad had to be on its way out. Boy, was I wrong.

Here we are in the twenty-first century, and Harley has now installed more Keihin CV-style carbs on its motorcycles than any other type, and with good reason.

The CV piston maintains a constant flow rate over the main jetting circuit, dependent on the air needs of the motor. Maintaining a constant flow rate at the jet does three things:

1. It meters fuel more accurately.

2. It can improve gas mileage.

3. Most importantly, it keeps the fellows at the EPA happy by minimizing pollution.

To its credit, the stock Keihin (when fixed) is a good carburetor. The only problem is the 40-millimeter size (really only 38.5 millimeters), which is too small for high-rpm use on big-inch motors.

Out of all of the carburetor brands on the market, I have the most experience installing, tuning, and modifying the S&S brand. I first started running S&S L-series carbs back in the 1970s, and I'm still running a 30-plus-year-old S&S GBL L-series gas carb on my 1959 XLCH. It works as great as it did when I installed it back in 1975. That's how reliable S&S carbs can be!

From the L-series, I moved up to the Super B and Super D. Now, it's mostly the Super E and G carbs that are used on the street.

There are a number of reasons why I like S&S carburetors. They're simple; they're reliable; they come as a complete kit; they are easy to tune; and they're fairly priced. About the only negative thing I can say about them is they have only a limited number of tuning circuits. We'll talk about adding tuning circuits to S&S carburetors later.

In addressing carburetors, I'll give you some general information that relates to all of them. But specifically, I'll only deal with stock Harley carbs, made by Keihin, and S&S Super carburetors. There are, of course, many other great carburetors on the market in addition to these two brands. For example, the excellent Mikuni HRS carbs. They are highly tunable, come in a variety of sizes, and work very well for performance use.

JETTING FOR ALTITUDE

As you go up in elevation, two things happen to a carburetor on a naturally aspirated engine: power goes down and your air/fuel mixture becomes richer. These things happen because air is less dense at higher elevations, meaning there are less oxygen molecules available for the combustion process.

There is only one way to make good power at high elevations, and that's with a power adder like a turbocharger.

When I had to jet for variable-elevation riding, I would

The SU CV carburetor: In the early days, it was originally designed for imported sports cars, but was adapted to V-twin intake manifolds. In the hands of professional racers like Carl Morrow of Carl's Speed Shop fame, it worked quite well. Carl liked the CV-type carburetor so much, he designed his own; it's called the Typhoon.

One of the downsides of running the SU was its large size. The carburetor on the right is an original stock Harley-Davidson Linkirt model DC carburetor of the same era. This particular DC carb is the larger model 12.

This is the front head from my Twin Cam project bike. It features Branch Flowmetric's famous bathtub chamber and has the Branch number 4 configuration, set up for maximum flow and velocity for a 95-inch motor. I have placed a gasket on the head so you can see the very generous squish band this chamber creates.

always jet for the lower elevation, because as I moved to higher elevations, my air/fuel mixture got richer.

If your engine is jetted rich, the worse thing that can happen is that it will become sluggish and possibly foul your spark plugs.

On the other hand, if you jet for the higher elevation, your mixture becomes leaner as you go down in altitude. As the mixture gets leaner, your motor will begin to run hotter. The first sign of this may be popping through the carburetor. If the motor's temperature continues to rise until it's over the safe level, catastrophic engine damage can occur. Now you know why sensor-driven computer-controlled fuel-injection systems really shine when you're dealing with elevation changes.

With S&S Super E and G carbs, you can adjust some of the richness out of the intermediate circuit by leaning out your idle mixture (turn the screw clockwise), as they are the same circuit. This may be all you need to do to correct the mixture from idle to 3,000 rpm, which is the normal operating range of your motor, anyway. Don't forget to readjust your idle mixture on the way back down.

EFFECTS OF BAROMETRIC PRESSURE

Barometric pressure and elevation have a lot in common, because they both relate to air density. Barometric pressure is expressed in either millibars or inches of mercury, and is measured by the distance that the given air pressure can push (usually) liquid mercury up a tube.

Most people think that as the piston moves down the cylinder on the intake stroke, it is sucking air and fuel into the cylinder. This is close to being true, but does not really explain what's happening. Here's the correct way to look at it. As the piston moves down the bore on the intake stroke, it creates a negative pressure area in the cylinder when compared to the atmospheric pressure outside of the cylinder, which is normally about 14.7 psi.

The difference between the outside air pressure and negative pressure inside the cylinder regulates the force of the incoming air during cylinder refill. So, if the barometric pressure is high on the outside of the cylinder, the cylinder refill will be greater than the rate you'd experience if the barometric pressure were lower.

In other words, you can make more power with high barometric pressure, due to increased cylinder refill. I keep a barograph near my shop and check it every time I go riding, and I've put little code marks on it. It's my code for: "Harleys go slow, Harleys go fast, Harleys go really fast." Remember, we shouldn't take ourselves too seriously. After all, we're in this for the fun!

In addition to air pressure, humidity also affects power. The less humidity there is, the more power you'll make.

CHANGES IN AIR TEMPERATURE

Temperature changes affect your air/fuel mixture because the density of the air changes along with the temperature.

Colder air is denser than warm air and will make your air/fuel mixture leaner. Warm air is less dense than cold air, and will cause your mixture to become richer. Just adjusting your idle mixture screw will usually correct this condition for normal riding, when your rpm are mostly below 3,000.

AIR/FUEL RATIOS AND BRAKE-SPECIFIC FUEL CONSUMPTION (BSFC)

The two most important things that affect BSFC are mixture turbulence and combustion chamber shape. The stoichiometric (or chemically perfect) air/fuel ratio is 14.7 parts air to one part fuel, or 14.7:1.

To produce the most power, every oxygen molecule must link up with a fuel molecule to burn and create power. Any unused oxygen molecules—ones that do not link up with fuel molecules and burn during the power stroke—end up as lost potential power exiting the exhaust port.

Air only holds so much oxygen, normally 21 percent. So if we can't add more oxygen to the air (actually we can with NO2, but we'll talk about later), at least we can try to ensure that every available oxygen molecule will find a fuel molecule and be consumed to make power.

We do this by increasing the amount of fuel in the air/fuel ratio. Air/fuel ratios can be as high as 12.0:1 and as low as 14.0:1. Of course, doing this may cause a higher amount of unburned fuel to exit the cylinder and be wasted, but that's the cost of making power. The way we reduce the amount of wasted fuel is by improving combustion efficiency. For maximum power, try for a ratio between 12.7:1 and 13.2:1. Remember, you always tune for maximum power, not for the best BSFC.

To improve combustion efficiency, a well-designed combustion chamber (like a bathtub chamber) with good turbulence (squish bands) will be required. It should also help lower the required air/fuel ratio and improve BSFC. A well-designed, high-performance street engine can, and often will

(if done correctly), get better highway gas mileage than a stock motor.

Here's an example: My 95-inch Dyna puts out about 100 horsepower and 100 lb-ft of torque, and the last time I checked the mileage I was getting about 50 highway miles to 1 gallon of 90 octane pump gas using an S&S Super E carb. S&S recommends that this motor should have a 0.031- or 0.0295-inch intermediate jet. This motor's combustion chamber is very efficient, though, with an extremely large squish band set up very tightly at only 0.025 inch, so it only requires a small 0.0265-inch intermediate jet. This is three jet sizes smaller than the recommended 0.031.

This motor also requires a small 0.068-inch main jet to achieve maximum top-end power on the dyno. The benefits of a well-designed combustion chamber are an increase in power and fuel economy.

AIR/FUEL RATIO METER

When the average person puts his bike on the dyno, he usually just wants to see big horsepower numbers for bragging rights. You know, the mine's-bigger-than-yours thing. The street performance guy, on the other hand, puts his bike on a dyno so he can tune it. To tell the truth, after running our bikes on the dyno, we hardcore performance guys usually start by saying, "I know my motor can do better than that!" In the end, if the motor was designed, built, and tuned right, the mine's-bigger-than-yours thing will take care of itself.

Would you believe me if I told you that for around $300 you could install a device on your bike that can and does work almost as good as a rear-wheel dyno to tune your carburetor? And you can use it all the time and every time you ride? You probably wouldn't believe me, but there is such a device.

Unless you have a tunable ignition and/or exhaust system, you're on the dyno to power tune your carburetor. Now you can use an air/fuel ratio meter to tune your carburetor without paying the man for time on the dyno. We know how expensive dyno time can be. The last time I tuned my main jet in Anchorage, I was charged $160 for only 30 minutes of dyno time. This was in addition to the cost of driving 230 miles to get to the dyno and back.

The air/fuel ratio meter consists of a display meter and an oxygen sensor that connects to your exhaust pipe. It constantly monitors the unburned oxygen exiting your exhaust port. Remember that unburned oxygen is lost power! The oxygen sensor, also called a Lambda sensor, is a major component of the closed-loop electronic fuel injection (EFI) system (which will be discussed later in this chapter).

Air/fuel ratio meters are extremely easy to connect. One wire goes to a switched positive power source, one wire goes to the battery's negative terminal, and one wire goes to the sensor. Tip: Always connect the negative ground wire directly to the battery, not the frame, to prevent picking up trace voltage from other sources.

You will need to drill a hole in your exhaust pipe and weld in a bung fitting so the oxygen sensor has something to screw into. Preferably, you want the sensor mounted as close to the exhaust port as possible, both to obtain the best reading and because the sensor doesn't start to operate until it reaches 600 degrees Fahrenheit. When installed correctly, the meters are very accurate, quick acting, and easy to use.

Let's look at the air/fuel ratio meter from RB Racing in Gardena, California, (310) 515-5720.

RB Racing's meter consists of a small 2-inch round gauge that is mounted somewhere in clear view. The oxygen sensor is made by Bosch. The meter has a series of 10 differently colored LED lights—green, yellow, orange, and red—for easy reading that dim automatically when it gets dark. The 10 LEDs cover the air/fuel ratio range from 17.1:1 (lean) to 12.1:1 (rich). Quality meters dis-

Here you can see how I mounted the gauges onto the Twin Cam project bike. The gauge cups are modified automotive gauge cups. The gauge on the right is the air/fuel ratio meter, which tells me what's happening on the exhaust side of the cylinder head. The gauge on the left is a vacuum meter, and it tells me what's going on in the intake side of the head. The gauges work hand in hand so you can dial in the perfect fuel curve.

play changes in air/fuel ratios almost instantaneously. Cheaper meters may not work fast enough, and the information may be unreliable. For these reasons, you should always buy a quality meter.

By monitoring the meter as you ride, you can see if your carburetor is jetted correctly over the entire operational range. If it is not, you can use the meter to correct the air/fuel mixture through jet changes on your carburetor. You can also use it to calibrate the idle mixture, intermediate jet, main jet air bleed, main jet, accelerator pump circuit, and, if installed, ThunderJet(s).

TUNING WITH AN AIR/FUEL RATIO METER

For tuning purposes, carburetors work in two modes: steady state and transient state.

Steady state is operating at a fixed speed and load (like doing a steady 55 miles per hour in fifth gear). When running in a steady state, you can use a leaner mixture closer to the chemically perfect ratio of 14.7:1.

Transient state is accelerating, load changing, or decelerating. Increasing the load and accelerating requires a richer mixture than a steady state, while decelerating has a leaner mixture.

Here are some ballpark numbers that the air/fuel ratio meter should display if your carburetor is jetted correctly. Remember each motor is different, and so is each of its fuel requirements.

Cold startup	=	10.3:1 to 11.1:1
Idling	=	12.25:1 to 13.5:1
Steady-state load	=	13.4:1 to 14.0:1
Acceleration heavy load	=	12.5:1 to 13.2:1
Deceleration	=	never leaner than 17.1:1

Unless the dyno numbers tell you differently, don't go richer (lower) than a 12.5:1 air/fuel ratio for maximum power. Personally, I run my project bike at 13:1.

Note: You cannot use leaded gas or gas additives unless the additives are safe for oxygen meters; otherwise they can destroy it. Nor will oxygen sensors work with nitrous oxide. If treated properly, on average your oxygen sensor probe should last 50,000-plus miles. If you're going to run leaded racing gas or nitrous, remove the sensor and install the plug that comes with most kits.

Unless you run a self-heated sensor, you may not be able to see your cold-start mixture ratio, as the sensor must be heated to 600-plus degrees Fahrenheit before it reads correctly. On my bike the gauge starts operating after about 30 seconds.

Once your meter is installed, it's always a good idea to run your bike on a dyno to verify the correct air/fuel ratio at which your bike makes its maximum power.

In addition to RB Racing, you can also get air/fuel ratio meters from K&N Engineering, Riverside, California, (800) 858-3333, and TWM Induction, Goleta, California, (805) 967-9478.

This is how I mounted the sensor to the Twin Cam test bike's front exhaust pipe. I painted the sensor black to make it inconspicuous and painted the weld with 1,500-degree aluminum to help prevent rust.

To make a long story short, if you're really serious about carburetor tuning, you need an air/fuel ratio meter.

PERSONAL EXPERIENCE

As you'll read later, after finding myself with a very bad fuel curve, I broke down and purchased the air/fuel ratio meter kit from RB Racing. I installed the sensor about 1 1/2 inches from the front cylinder's exhaust port using a set of the new Rinehart Racing pipes.

Drilling the pipe and welding the bung for the sensor was pretty straightforward; I just had to make sure the sensor clears the frame and everything else. Believe it or not, the hardest part of the whole installation was finding something to mount the gauge into, then mounting it on the bike so it wouldn't affect the bikes aesthetics. The meter also has a bright event light on it; for racing it could be used as a shift light. Finding neutral on a Harley can sometimes be a pain, so I wired the event light to come on when the transmission is in neutral.

What do I think about the air/fuel ratio meter kit? It works great and made jetting my carburetor a breeze. Considering how expensive dyno time is, the $295 the kit cost was money well spent. If I make changes to the motor, I don't need to pay the dyno guy anymore because I now have the same tool he uses to tune the air/fuel mixture. Now I can see what my air/fuel ratio is doing every second the motor is running. If you're serious about going fast and tuning a carburetor or fuel injection system, the air/fuel ratio meter is a very wise investment.

For performance work, you don't want to clog and block your exhaust pipe with the tip of the sensor. Here's what I do:

Here you can see the parts I used to install the sensor. I bent the washer to the shape of the pipe, then welded the bung to the washer. I then fish-plate welded the washer to the exhaust pipe.

Screw the sensor into the bung. Measure the distance from the base of the bung to the tip of the sensor. You will only want about 1/2 inch of the sensor tip sticking into the exhaust pipe. Do the math and find out how thick a washer or spacer you'll need to accomplish this. Then locate a piece of junk pipe that's about the same size as the outside of the exhaust pipe. Bend the washer so it fits flush against the exhaust pipe and weld the bung to the washer. Next, drill a hole in the exhaust pipe where you want to mount the sensor. As the washer will be larger than the bung, the hole you make in the pipe should be almost as large as the outside diameter of the bung. Then fish-plate weld the washer to the exhaust pipe. This gives the sensor a large area, or pocket, to analyze the exhaust gases. Lastly, screw in the sensor and make sure you use high-heat anti-seize compound on the sensor's threads.

SENSOR WARNING

I had a brand-new, still-in-the-box General Motors (GM) automobile oxygen sensor sitting in the shop. The GM sensor is a little smaller in overall size than the Bosch sensor that came with the air/fuel ratio meter kit. To me, a smaller oxygen sensor means it's easier to hide. So for the heck of it, I removed the kit's large Bosch sensor, installed the GM sensor, and started the motor. Big mistake! This motor likes to idle warm at 13.0:1. With the GM sensor installed, the gauge was reading between 16:1 and 16.5:1! We're talking melted pistons at a ratio this lean! I reinstalled the original Bosch sensor that came with the kit and it was back to 13.0:1.

This is why I highly recommend you save the box your sensor kit came in, or at least write down the brand name and part number for the sensor that came with the kit. If you ever need to replace the sensor, to be on the safe side and always replace it with the exact same type.

ELECTRONIC FUEL INJECTION (EFI)

Depending on how efficiently, or inefficiently, your carburetor is metering fuel, a high-performance EFI system could produce a 15–25 percent increase across the board in both torque and horsepower. Unfortunately, to many old-time performance people, EFI is some kind of complicated, unreliable, dark-art device that should be avoided at all costs. If you gave them a bike with EFI on it, they would rip it off and install a carburetor. That's too bad, because nothing could be further from the truth. EFI is the best thing since sliced bread for performance applications.

HOW DOES EFI WORK?

When you look at the components that make up an EFI system, the whole thing looks complicated. Luckily, all EFI systems basically work the same way, and once you understand how one works, none of them should be intimidating.

EFI systems inject fuel through nozzles, under pressure (44–50 psi), and directly into the intake tract. The closer the injector is to the intake valve, the better. The brain of the unit is the electronic control unit (ECU); it's basically a microprocessor (or computer) and controls the amount of fuel that's injected. The ECU is connected to various engine sensors. Depending on the system, it could use any or all of the following sensors:

- Crankshaft position sensor
- Throttle position sensor
- Rpm sensor
- Manifold absolute pressure (MAP) sensor
- Engine temperature sensor
- Atmospheric pressure sensor
- Air temperature sensor
- Oxygen sensor

Your ECU takes real-time information from the sensors and processes it by comparing the incoming information to a pre-programmed fuel map. Then it delivers precise fuel metering through the injectors for hundreds of possible operating conditions. For metering fuel over the entire operating range of your motor, the best-tuned carburetor could only come close to the accuracy of an EFI system.

There are two basic types of EFI systems: open loop and closed loop.

OPEN-LOOP SYSTEM

In these systems, the ECU operates in the stand-alone mode and receives data from any of the sensors mentioned in the previous section, except for the oxygen sensor. It then compares that information to a fixed pre-programmed fuel map (or program) and tells the injectors how much fuel to deliver to the intake tract. Until recently, both of the stock Harley EFI units were stand-alone open-loop systems.

CLOSED-LOOP SYSTEM

These systems do what an open-loop system does, then go beyond that. Closed-loop systems use an oxygen sensor mounted in the exhaust pipe to monitor oxygen content in the exhaust gases. It sends this information back to the ECU, which compares the real-time oxygen data with what the optimum oxygen content should be. If the real-time information shows the levels are incorrect, the ECU will adjust the fuel delivery amount to correct the air/fuel ratio. There is virtually no lag time for the correction.

Because the closed-loop system is self-correcting, you can see why it is superior to the open-loop system. Of the two, the closed-loop system is the best choice for performance work.

Some of the bad press regarding EFI systems on V-twins came from Harley's first EFI system. That system used the Magneti-Marelli injector and consisted of dual 38-millimeter throttle bodies using a split runner system. (Except for the single runners on the XR-1000, this was the first time Harley used a split runner system on a street production bike.)

Harley called this system a twin-runner 38-millimeter sequential-port EFI. This open-style EFI system worked very well for its intended use.

But for performance use it was undesirable because it restricted airflow and there was no way to reprogram the ECU. Unfortunately, there were no performance programmable read-only memory (PROM) chips available to change the fuel map. And if you can't change the fuel map, you can't make any changes to the bike.

The K&N Power Commander addresses changing the parameters in the ECU. It allows you to make changes to the bike, but still does not change the airflow restriction problem.

Harley has now come out with the new optional Delphi

single-throat 45-millimeter EFI system, which I haven't had a chance to evaluate yet. Hopefully, it will flow more air than the 38-millimeter system. If teamed up with the Power Commander III, the new Delphi EFI system should easily outperform motors running the stock Keihin carbs.

THE NEW DELPHI EFI

The new Delphi fuel-injection system has plugged the hole that the older system had. The new system has an oxygen sensor in the exhaust pipe, so it's a closed-loop system. By having this sensor, the ECU can adjust fuel delivery instantaneously by identifying the contents of the exhaust gases exiting the cylinder head. A closed-loop system is far superior for performance use, so we should capitalize on how we can use it.

First, let's start with a reality check. We must remember that the Motor Company must comply with tight EPA air pollution regulations. So to meet these regulations, it may have switched over to a closed-loop system to produce cleaner-burning engines. After all, this was one of the prime motivators for developing the new Twin Cam engine.

As I truly believe that any stock motor can be improved, we'll take a closer look at this new EFI system and see what we have to work with.

By the time you're done with this chapter, you'll spot two required modifications right away: the ECU and the air cleaner. The ECU will limit the amount of fuel the injectors will deliver and the air cleaner will restrict the amount of air that can enter the fuel-injection body. So we will need to replace the air cleaner with a high-flow unit and find a device that will interface with the ECU and allow us to adjust the fuel delivery to meet our modified motor's air/fuel requirements. By the time you read this, you will have many aftermarket devices to choose from that will do just this.

You'll also want to look at Chapter 8, Do It Yourself at Home Head Fix, where I will explain how to improve the flow characteristics of the induction tract and how to blend manifolds to head ports. The same rules that apply to carburetor intake tracts also apply to EFI tracts.

SO WHAT CAN I EXPECT?

If tuned correctly, you'll end up with a fuel delivery system that is light years ahead of our old beloved carburetors. Why? Well, technology is the answer, and it may intimidate some of us old-timers because we like to turn screws, change jets, and beat on things with hammers. With EFI, those days are gone! Now we have to tune computer components with other computers. Sadly, screwdrivers are becoming a thing of the past.

EFI is not that hard to deal with once you understand how it works and how to adjust it correctly. You will be rewarded for embracing this new motorcycle technology. If that's not enough motivation, just remember what happened to the dinosaurs.

WHAT ARE THE EXPERTS DOING WITH THIS?

To sum it up, two words: good things. Branch Flowmetrics, using its components and the stock retuned EFI system, was able to produce motors in the 100-lb-ft and 100-horsepower range. Those are good numbers with the stock EFI parts.

WHAT ABOUT THE STOCK EFI AND BIG MOTORS?

Sorry, but it's time to take out your wallet. On really big motors the stock parts won't cut it here. Why? They can't flow enough air or deliver enough fuel to feed big-inch motors. If you're looking at big-inch motors and you want them to keep building power up to or past the 6,000-rpm range, you will need the following: a larger-than-stock throttle body and intake manifold; larger high-capacity fuel injectors; and a fuel pump that can handle and produce both higher fuel volume and pressure.

EFI AND EXHAUST SYSTEMS

Earlier in this chapter, I showed you how I installed the 14-millimeter bung on the project bike's front exhaust pipe, and I will admit my process was a little labor intensive. Now that the new closed-loop EFI systems are commonplace, the aftermarket has started installing the bung needed to mount the oxygen sensor onto the pipes before you buy them. Very recently, I purchased a new set of Rinehart Racing pipes, and there was the bung ready to go.

Unfortunately for me, the bung was located about a foot from the exhaust port. I prefer to have my air/fuel ratio meter as close to the exhaust port as I can possibly get it. The situation I'm concerned about is called mixture delusion—when the air outside of the exhaust system mixes with the exhaust gases after the exhaust pulse exits the pipe. I moved the meter to the new location dictated by Rinehart and found that as long as the motor was turning 2,000-plus rpm, the air/fuel ratio meter works quite accurately. At idle, though, the meter jumped all over the place because of the mixture delusion, but, it was a small price to pay to avoid the hassle of cutting the pipe and welding in the bung. Besides, idle is what your motor does when you're not making power. So really, it's unimportant in the grand scheme of our goal to make more power.

POWER COMMANDER

The Power Commander II by Dynojet is for the Magneti-Marelli system, and the Power Commander III is for the new Delphi EFI system. By the time you read this, there should be numerous systems to choose from.

TO SUM UP EFI

Even with my bag of tricks to modify tuning circuits on my beloved S&S carburetors, I know that the best I can hope for is to get it really close to where it should be, because the carburetor is a fixed mechanical device. Once the jets are set, it meters the fuel the same way all the time. It can't adjust its metering to correct fuel delivery for environmental changes in barometric pressure, altitude, temperature, humidity, different grades of fuel, etc. But a closed-loop EFI system can do all this.

It constantly monitors and changes the fuel delivery to ensure you are getting maximum performance all of the time.

So I'm now looking into RB Racing's high-performance V-twin EFI system. After 30 years, I may finally be ready to remove my S&S carburetor and install the future of high-performance fuel delivery. The downside to this system is that it is very expensive, in the $2,300 range, so the price will keep it out of most people's budgets.

NITROUS OXIDE—IT'S NO LAUGHING MATTER

Pros: How much boost can you get from N2O? A 50 percent increase is possible with the right combination.

One of the nice things about nitrous oxide is that it will work very well on a motor that is primarily stock. You can save the money that most people spend on cams, headwork, high compression pistons, etc., by just buying a nitrous system. After installing the nitrous system with a free-flowing exhaust system, just open the throttle, push the button, and hang on.

If you want to run nitrous oxide, I recommend that you purchase a complete quality system from a company that has a proven track record with nitrous systems, like Nitrous Oxide Systems (NOS) of Cypress, California, (714) 821-0580.

Cons: Nitrous requires you to mount a bulky N2O storage bottle on your bike.

The bottles tend to empty in a very short space of time. Depending on the bottle size, maybe only a few passes.

If you screw up big-time with nitrous oxide, you will blow your motor into many small pieces.

ABOUT NITROUS OXIDE . . .

Nitrous oxide, or "squeeze," as it's often called in the performance world, is the same stuff the dentists use to make your visit to their office a bit more pleasurable. First, let's start off with what nitrous oxide isn't. Some people believe that it is an extremely dangerous volatile chemical, right up there with nitromethane and dynamite. Those comparisons are unjust.

In reality, as its name implies, nitrous oxide belongs to a group of chemicals called oxidizers, which means that when it reacts to something, it releases oxygen. For our use in making power, N2O reacts to heat and being compressed or squeezed, as in its nickname, N2O is a simple three-part molecule containing two parts of nitrogen (N2) and one part oxygen (O), or 67 percent nitrogen and 33 percent oxygen. The air around you only contains 21 percent oxygen, 78 percent nitrogen, and a 1 percent mixture of other gases.

Remember when I said air has just 21 percent oxygen and you can't change that fact? Well, running nitrous oxide will. That's because N2O contains roughly 1.6 times more oxygen, by volume, than normal air, and if we have more oxygen in our cylinders, we can add and burn more fuel. Therefore, we can produce more heat, and more heat means more power.

To get N2O to release its 33 percent oxygen content, all we have to do is inject it into the intake tract or the cylinder. On the compression stroke, the N2O will be heated

and compressed. The molecules will then break down and release oxygen.

Additionally, nitrous is stored under pressure, and when it's released into the low pressure of the intake tract, the gas is very cold. As cold air is denser than warm air, it will generate more power.

If we just ran the nitrous oxide by itself, it would create a dangerously over-lean condition. So when we inject the nitrous, we have to inject the correct amount of extra fuel along with it to get the correct air/fuel ratio. Failing to do so will cause catastrophic engine damage.

I've just touched on the very basics of running nitrous oxide. If you are really considering running N2O, you should contact some system manufacturers or buy a book that explains in detail how the systems work and what is required to install them properly.

SUPERCHARGER AND TURBOCHARGER

The two main mechanical power adders are the supercharger, or blower, and the turbocharger, or turbo. Both blowers and turbos can make an astounding amount of extra power.

The downside to either of these power adders is that most people buy Harleys or V-twin clones for their looks. After you've installed all of the plumbing required to operate a turbo, or all of the bulky stuff for a blower, you've lost the clean lines and style of the Harley motor. Looks often mean everything when it comes to Harleys!

Superchargers are generally run off the motor's crankshaft by gears or belts. Because you must use engine power to turn the supercharger, it causes parasitic loss, which means driving it robs some power from the rear wheel. But it produces lots of extra power, so who cares? The only personal experience I've had with blowers has been on marine diesel engines, not V-twins. Although I have a firm understanding of their operation and could waste considerable time discussing them, I am, instead, going jump into my favorite power adder—the turbo.

The turbocharger is the most logical choice of the two for street performance use. I call turbochargers "free horsepower" because they utilize otherwise wasted exhaust gas to power them.

Depending on your motor's thermal efficiency, only about one-third of the heat energy you create is used to force the piston down the cylinder, and the rest is lost through heat absorption or friction, or is wasted out your exhaust pipe.

If captured, however, these exhaust gases still contain a lot of heat energy. Turbos capture and utilize this heat energy to drive the vanes in the turbocharger; the rotating vanes then force more air/fuel mixture into your cylinders, which means you get more power.

Turbochargers are contained in a housing that is divided into two parts and includes two sets of rotating vanes, or impellers.

The exhaust gases drive the vanes in the exhaust section, and a shaft connects the exhaust section to the intake section. The intake side of the turbo draws air in and then pressurizes it before sending it into the intake tract. The rpm of the motor and the volume of exhaust gases being produced to spin the vanes regulate the amount of boost pressure the turbo can provide.

To regulate the desired amount of boost, a physical device called a waste gate is used. In addition to the waste gate, another safety device called a pop-off valve is often used to protect the system from over pressurization. A mechanical failure that results in over pressurization on the intake side of the turbo will cause severe engine damage.

Turbo lag is the time it takes for the velocity of the air/fuel mixture to catch up with the volume demand. Turbo lag used to be a big problem with turbos on V-twin motors. In the early days, using the wrong size of turbo, usually ones that were too big, was the main cause of this.

Impeller vane design also played a big part in turbo lag, but the new variable-vane turbos are great and have eliminated much of the turbo lag caused by the old-style vanes. Because there are turbochargers now specially made for V-twin motors, thus their size is properly matched, turbo lag is virtually a thing of the past.

There are two basic types turbochargers, the draw-though and the blow-through.

The draw-through system brings air through the carburetor first, and then the air goes through the turbo and into the cylinder heads. The Air Forced 1 turbo system, which used to be sold by RC Components, was a draw-through type turbo system.

Blow-through systems bring air through the turbo first, and then blow the air into the carburetor and into the heads. The popular Aerocharger is a blow-through type system.

There are many important advantages and disadvantages to both of these systems, and covering them here would require considerable space. So, if you are considering running a turbo, I recommend that you buy a book on turbos and become familiar with all aspects of their operation before choosing a system. Jeff Hartman's Turbocharging Performance Handbook is the most recent; there's also Corky Bell's Maximum Boost: Designing, Testing and Installing Turbocharger Systems, and the classic Turbochargers by Hugh MacInnes.

Here are a few considerations to keep in mind while reading your turbo book.

First, you have to mount the damn thing. One of the more obvious mounting problems is that your legs can't occupy the same space as the turbocharger and all of its plumbing. Besides, these suckers get hot and there is a lot of exposed surface area on them. Touching an operating turbo with any part of your body can be quite painful and is not recommended.

No matter which system you choose, to run more than 10 psi of boost you will need an electric fuel pump to supply enough fuel to the carburetor. Full throttle operation requires about 4 psi, and going above that causes many carburetors to run into metering problems. Your electric fuel pump may also require extra fuel fittings on your fuel system or fuel tank.

Most turbos require a separate and adequate supply of clean circulating motor oil for cooling and lubrication, so you may need to find a supply source for this oil. There are a few self-lubricating turbos systems that do not require a separate oil supply.

Motorcycles that run turbos often utilize carburetors for fuel delivery. Due to their demanding fuel requirements, turbochargers—like naturally aspirated motors—will always be able to perform better with EFI than with a carburetor.

Another problem that severely affects a turbo's potential performance is the fact that incoming air is excessively heated as it passes through the extremely hot turbocharger.

Hot air is less dense than cold air, so it severely diminishes the turbo's potential power output. Anything you can do to cool the air after it goes through the turbo housing is worth consideration. Over the years, people have gone to great lengths to correct this problem, sometimes with success, other times meeting with failure. Trying to cool down this air is a logistical pain in the butt! The device used to cool the air charge is called an intercooler.

Of the many V-twin-specific turbo systems I have seen, I liked the simplicity of the R.C. Components Air Forced 1 draw-through system. It was one of the cleanest and least complicated looking systems available. Unfortunately, it is no longer being produced. Maybe you can find one just sitting around somewhere.

Just as I like fuel injection, I really like turbocharging, and I wish I had a bike that I could devote just to turbocharging. Maybe someday I will!

Anyway, if I were asked what kind of V-twin street bike powerplant I would build to put the fear of God into those multicylinder imported sportbikes, it would be a light bike, like a Twin Cam Dyna or an even lighter bike like the Sportster. It would displace at least 100 inches, with a 4-inch or larger bore and a short 4-inch stroke. The short stroke would allow for fast revving without causing piston damage. The motor would be designed to run at a sustained 7,000 rpm running through a six-speed gearbox.

For fuel, it would be turbocharged, running about 10 psi of boost with an intercooler that would be adjustable up to 15 psi if needed, and it would have a closed-loop EFI system. I might run some squeeze too, but that might be overkill. If done correctly, this combination could produce an awesome torque band. If you could produce 150 lb-ft of torque at 7,000 rpm, you'd be looking at 200 horsepower!

If you're going to do something like this, invest in a good set of brakes, buy lots of rear tires, and double your life insurance.

RAM AIR INDUCTION

There has been a recent trend in the manufacture and use of expensive air cleaner assemblies that resemble ram air induction devices. This trend is prolific enough to warrant a factual explanation of what ram air actually does and, more importantly, what it does not do.

I hate to see people waste their money and, in presenting this information, I realize I will upset a few people and equipment manufacturers, so I will apologize now if the truth

This is the backing plate of the excellent, no-hype S&S air cleaner. It has all the elements we're looking for to make the air flow into the carburetor in a smooth, linear fashion. The backing plate has a large-radius entryway that increases the size of the carburetor's throat area. The throttle plate on this carb has been modified (drilled).

The cover protects the airflow from being disrupted by buffeting effects of wind, and the directional cone helps guide the airflow into the center of the carburetor's throat.

hurts. At the very beginning of this book, I said some things work and some things just cost you money. Unfortunately, many of these devices sold may fall into the latter category.

There has been a great deal of research and development work on the subject of motorcycle ram air induction. Japanese sportbike manufacturers know a few things about making bikes go really fast. Led by Kawasaki, they put a lot of time and yen into developing truly sophisticated ram air induction systems. Two American companies, WesTech and

Airtech, have also devoted a considerable amount of time designing truly efficient ram air systems.

These experts discovered that ram air can increase an engine's efficiency by a small amount, but this improvement only happens at extremely high speeds. Performance gains are negligible at speeds of less than 100 miles per hour.

Here's the maximum benefit you can expect from a highly efficient ram air induction system. At 100 miles per hour, you'll get about a 1.7 percent boost in atmospheric pressure. So, instead of the normal 14.7 psi entering your motor, you would be exposing your motor to an ambient air pressure of up to 14.8 psi. So, at 100 miles per hour, the best-designed ram air system will gain you about 0.1 psi. The benefit is tiny.

At 150 miles per hour you could raise the boost to about 2.5 percent above ambient, or 15.0 psi—a boost of 0.3 psi; still not much.

At 200 miles per hour, the potential boost would be up to 4.7 percent, and the ambient air pressure would be 15.4 psi, again up from 14.7 psi. This gain may sounds significant, but when you compare it to the 24.7 psi of pressure coming from a turbo running at only 10 psi of boost, it's not much.

So what do these numbers mean? In the real world at speeds below 100 miles per hour, there are almost no beneficial gains from ram air, and how often do you ride above 100 miles per hour?

On the other hand, here's another way to look at the potential benefits of ram air. Let's say you have a Japanese sportbike that can do 175 miles per hour without ram air. With the most sophisticated ram air system installed, the bike could now potentially achieve a maximum speed of 177.3 miles per hour, a 2.3-mile-per-hour gain. That may not sound like much, but to a professional racer, a 2.3-mile-per-hour gain is a big deal.

At speeds above 200 miles per hour, we'll realize some actual benefits from ram air. But when was the last time you had your bike up to 200 miles per hour?

Now let's talk about a naturally aspirated motor. On such a motor, we want the air to enter our carburetors in an organized, smooth, linear fashion.

Air cleaners like the S&S teardrop units are designed to do just that. We also know that at speeds of less than 100 miles per hour, there are negligible gains from ram air.

So, if you run one of these so-called ram air cleaners, you could actually be decreasing your power output. Here's why: When air enters the front of these things, the air inside the air cleaner can be tossed all over the place due to turbulence, which accomplishes exactly the opposite of what we want, because it disrupts the smooth linear progression of air entering the throat of our carburetor. And, the faster you go, the more turbulence there will be to disrupt things.

The bottom line is that most of these things will not increase power and, depending on how badly they disrupt the air steam flowing into your carburetor, they can actually cost you power.

Remember that lost power won't show up on the dyno, because on the dyno your bike is not moving! If you want to run one of these devices because you think they look cool, I can live with that. But please stop trying to tell me how much extra power you're getting from one of these things, because I do know that some things work and some things just cost you money.

CARBURETOR JET AIR BLEEDS

Here is a brief explanation of what carburetor jet air bleeds are and, more importantly, what they do.

Most carburetor jetting circuits are twofold. That is, they contain an air bleed and a fuel metering jet. The metering jet does just that: it meters the amount of fuel that can enter the jetting circuit and be discharged into the air stream.

The air bleed does three things. It controls when the fuel metering jet starts to deliver fuel to the circuit; it mixes (emul-

The main job of the emulsion tube is to mix (or atomize) air and fuel together before the components are introduced to the carburetor's air stream.

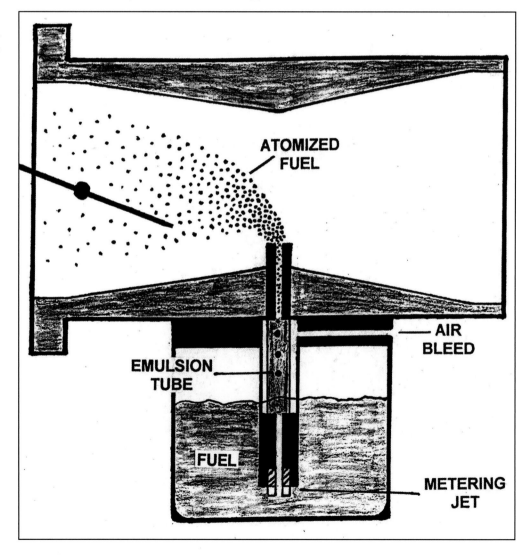

ATOMIZED FUEL

AIR BLEED

EMULSION TUBE

FUEL

METERING JET

sifies) the air and fuel together to make the mixture's viscosity lighter; and, in the case of the main jet, it provides an air correction factor to help prevent over-richening of the mixture during transition.

AND NOW, A BIT MORE DETAIL . . .

When the signal is presented to the jetting circuit (in the case of the low-speed jet, the signal is usually vacuum), it will first start to flow air from the air bleed through the emulsion tube and into the carburetor's throat. The size of the air bleed controls how strong the vacuum signal must be before it allows fuel to start flowing into the air stream. This is due to the fact that air is lighter than fuel, and it can pass through the jet's circuit easier.

Therefore, when the signal at the jet is increased to a predictable point, fuel also starts to pass through the emulsion tube and into the carburetor's air stream, so by changing the size of the air bleed, we can control when the jet starts to deliver fuel. More about this later.

The second job of an air bleed is to mix, or emulsify, the air and fuel together. This is done with a device called an emulsion tube. If we were to allow only fuel to pass into the carburetor's air stream, it would look like water being discharged from the end of a garden hose. In this condition, the fuel would be entering the air stream in large and heavy droplets, which would cause the fuel to fall out of the air stream. If this happened, the fuel would create puddles in the carburetor

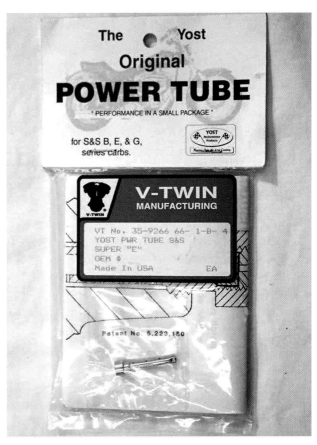

On the left is an original stock Harley-Davidson Linkirt model DC carburetor. This is the larger model 12 and was stock equipment on Harley Big Twins and Sportsters until 1965. A smaller version was used on the 45-inch flatheads. The design of the carburetor was fairly simple, and it worked well. The model DC carb was used somewhat successfully for racing, but its main drawback was its small size; because of this, the carb's throat was sometimes bored larger. S&S Cycle fixed that problem when it released its L-series carburetors.

and the intake manifold, both of which are bad things.

So to prevent this, we'll use an air bleed and an emulsion tube to mix the air and fuel together before we allow it to enter the carburetor's air stream. Instead of a garden hose–type discharge, we have a finer aerosol-like mist.

In this state, the fuel's viscosity is lighter, so it will flow easier and respond quicker to signal changes. This lighter and finely distributed fuel will do a better job of resisting separation from the air stream on its way to the cylinder heads. Logic dictates that when the fuel is broken down into a mist and mixed with air before it enters the carburetor's air stream, we get a better result. We accomplish this by using an emulsion tube.

EMULSION TUBES

The job of an emulsion tube is to mix air and fuel together before the components enter the carburetor's air stream. Racers, especially drag racers, have been modifying emulsion tubes for years. When done correctly, it can yield small but worthwhile power gains.

The downside of the process is the tedious work required to find the precise combination that increases power instead of deceasing power. There's a lot more to the process than just increasing the size, number, or location of holes in the emulsion tube. For example, racers spend hours testing different combinations to find something that works, because it may mean the difference between winning and losing. For the street performance bike, this time-consuming effort is often not warranted and usually above the ability of an average rider.

S&S Cycle's L-series carb was its answer to the small size of the model DC carburetor. The L went straight to the drag strip and started S&S's reputation for building winning carburetors. This particular one is a model GBL and has a 1 3/4-inch throat. It has been mixing air and fuel together on my 1959 XLCH for almost 30 years! If you look under the intake manifold, you can see one of the two single-fire ignition modules.

POWER TUBES

If modifying the emulsion tube is beyond the ability of the average rider, is there anything you can do to improve the performance of emulsion tubes? Yes, you can try the Yost Power Tube. Bob Yost invested a great deal of time designing and testing his drop-in power tube kits. At present, he has emulsion power tubes for S&S, Keihin, and Mikuni brand carburetors.

I am often asked if these power tubes will increase a bike's power output. I always answer honestly: I don't know. Unlike Yost, I have not personally conducted before-and-after dyno testing of the tubes. I have used these tubes in two of my bikes. I would even try one on my 1959 Sporty, but Yost does not make a power tube for my 30-year-old S&S L-series gas carb.

Despite my lack of personal dyno testing, I can still present an overview and my opinion about their operation, based on the theory of making power. We already discussed the benefits of a highly atomized fuel mixture, which include the fuel flowing easier and responding quicker to signal changes, and one of the most important benefits is the fact that the mixture will be less susceptible to fuel separation. These benefits alone warrant the use of power tubes.

From a theory standpoint, the answer of making more power is not as clear. Most of the homogenizing of the air/fuel mixture takes place inside the cylinder head and is caused by effective squish band turbulence during the compression process, as well as from mixture swirl and tumbling as the mixture enters the cylinders. Combustion chamber design can also play a small role in causing mixture turbulence.

If your motor's squish band is set up correctly, it is debatable how much, if any, additional mixing, or homogenizing, will be achieved. Of course, if your motor does not have effective squish, the benefits from power tubes may be more pronounced.

One benefit that I've noticed with Yost power tubes that is not used in their marketing pitch is a slight increase in fuel economy from the main jet circuit. After installing a power tube, I have often found that a smaller main jet may be required.

In conclusion, there is nothing in the design or operation of the power tube that should cause a decrease in performance; if anything, the opposite should happen. If you want to run one of these power tubes, by all means do so. Remember, Yost sells a bunch of these things and I have utilized them as well.

S&S SUPER E AND G AND OTHER BUTTERFLY-STYLE CARBURETOR TUNING NOTES

Carb sizes, Venturi comparison, stock H-D compared to S&S Super E and G carbs:

The stock Keihin
38.5 millimeters = 1.4687 inches
Area = 1.6933 square inches

S&S Super E
39.6 millimeters = 1.5625 inches
Area = 1.9165 square inches

S&S Super G
44.5 millimeters = 1.750 inches
Area = 2.4040 square inches

S&S SUPER E
JETTING—MY RECOMMENDATIONS

Note that results from these numbers create a leaner mixture than is usually listed in books.

Efficient combustion chamber: 0.0280–0.0295-inch intermediate, 0.070-inch main

Inefficient combustion chamber (Hemi): 0.031-inch intermediate, 0.070–0.072-inch main

S&S jets are size rated in inches: 295 = 0.0295 inch; 31 jet = 0.031 inch; 70 = 0.070 inch; 72 = 0.072 inch S&S intermediate jet size = drill bit size 28 = 70 drill, 295 = 69 drill (really 0.0292 inch), 31 = 68 drill

Should you modify your main jet air bleed? Yes, because you can fix the over-rich condition that often happens between 3,000 and 3,500 rpm.

S&S INTERMEDIATE JET

Tuning the intermediate jet is relatively easy. When using the seat-of-your-pants method to tune the S&S Super E or G intermediate jet, always turn the accelerator pump off before you start to tune the circuit. The correct jet will do the following: When you slowly roll the throttle on the bike, it should smoothly accelerate. If it hesitates or spits through the carb when doing this, the jet is too lean.

Next, give the throttle a sudden, small, quick twist open (say one-quarter turn). The motor should hesitate or stumble before it catches up with the vacuum signal. If the motor does not hesitate at all, but smoothly accelerates when you do this, the jet is too big.

When you've found the jet that accelerates smoothly on a slow roll on, and hesitates a bit on a short, quick opening, you have located the correct jet and can now adjust your accelerator pump to eliminate the quick throttle opening hesitation. Use only the minimum amount of accelerator pump required to make this hesitation go away. Too much accelerator pump will waste gas and foul spark plugs.

The number of turns out on the idle mixture screw will give you a good indication as to the proper intermediate jet size. S&S recommends one to one-and-one-half turns out. I've found that approximately one turn or less out will give you a truer indication of the proper intermediate jet size. This is especially true if you are modifying the main jet air bleed circuit. If you modify the main jet air bleed, you are correcting the over-rich condition at the transition point, which is the point where one jetting circuit stops delivering fuel and another jet takes over the control of fuel delivery. Now you can utilize a larger intermediate jet, if needed, for more power in the midrange—from idle to 3,500 rpm.

S&S MAIN JET

You can spend hours trying to do this by the seat-of-your-pants method and you may even get it right. Or you can spend some money and get it exactly right through dyno tuning.

I always recommend dyno tuning the main jet, because the average riders need a 10 percent power change (good or bad) before they can feel it by the seat of their pants, while the dyno's computer can recognize a change as small as 1 percent.

Remember that when you run your bike on a rear-wheel dyno, don't automatically believe the numbers you receive. I witnessed two Harleys being run on a dyno, one right after the other at an Anchorage motorcycle shop. Both owners forked over hard-earned money for the printed results, and both owners walked away with false readings of 7 percent over their correct power values. The sad thing was that neither of these fellows knew that they had just been had.

So how did this happen? The operator used a false barometric reading that was almost 80 millibars lower than the correct pressure. There are a number of reasons why this can happen:

1. The operator may have been lazy and just didn't bother to enter vital information.

2. The operator was not properly trained or didn't really care if the information was correct or not.

3. The operator deliberately wanted to get higher-than-correct values.

Reason number 3 requires the operator do something deliberately; having witnessed it, I'll vote for reasons 1 & 2 as more likely. Will the dyno owner refund the money? Maybe when pigs fly, and I don't mean when Harleys go fast!

Arm yourself with information. The V-Twin Tuner's Handbook, Volume Two, by D. William Denish, has an excellent and extensive section on what every bike owner should know before going to the dyno shop. The book is cheaper than a dyno test, so buy and read the book first. If the bike owners we discussed earlier had read Denish's book, red lights should have started flashing when they saw a correction value of 1.07 percent, considering the dyno runs were done on a nice, dry, sunny day at sea level with an air temp of 70 degrees Fahrenheit. While we're on the subject, if you're really serious about V-twin performance, buy every book that Denish has written or will write in the future!

Back to S&S Super carburetors. The stock main jet air bleed on S&S Super B, E, and G carbs are 0.042 inch. The D carb had a 0.040-inch fixed air bleed, but now it comes with an adjustable main jet air bleed.

Enlarging the main jet air bleed causes a delay (in rpm) when the main jet starts delivering fuel. It will also lean-out the main jet circuit. Because of this, you may need to run a

In the center of this photo, you can see where the stock air bleed has been plugged. I used an Allen plug with blue Loctite on the threads.

Here you can see where the adjustable main jet air bleed is installed. The location is the same for both S&S Super E and G carbs.

larger main jet when using an adjustable air bleed, compared to what is needed with the fixed 0.042-inch main jet air bleed.

Why do you want an adjustable main jet air bleed? On an S&S carb, the intermediate jet supplies fuel from idle to approximately 3,500 rpm. The main jet begins supplying fuel at approximately 3,000 rpm and continues to redline. So if both jets are supplying fuel at the same time from 3,000 to 3,500 rpm, an over-rich condition will occur at the transition point between the two jet circuits. The dip in power from this over-rich condition between 3,000 and 3,500 rpm is very apparent when looking at a dyno-chart printout.

Ideally, you want to enlarge the main jet's air bleed (which delays when the main jet starts delivering fuel) so it doesn't start delivering fuel until the intermediate jet is just about ready to stop delivering fuel. With an adjustable main jet air bleed, you can correct the power loss caused be the over-richness at the transition point.

If you enlarge the main jet air bleed too much, though, the exact opposite will happen, and it will create a lean spot at the transition point. Remember that a lean condition is more dangerous to the motor than a rich condition!

Bob Yost, or one of his employees, told me that he recommends over-drilling the stock 0.042-inch main jet air bleed hole to 0.0465 inch by using a 56 drill bit. I consider this a safe and conservative starting point. Personally, I have been routinely over-drilling the air bleed to 0.052 inch using a 55 drill bit with satisfactory results in 80-plus-inch motors.

Remember, if you increase the size of main jet air bleed and still see a large dip in power between 3,000 and 3,500 rpm, you have some more drilling to do.

If you screw things up or are not happy with the results, you can always solder over the air bleed hole and drill it with a 0.042-inch drill bit, and you will be back to stock.

S&S ADJUSTABLE AIR BLEED

To make the main jet's air bleed circuit on an S&S Super E or G carburetor adjustable, you must first locate and plug the stock main jet's air bleed hole, either with a 10x32 (or smaller) Allen set screw or by soldering it closed. The location of the main jet air bleed hole is on the inside of the carb's body, above the float bowl. The air bleed's location is illustrated in the S&S instruction book that came with your carb.

On the outside of the carb's body, above and left of the S&S logo, locate the pressed-in plug that is in the main jet's air passageway. Drill and tap the plug in the main jet's air passage using a 5x0.8-millimeter tap. You can now use Mikuni (round) main jets to adjust the point where the main jet starts supplying fuel.

The air bleed for a stock S&S emulsion tube should require a jet size of 130 to 170, or 0.055 to 0.067 inch. If you're not happy with the results, just install a 0.042-inch jet (105) in your new air bleed hole, and you're back to stock.

The intermediate, or low-speed, jetting circuit has its own separate air bleed. When you modify the main jet's air bleed circuit, it does not affect the air bleed of the intermediate jet.

Jet Conversion Formula
To convert Mikuni main jets to inches:
jet size number x 0.0003937 = inches
130 x 0.0003937 = 0.055 inch

THUNDERJETS (T-JETS)
ThunderJets, or T-Jets, are designed to supplement and work with the main jet. The S&S main jet has to supply and meter the fuel between 3,000 to 6,000-plus rpm. This is not an easy job for one jetting circuit to do!

Remember, the best and easiest way to tune a main jet is on a rear-wheel dyno. When a dyno is used, the turner often concentrates on the very top of the rpm range, trying to squeeze out that last drop of horsepower for the customer. Here's the problem: If you just jet for the top-end of the main jet's range, you can cause the bottom of the jet's range to be too rich, and that's why ThunderJets can save the day.

One or more T-Jets can be added to the carb to smooth out the main jet's operating range and correct the over-rich condition that can happen when it starts delivering fuel.

T-Jets work almost the same way as the S&S main jet. It has a fuel pickup in the float bowl, an air bleed to regulate when it begins delivering fuel, and a fuel jet to meter how much fuel it actually delivers.

With a T-jet installed, you can correct the over-rich problem that happens at the low end of the main jet's range.

By using a smaller main jet, you can now tune your main jet and its air bleed to produce the most power between 3,000 and 4,500 rpm. From 4,500 rpm to redline, you will use the T-Jet's air bleed and the T-Jet's fuel jet to supplement the main jet's fuel delivery to obtain the most power on the top end.

The stock carb had only three tuning adjustments and the accelerator pump. To illustrate what you can make happen, let's look at an S&S carb that has an adjustable main jet air bleed and a T-Jet. With this combination you will now have a total of six tuning adjustments, which will look like this:

- Idle mixture screw controls the idle mixture.

- Intermediate jet controls the mixture from off idle to 3,500 rpm.

- Main jet air bleed controls when the main jet will start delivering fuel.

- Main jet controls the mixture from 3,500 to 4,500–5,000 rpm.

- T-Jet and T-Jet air bleed supplements the main jet in controlling the mixture from 4,500–5,000 to redline.

- Accelerator pump corrects lean spots during rapid acceleration transitions.

With six tuning circuits to control the mixture, the simplistic S&S carb now becomes a highly tunable fuel metering device over the entire rpm range.

Personally, I don't think tuning S&S main jet air bleeds or T-Jets is that hard to do, but that's me. Some dyno operators may have never tuned one of these things before, and you don't want an operator learning at your expense! So I recommend that you seek out a dyno operator who is experienced in tuning S&S main jet air bleeds and T-Jets. The main problem with tuning these jets is just that it takes time, and time on the dyno is money!

Tuning air bleeds and T-Jets could take hours. An inexperienced tuner will take longer and cost you a fortune, and the final job will probably be questionable. Experienced tuners, like the people at Zipper's Performance, have years of experience tuning these circuits. If you want your money's worth and a good tuning job, they're the kind of people you want tuning your bike.

When dealing with jets, consider the fact that a jet with a radius entryway (or orifice) can flow up to 20 percent more fuel than a jet with a sharp edge. For the sake of consistency, never mix jet brands. Always use like jets from the same manufacturer whenever possible.

When using a small to midsize butterfly carb (S&S types) on a large displacement motor, you may have to open the butterfly plate beyond the idle jet's transfer hole(s) to supply enough air and keep the motor running. If your idle circuit jet does not appear to be working, or your motor stumbles or hesitates off idle, you can try to correct this by drilling a 0.060–0.125-inch hole in the butterfly plate a quarter of the way down from the top of the plate. This should help increase the signal at the idle jet hole. Start small and work up in size. If it does not correct the problem, you can always solder the hole closed. I have used this drilled butterfly setup on a big-inch motor, and it has helped smooth the idling quality.

When tuning different jetting circuits on carburetors that have butterfly plates (S&S and Keihin CV), please note that different jetting circuits respond to, and are activated by, different signals. Low and intermediate jet circuits get their signals from, and respond to, vacuum pressure between the butterfly plate and the carb body, where the jetting circuits are located.

The main jetting circuit does not rely on vacuum pressure.

Instead, it receives its signal from airflow across the venturi, where the main jet's discharge tube is located. This is the same principle that gives an airplane's wing lift.

Butterfly-style carburetors that use a butterfly plate larger than the venturi, like the S&S Supers, can flow more air than carburetors with a plate that is the same size as the venturi, like the Keihin CV.

All final jetting adjustments should be made when the engine and oil have reached normal operating temperature, as adjusting jets on a cold motor will cause them to be too rich when the motor does reach it.

CARBURETOR FLOW RATES

Automotive carburetors are marketed according to flow rates, which are extremely useful to automotive performance enthusiasts when choosing the correct size carburetor to meet their performance requirements. Unfortunately, motorcycle carburetors are not flow rated, so motorcyclists have a harder job of choosing the correct size carburetor for their needs. To help you select the right carb, I have included a flow list that I obtained from S&S Cycle. I have no way of knowing how the different systems were flow tested.

	Cfm at 10 inches of H2O
S&S G carb 2 1/16 inches	
Carb and air cleaner with S&S filter	217.4
Carb and air cleaner with K&N filter	225.0*
Carb and air cleaner without filter	233.2
Carb with back plate only	238.7
Carb with long air horn	240.1
S&S E carb 1 7/8 inches	
Carb and air cleaner with S&S filter	178.0
Carb and air cleaner with K&N filter	185.0*
Carb and air cleaner without filter	194.8
Carb with back plate only	194.8
Carb with long air horn	194.8
S&S B carb 1 7/8 inches	
Carb and air cleaner with S&S filter	156.0
Carb and air cleaner without filter	176.0
Carb with back plate only	179.0
Carb with long air horn	180.0
S&S D carb 2 1/4 inches	
Carb and air cleaner with S&S filter	200.0
Carb and air cleaner without filter	268.0
Carb with back plate only	279.0
Carb with long air horn	279.0
Mikuni carbs	
HS40 40-millimeter without air cleaner	147.0
HSR42 42-millimeter without air cleaner	201.0
HSR45 45-millimeter without air cleaner	227.0

* My guess on flow rate using the excellent K&N air filter.

TO SUM THINGS UP ON SIZE

Ideally, you want a carburetor that flows just a little over your engine's maximum flow requirement. If the carburetor is too small, it will cost you top-end power, and if it's too large it can cause poor low-speed throttle response and poor low-speed drivability.

Probably 90 percent of the people who purchase aftermarket carburetors end up with one that is too big for their motor's airflow requirements.

How much will your low-speed drivability be impacted by a carb that is too large? The largest-displacement motor I have right now is 95 inches, and this motor is highly modified. It has high-flowing Branch 4 heads, which are set up for maximum flow and velocity for a 95-inch motor.

The cam has a 0.550-inch lift and 250 degrees of duration. Due to the installed cam and head combination, this motor will run out of airflow around 6,000 rpm, so that is its redline. After entering all the correct flow data in Accelerator's flow

Here you can see where I drilled the butterfly plate to help the idle circuit on a large displacement motor.

This is the excellent K&N air filter. I highly recommend that you always run one of these cotton gauze-type elements on anything that has an air filter.

Stock Keihin carburetors work well on older Big Twins and Sportsters, but will need to be re-jetted for use on an inefficient combustion chamber design like a hemi. Stock Keihin carburetors are often replaced with an aftermarket unit on newer bikes, so chances are you can pick one up at a reasonable price and upgrade the mixer on your older bike. You will need to use an adapter to mount the Keihin on older-style intake manifolds.

math feature, I found that this motor will require a carburetor that will flow 143 cfm for street performance use and 185 cfm for racing use, both at 10 inches of H2O. Now compare this motor's required airflow requirements to the flow chart.

The chart reveals that the smaller of the two most popular S&S carbs, Super E, should meet the flow requirements for the racing value of 185 cfm for my Twin Cam. Note that this bike is used as a daily rider, not for racing. Can you guess which carburetor is on my modified 95-inch motor? It has an S&S Super E and breathes through a K&N air filter.

If I had designed this motor to redline at 7,000 instead of 6,000 rpm, the smaller E carb would cause it to lose top-end performance. If I were to stick with the S&S brand, I would go with the larger G carb, as it flows close to 40 cfm more air than the E carb.

How many people do you know who are running an S&S E carb on a stock 883 or 1200 Sportster, or are running a G carb on and 80-inch Evo? They're in no danger of running a carburetor that is too small, are they?

Remember we deal in compromises. That is why I used the word "should" three paragraphs ago. On the Twin Cam proj-ect bike, I have installed two gauges to tune this bike. The air/fuel ratio meter on the exhaust side monitors the exhaust gases so I can correctly jet the carb. The vacuum gauge tells me what's happening on the intake side of the motor to aid in matching its flow requirements. Using the information provided previously, the S&S E should meet the airflow requirements of this motor combination. But does it?

Well, the vacuum gauge tells me slightly different information. When I open the throttle plate in the carb wide open, the vacuum pressure goes to zero as it should, but when the motor reaches 5,000 rpm, the needle on the vacuum gauge starts to move a little. By the time I hit the rev limiter at 6,200 rpm, the vacuum gauge is showing 2 inches of vacuum. This tells me two things:

1. The project motor is doing just what it was designed to do by flowing a large volume of air through the motor to make maximum power.

2. The S&S Super E is just a little small for this particular motor combination.

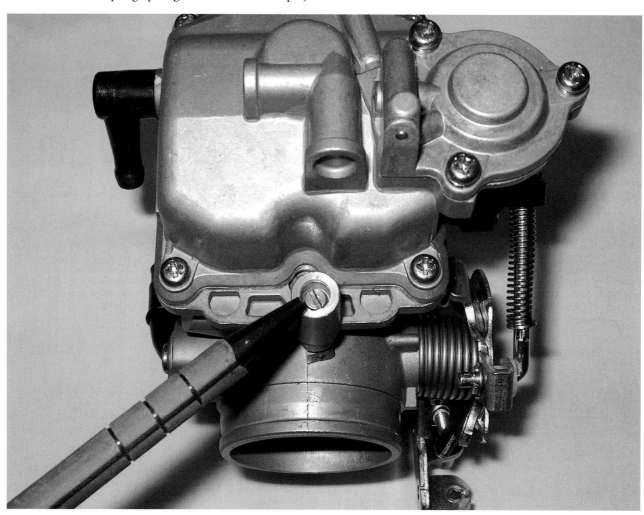

This idle mixture screw was hidden under a pressed-in plug. The plug, obviously, has been removed.

This is why the gauge is reading 2 inches of vacuum at 6,200 rpm. Ideally the needle should not start fluctuating until I get close to 6,000 rpm.

Automatically, we would say that this motor needs a bigger carb, like the S&S Super G, and we would be right. But remember what I said about the tuning problems of running a carb that is too big for the motor combination. I will prove this fact later in the book after we experiment with the larger G carb on the project bike. To give you a hint of what's to come, the project bike still runs the S&S E. Remember, the project bike is a performance street bike, not a drag bike. The E carb keeps both the motor and me happy, the most important reason why we often have to return to that word "compromise."

STOCK 40-MILLIMETER
KEIHIN CONSTANT-VELOCITY CARBURETOR

The stock Harley carburetor is the Keihin constant-velocity carb (actually, it's really a constant-vacuum carb, but who cares?) and is often one of the first stock items to go in the used-but-still-good pile. That's a shame!

You would serve yourself better and save money if you just fixed the stock carb along with the stock exhaust system. But by all means, fix—or even better, lose—the stock air cleaner. There are much better air cleaners out there. The Screamin' Eagle K&N combo is hard to beat; also, I've always been fond of, and gotten good results from, S&S teardrop units running high-flow K&N air filters.

Here's a plug for K&N air filters: If K&N makes an air filter that fits the air cleaner you're running, please do yourself a favor and install one. Yes, it's expensive, but it's the best and last air filter you'll ever need to buy.

There I go again. Let's get back to the Keihin carb. Compared to past Harley carbs, the Keihin CV carb is really good. Its only major problem is the stock low-speed EPA lean jetting, and the fact that its bore is rather small and flow restricted if used on a large-displacement motor.

When re-jetted and used within its flow limitations, it's a very good carburetor. For those who like and understand how to tune the Keihin, Harley's Screamin' Eagle line has 44- and 48-millimeter big-bore versions of the Keihin CV carb that address the stock 40-millimeter (really only 38.6) Keihin's flow limitation problem.

Even though I love my crude and oh-so-simple S&S carbs, both the Keihin big-bore CV and the Mikuni HRS series carbs are extremely accurate fuel metering devices in the hands of an expert tuner. I have no problem recommending the use of either of them.

About the only negative thing I can say about the Keihin and other CV-style carburetors is that, due to their design, their on-throttle response can be described as smooth, rather than the sudden and abrupt acceleration response you get from other designs. This is not necessarily bad; it's just that I really notice the difference.

MY PERSONAL-USAGE RECOMMENDATIONS
FOR THE KEIHIN 40-MILLIMETER CARB

They're okay for performance use on 55-inch Sportsters and mild-performance use on 74-inch Sportsters and Big Twins.

They're okay for mild-performance work on 80-inch Evo motors, but not the best for true high-performance work on 80-inch Evos, because they do not supply enough air for high-rpm use.

They're marginal for performance work on the TC-88, because they will run out of airflow at, or before, reaching the rev limiter at 5,700 rpm.

They're too small for performance work on the 95-inch Twin Cam, because they will run out of airflow long before reaching the rev limiter, limiting the ability of making any real top-end power.

STOCK JETTING

Stock factory EPA jetting is too lean at the low-speed jet, and is often too rich at the high-speed jet. If you open up your air cleaner and exhaust, the low-speed lean jetting problem will become worse.

KEIHIN IDLE MIXTURE SCREW

The idle mixture screw on stock Keihin carburetors is preset at the factory, and then covered with a tamper-resistant plug.

The idle mixture is almost always adjusted too lean because of EPA regulations. To fix this lean condition and properly adjust the idle mixture, the first thing you need to do is tamper with the tamper-resistant plug. Removing the plug is easy. You will need a drill, a drill bit, a 10 sheet metal screw, and a pair of pliers.

First, drill a hole in the center of the plug that is slightly smaller than the sheet metal screw. Be very careful when you drill the plug. You want to stop as soon as you get through the plug. If you run the drill bit in too far, you can ruin the idle mixture screw. Insert the sheet metal screw into the plug, turn it about two turns, then grab the top of the screw with the pliers, and pull the plug out.

You can now adjust the idle mixture. Gently turn the screw in clockwise until it touches the seat, then back the screw out three full turns. This will be close enough to start the bike. After the motor is hot, adjust the mixture screw to achieve the best idle. Remember, when you run any adjustable mixture needle jet against its seat, always do it gently and stop as soon as it touches the seat. If you apply too much pressure to the screw when it bottoms out, you can permanently damage the seat.

Now, turn the screw in until the motor starts to die. This is the too-lean position. Make note of the screw's position. Next, back the screw out until the motor starts to die again. This is the too-rich position. Again, note the position of the screw. Set the idle mixture screw so it's directly between these two positions and you're ready to go.

If the idle mixture screw requires three or more turns out to achieve the best idle, chances are that your low-speed jet is too lean, so try going up one jet size.

KEIHIN JETTING RECOMMENDATIONS

For the Sportster, I usually use a 45 slow-speed jet. If gas mileage is of major concern, you may be able to get by with a 44 slow jet. I use a 160 or 170 main jet.

The stock TC-88 jet sizes for the model year 2000 are a 45 (0.0177-inch) slow jet and a 180 (0.0708-inch) main jet. The main jet on the 2001 models is a 190 (0.075-inch).

My TC-88 slow-speed jet choices range from a 45 (stock) to a 50. The 48 jet has been reported to work well with mild-performance upgrades. On the 80-inch Evo, the 45 and 46 slow jet has often worked well for me.

I have noticed that motors that have properly set-up squish bands will often get by with smaller jets, since properly set-up squish bands do a better job of mixing the oxygen and fuel molecules together.

Jet size numbers to inches:
42 = 0.0165 inch
43 = 0.0169 inch
44 = 0.0173 inch
45 = 0.0177 inch
46 = 0.0181 inch
47 = 0.0185 inch
48 = 0.0189 inch
49 = 0.0193 inch
50 = 0.0197 inch

As always, all final jetting adjustments should be made when the engine and oil have reached normal operating temperature.

CV DIAGNOSTIC TIPS

When changing jets, change by one increment at a time. When changing needle jet position, change by one notch at a time. When changing idle screw positions, change by one-eighth turn at a time.

If the carb pops or coughs when operating at low, steady rpm, the slow-speed jet may be too small. Increase the slow-speed jet by one size.

If the bike hesitates or breaks up and/or if the carb spits or coughs under normal acceleration through the gears, the needle jet for the main jet may be too low, causing a lean condition. Raise the needle jet up by one notch by moving the C-clip down one notch.

When running at higher rpm, if the motor hesitates, stumbles, or coughs through the carb under hard acceleration, the main jet may be too small. Increase main jet by one size.

When stopped and idling, if the motor idles rough and/or sometimes dies, the idle mixture is not set correctly or the idle speed is set too low. Adjust idle mixture and/or idle speed.

If the motor feels sluggish and weak, puffs black smoke from your exhaust pipes, or fouls your spark plugs, one or more of the jets are too rich. Try leaner jet settings.

MORE CV TIPS

To improve the CV piston's response to required airflow demand, drill out the vacuum porthole on the bottom of the piston behind the needle jet hole to 0.120 inch, or a 31 drill bit. I recommend you don't drill the vacuum hole any larger. Also, don't enlarge the hole in the piston that the needle jet fits through. Installing a lighter spring will also help piston response action.

Enlarging the piston's vacuum hole and/or changing the piston's spring to a lighter version gets mixed reviews from

If done correctly, your finished CV piston should look like this.

Although the stock air cleaner's performance can be improved, replacing it with a high-flowing aftermarket unit will provide the best results.

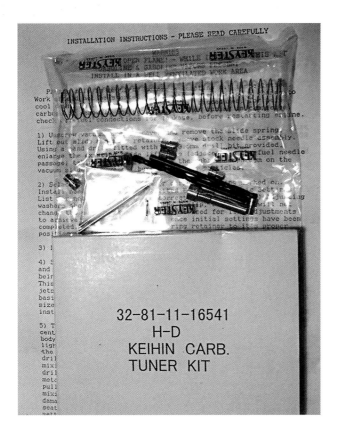

This is the recalibration kit made by Kinetic-Karb. I use this kit regularly: it is complete and priced right. It will fix your carburetor, but you won't get a cool decal for your toolbox. This kit came from V-Twin Manufacturing.

tuners. I have been doing this regularly and the carburetors seem to respond quicker to throttle changes. After making this modification, people will often tell me that their bike feels crisper or snappier when they lay the throttle on.

Some tuners don't recommend running a lighter spring, as they say it can lead to CV piston surging or fluttering. Most tuners do agree that enlarging the piston vacuum hole is a good idea. The best I can recommend is to follow whatever instructions your kit requires, and good luck!

To increase airflow at the CV piston, I like to radius and polish the bottom outside edge of the CV piston. Be careful not to remove too much material, because you could ruin the CV piston if you grind a hole in it. This is one of the tricks that Zipper's Performance does when it modifies your CV carb.

If you accidentally grind a small hole in the piston, you may be able to save it with a small spot of solder.

STOCK HARLEY AIR CLEANERS

The stock air cleaner was designed for double duty as a muffler first and an air cleaner second.

The muffler portion muffles induction noise and restricts its ability to flow adequate air volume. The air cleaner part removes contaminants.

Although the stock air cleaner can be modified to flow a lit-

tle more air, it's best to replace the stock unit with an aftermarket high-flow unit. No matter which brand of air cleaner you use, always use a high-flow K&N-style pleated-gauze filter element. The only thing that can outflow it is having no air filter at all.

I have pointed out how the cotton gauze (K&N-type) air filters are top performers when it comes to flowing air, but to keep these filters working at their best, they will need to be cleaned occasionally.

There are specialty cleaners that are made just for cleaning cotton gauze filters. If you decide to go this route, just follow the instructions on the bottle.

The good news is you don't have to buy the specialty cleaners; household cleaners like 409 will work fine.

Here's how: Thoroughly saturate the gauze with the cleaner and let it soak for 10 to 15 minutes. Then wash the cleaner from the filter using a low-pressure water source (like a sink faucet). Always apply the water from inside the filter, so it flows from the inside to the outside. After all, we're not trying to drive the dirt deeper into the filter.

If you choose to dry the air filter using compressed air from an air hose, go easy; using too much air pressure and applying it too closely will destroy your expensive filter. Just like with the water, you should directed the air from the inside out.

When the filter is clean and dry, re-oil it. Remember, cotton gauze filters use oil specifically made for them; if you use oil designed for foam fileters, you will render your gauze filter useless. The filter is sufficiently oiled when the entire gauze element turns the color of the oil. Example: K&N's oil is reddish in color, so the entire gauze should turn red. I love to save money, but I don't skimp on the filter oil!

JET KITS FOR CV CARBS

Numerous tuner kits are available for the Keihin carburetor, such as big name-brand kits from Dynojet and Yost, as well as kits from lesser-known manufacturers. As a rule, they all address the same EPA-mandated lean jetting problems of the stock carb. Each kit maker has its own way of doing things, so unless you really understand the fine workings of the Keihin tuning circuits, never mix different brands of carb kits together.

Here's another way to save some money: You can go with one of the expensive name-brand kits, or you could buy the generic Kinetic-Karb CV tuner kit from V-Twin Manufacturing. It does about the same thing as the expensive brands, but it will cost you a lot less money.

Unfortunately, the Kinetic-Karb kit doesn't come with a cool decal, so if you really must have the decal to go fast, and you're willing to shell out an extra $40 or $50 for it, then go with one of the name-brand kits. Your carburetor may not perform any better, but that decal will sure look nice on your toolbox. The choice is yours.

MORE KEIHIN CV JETTING NOTES AND TIPS

I recently installed two CV tuner kits made by Kinetic-Karb on a pair of TC-88B motors. The motors were all stock except for high-flowing air cleaners with K&N air filters and stock gutted mufflers.

After the kits were installed, I ended up with a 46 slow jet for good gas mileage. The idle mixture screw was set at three turns out with a 190 main jet.

The kit recommended a 160 as the basic main jet, with the 170 jet being optional. I was somewhat surprised that both carbs ended up needing the large stock 190 main jet. I believe that further tuning is required on the main jetting circuits of both carburetors.

Personally, I feel that a 190 main jet is big considering the size of these carburetors. It has an orifice of 0.075 inch, and it should be able to pass gallons of fuel into the air stream. Therefore, something must be restricting the flow of fuel through this jet, and that something has to be the main jet needle.

If you have to run an excessively large main jet in a Keihin or similar carburetor that has a main jet needle, this may be an indication that the jet needle is not set at the proper height or that the jet needle is the wrong shape. In this particular application, the correct jet needle profile was used. The kit recommends that the C-clip be placed on the third groove from the top of the jet needle and that no tuning washers be used.

If we were to raise the jet needle by lowering the C-clip by one or more grooves, we may find that a smaller 170 or 180 main jet works satisfactorily. Another way to enhance the richness of the main jetting circuit would be to place one or more of the tuning washers under the C-clip on the jet needle.

The point I'm trying to make here is that when you're tuning a carburetor that has both a main jet and a main jet needle, you have two things you can adjust. So don't just deal with the metering jet and forget that you may also have to adjust the main jet needle position. Most people don't give the jet needle height any thought, but it can make a big difference.

The owners of both of these bikes said they were considering a 200 main jet! I tried to explain that they don't need to spend money on a new main jet. They should first try raising the main jet needle, which would cause the main jet circuit to become richer.

THE CV JET NEEDLE PROBLEM

To work on a Keihin carburetor, it's important to know the terminology, which can get a little confusing with jet needles and needle jets. The nail-shaped rod that hangs off the bottom of the vacuum piston is the jet needle. The tube that the jet needle fits into on the floor of the carburetor is called the needle jet. At the bottom of the needle jet is the main jet. Although the needle jet and the main jet are connected together, for tuning purposes they are two separate circuits.

It has been my observation that too many people overlook the importance of the jet needle in the Keihin carb. For instance, someone will install a recalibration kit in his stock Keihin carb. The instructions may tell the owner to install the C-clip in the third groove from the bottom of the jet needle. So the owner installs the C-clip in the proper groove, changes the jets, drills the piston, installs

the lighter piston spring, and re-installs the carburetor.

If the carb does respond properly, the owner jumps right in and starts adjusting the idle mixture screw and changing jets. But the owner leaves the C-clip on the jet needle in the same position it was in when he first installed the kit.

If you run a Keihin or any carburetor that has a combination of a jet needle and a needle jet, it is extremely important that you understand that the jet needle, its shape, and its set height are the key factors to achieving proper carburetor tuning.

The Keihin carburetor has a throttle plate, or butterfly. The throttle plate does two things. It meters how much air can flow through the carburetor, and, at slow speeds, it controls the fuel mixture for the low-speed circuit. The position of the throttle plate has nothing physically to do with the height of the CV piston. The amount of vacuum and airflow through the carburetor controls that.

When the CV piston starts to rise from its seat, it starts taking over control of the air/fuel mixture. When the piston and jet needle are lifted to a height of about one-quarter open, and until the piston is about three-quarters open, the jet needle and the needle jet are controlling the entire air/fuel ratio. The low-speed jet and the main jet have almost no influence in this range. The size of the main jet does not come into play until the CV piston is lifted three-quarters or more open. In theory, your carburetor should run normally with no main jet at all until the CV piston reaches a height of more than three-quarters open.

My point is that if you're going to tune a Keihin carburetor, you're going to have to deal with the jet needle. It's the jet needle and needle jet that control the fuel for a large portion of the carburetor's operating range. At the end of this chapter, you'll find a few air/fuel ratio graphs that may help you to understand this a little better.

There are several different taper profiles of main jet needles, and every kit seems to use something different. This is another good reason why you should never mix kit parts unless you know what you are doing.

Most stock main jet needles are too large in diameter at the top end (fat end) of the needle, and this will cause the motor to run lean at lower rpm when the slide is nearly closed.

This is also the location where the needle resides during normal cruising speeds. If you try to correct this by installing a larger main jet or raising the jet needle's height, you will correct this low rpm lean mixture problem to some degree. However, your carburetor will now be entirely too rich when the needle rises up higher in the emulsion tube. This over-rich condition will cause sluggish performance, create a power loss at higher rpm, and will waste lots of fuel. At today's fuel prices, wasting fuel is a bad idea.

As an example, I get good results on modified 1200-cc Sportsters by running a 45 low-speed jet. Sometimes, even a smaller 44 will work well with a properly set-up squish band. Some questionable tuners are running 48 and 50 low-speed jets in 1200-cc Sportsters.

I recently read an article on an 883-to-1200-cc conversion that one of the V-twin performance magazines (I'll withhold the name to protect the guilty) performed for a feature story. It said: "We later installed a 50 slow jet to correctly jet the carburetor." If you need to run a large 50 slow speed jet, chances are that you either have one of the world's most inefficient combustion chambers, or you have a needle jet profile problem.

CV JET NEEDLE FIX

If you are going to run the stock CV emulsion tube (the tube that the main jet screws into, and the needle jet slides through), one fix that seems to work well is to use the stock CV jet needle (H-D part 27094-88) that was used on the early 1988–1989 1200-cc Sportsters.

This jet needle has a better profile at the top end and often corrects the low-rpm lean mixture problem. If you are going with one of the many aftermarket recalibration kits, hopefully its manufacturer has addressed this common problem.

GAS MILEAGE

Remember that intermediate, or slow-speed, jets have a major impact on your fuel consumption, good or bad. These jet circuits are what supply the fuel delivery for about 95 percent of the time you're riding.

So if fuel consumption and gas mileage are a concern, keep that in mind when setting up your jets. If you're only getting mileage in the 30-miles-per-gallon range, chances are that your intermediate jet circuits are too rich!

A properly tuned motor with a well-designed combustion chamber and good squish band turbulence will not only increase your gas mileage, but also your engine's efficiency and power.

A CLOSING THOUGHT ON TUNING

Correctly tuning a carburetor is easy to do, once you know how to do it. Sadly, many bike shops are not very good at this. A fuel delivery system that is properly tuned to measure precisely the correct amount of fuel from idle to redline is a joy to ride. But, if incorrectly tuned, your bike will perform poorly and you will be at a disadvantage from a power standpoint.

A CLOSING THOUGHT ON JETTING

There seems to be a general misconception that if you make a performance modification, you will automatically need to install richer jets in your carburetor.

Many performance magazine articles tell you that, after they completed the modifications, they had to install a slow speed jet one size larger, and a main jet two sizes larger, to correct the fuel mixture.

This gives people the idea that one must install larger jets after making a performance modification. My question is this: If they were trying to increase the motor's performance, how did they manage to screw up the air/fuel ratio in the process?

I often tell people that if their air/fuel ratio was adjusted properly before the modification, yet they have to install richer jets afterwards, they've obviously done something wrong.

When I perform a power modification correctly, if any jet change is required, I'd expect it to need smaller jets. If my modification does require richer jets, I'm somewhat disappointed, because I've obviously altered my combustion efficiency.

LET'S DISCUSS WHERE I'M GOING WITH THIS . . .

By now, you should have a better understanding of the subject of mixing air and fuel together to make power. We've discussed the operation of jetting circuits, and more importantly, what correct air/fuel ratios are.

We know that stock carburetors are jetted first to meet pollution restrictions and only secondarily to meet power requirements.

We know that stock carburetors often require jetting changes to deliver the proper air/fuel ratios to make maximum power.

And we know that pre-jetted aftermarket carburetors may require slight jetting changes to provide the correct air/fuel ratio to meet your motor's requirements.

For example, the S&S Super E carburetor that I started with on my modified 95-inch Twin Cam at sea level should require a 31 and 72 jet, but due to its high efficiency rate it only needs a little 26 and 68 to produce maximum power on the dyno.

We also know that different motor combinations yield different burn efficiency rates, and that the required air/fuel ratios will be directly dictated by the motor's efficiency at mixing those air and fuel molecules together. An efficient combustion chamber design will require a lower air/fuel ratio and have a better BSFC than an inefficient one.

And finally, once the carburetor is adjusted to provide the correct air/fuel ratio, the ratio will not change unless we change the motor's efficiency rate or the conditions of its operating environment.

For example, if you moved from Death Valley to the mile-high city of Denver, Colorado, that would be a definite environment change and would require a change to leaner jets.

Efficiency pertains to the ability of the motor to mix oxygen and fuel molecules together and consume all of the oxygen in the cylinder during the burn process. Any oxygen that is not consumed is lost potential power.

So here's my point: When you perform a performance modification, you should have two goals. Your first goal is a given: to flow more air through the motor. To increase your power output, you must get more air and fuel into the cylinders. This is a concept everyone accepts as the way to increase power output.

The next important goal is motor efficiency. Sadly, this concept is often overlooked. To increase the motor's efficiency, we must find ways to burn the air and fuel more efficiently in our cylinders. This can be accomplished through modifying squish bands, combustion chamber shapes, compression, and timing. Reducing motor and drivetrain parasitic loss due to friction also falls under the category of efficiency. Switching from petroleum-based oil to straight synthetic oil will help reduce parasitic loss.

If you only address flowing more air without increasing your motor's efficiency, you'll be doing yourself a great disservice, because you'll only receive a partial benefit from the modification.

Whenever I plan a power modification, I look for ways to increase combustion efficiency first. Removing the heads and properly setting up the squish bands are two of my first moves, and as it requires only time and a few gaskets, it's a relatively cheap way to improve combustion efficiency.

After you've made a power improvement, the required air/fuel ratio should not change if the ratio was correctly set prior to the modification. If you do have to increase jet sizes after the modification, the motor may be putting out more power, but you have decreased your motor's burn efficiency because it's requiring more fuel to burn the same percentage, or ratio, of oxygen.

If any jetting change is required when I perform a power improvement, it will usually be done to reduce jet size. If you have to change to smaller jets after the modification, you have maximized your power improvement, because you have not only increased flow rate, but you've also improved your burn efficiency rate.

This is the reason why properly set-up performance motors can, and often do, get better gas mileage than a stock motor with considerably less power. The bottom line: Don't automatically assume you have to install larger jets unless your air/fuel ratio meter or the dyno says their installation is required.

AIR/FUEL RATIO GRAPHS

The fastest, safest, and most accurate way to tune your carburetor or EFI system is to use a dynamometer with an exhaust gas analyzer. A dynamometer that doesn't have one will work, but you'll waste time using the trial-and-error method to figure out whether to go richer or leaner. If you don't have access to a dynamometer, the air/fuel ratio meter we discussed earlier is also a very helpful tool for tuning. You can also permanently mount the air/fuel ratio meter on your bike and monitor your air/fuel ratio all the time.

To give you an idea of what an exhaust gas analyzer graph looks like and how you can use it, I have recreated two real graphs

taken from a Dynojet Model 250 with an exhaust gas analyzer. I have also created a simulated graph illustration of what happens at the transition point on S&S Super E and G carburetors.

This air/fuel ratio graph is from the un-tuned Keihin carburetor from my wife's 883-to-1200-cc Sportster conversion recipe we'll cover in a later chapter.

Only the idle mixture and the low-speed jet have been tuned to the motor. The carburetor is a stock Keihin with the Yost Master recalibration kit installed. The jet needle and the main jet have not been tuned and are set at the kits recommended starting point. As stated earlier, I usually use the cheaper Kinetic-Karb recalibration kits, but I got a really good deal on this Yost Master kit from a guy who couldn't use it. It also gave me an excuse to try something different.

Most people roll the throttle open when they want to accelerate quickly. This allows the jetting circuits do their thing. Let's look at the graph. The first thing you'll notice is the dangerously over-lean condition between 2,000 and 3,000 rpm. I really wish they wouldn't do this because it doesn't simulate real-time use and you lose valuable tuning information. But this seems to be the normal drill. With the motor running at 2,000 rpm with a strong vacuum, the dyno operator yanks the throttle wide open, and the vacuum pressure instantly drops to zero. With no signal to the jets, you get no fuel from the jets. One of the benefits of the CV design is that it's somewhat forgiving when applying the throttle too fast. But with the motor only turning 2,000 rpm in a steady state, there's not much demand for airflow, due to the fact that the butterfly and the low-speed jet are supplying the mixture. The CV part of the carburetor will start to come into play only when the airflow requirements are increased. The Keihin does have an accelerator pump, but it's rather small and doesn't stand a chance of satisfying the fuel demand in a situation like this.

At 3,000 rpm the carb is starting to catch up with the fuel demand. The next important issue is the over-rich condition that's happening between 3,500 and 3,800 rpm. In this location the mixture is considerably rich at 12:1.

At 4,300 rpm the fuel curve settles in to a fairly even level

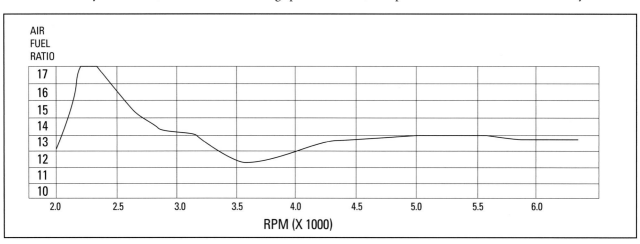

This air fuel ratio graph is from the un-tuned Keihin carburetor from my wife's 883 to 1200cc Sportster conversion recipe.

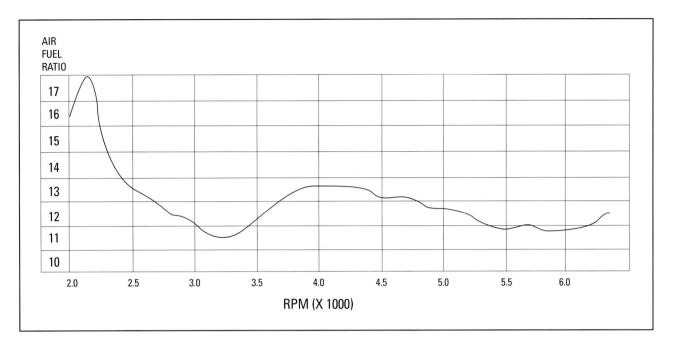

of 13.7:1 or 13.9:1, where it remains until the run is ended at 6,400 rpm. An average air/fuel ratio of 13.8:1 will produce good economy, but to make maximum power, the mixture should be made richer by about a full point to 12.8:1.

Okay boys and girls, you're at the end of the chapter on mixing air and fuel, so it's test time! Let's say that this is your carburetor's air/fuel ratio and you want to tune your motor for maximum power, what, if anything, would you do?

While you're thinking about your answer, let me tell you a true story about the graph you are looking at. I drove 130 miles to Anchorage to have this bike dyno tuned for maximum torque and horsepower. The normal cost for a dyno tune job is $160 plus parts and more if it takes the shop longer than an hour to do the tuning. I dropped the bike off at the shop a little before noon. I returned to the shop at the end of the day to pick the bike up. I asked the dyno guy if the bike was done being tuned. He said it was and that she's ready to go. I asked him what he changed. He said he didn't have to change anything because the bike's air/fuel ratio was already tuned perfectly and here's your bill for $160 for the work. I asked the dyno guy if I could have a copy of the dyno results, you know, a graph of torque and horsepower curves—the whole reason why I drove 130 miles to get there. He goes back into his dyno cell and comes out with a printout of the bike's torque and horsepower, but his printer was out of ink so you can only see about half of it. The air fuel/ratio graph you're looking at is part of the Dynojet 250's WinPEP program printout. Remember at the beginning I said I recreated these graphs? I had to so you could see them. Unlike the dyno guy, my printer has ink and I don't charge 160 bucks an hour.

Okay what's your answer? If you said you'd change nothing, you have the right qualifications and the shop in Anchorage would probably hire you as a dyno tuner.

There is no one correct answer. You look at the baseline air/fuel ratio graph and decide what jetting changes you can make to improve the air/fuel ratio that may help you make more power. You make the changes and then run the bike on the dyno until you find what combination of settings makes the most power. That's why it's called dyno tuning. Of course, if the bike is "perfect," like my bike supposedly was, you could skip all that effort and just collect the money.

After driving another 130 miles to get this perfectly tuned bike home, I grabbed some tools and took the carburetor apart. Yes, I know I just paid the dyno guy to do that. As you'll see, this bike gets great gas mileage and doesn't pop through the carburetor between 2,000 and 3,000 rpm, so to keep the good gas mileage, I left the 46 slow speed jet alone. First I lowered the jet needle two notches to try to correct the 12:1 over-rich condition occurring at 3,700 rpm. I removed the main jet and replaced it with the next size larger. The mixture from 4,500 to 6,400 rpm was too lean with an average around 13.8:1. My goal was to try to flatten out the fuel curve so it would be closer to 13:1 across the entire rpm range. Lowering the needle jet should fix the rich condition in the midrange and the main jet change should richen up the lean top end. Will the motor make more power now? My guess is it will, but to see it I'll need to pay the dyno guy again. As the bike is a blast as is, I think I'll just ride it instead!

OKAY, LET'S GO FROM NOT BAD TO FLAT-OUT UGLY

Look at the graph above. This mess is from early testing of my Twin Cam project bike using an S&S Super E carb with a fixed main jet air bleed enlarged to 0.0485 inch. Despite this miserable fuel curve, the motor still pumps out 100 lb-ft of torque at 4,000 rpm and runs great. God only knows what this motor would do with a tuned performance exhaust system and a proper fuel curve. But this is my project bike; its purpose is to test my different ideas to see what works and what doesn't. Obviously, this carburetor is not working correctly.

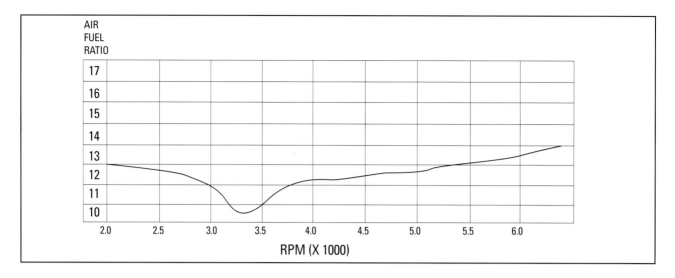

Normal air/fuel ratio graph you'd expect to see from a stock S&S E or G carb. Notice the dip between 3,000 & 3,500 rpm where the intermediate circuit and main jet are both working, causing an overly rich condition. An adjustable main jet air bleed will solve this.

How could someone write a performance book and have a fuel curve this messy? The reasons are simple: (1) I'm honest, and (2) until recently I did not have access to a dyno with an exhaust gas analyzer or an air/fuel ratio meter. My only tuning reference point was the torque and horsepower data from the dyno to tune this bike. Now that I've seen the fuel curve, I can also see where more power may be hidden.

The reason I say this fuel curve is a mess has nothing to do with what it looks like, although I'll admit it doesn't look very nice. The reason I say it's a mess has to do with where the fuel curve is lean and where it's rich. We can and will learn a lot from this fuel curve—not from the answers it will give us, but from the unanswered questions it will create.

First the carburetor: It is an S&S Super E, and the main jet air bleed has been enlarged from the stock 0.042 to 0.0485 inch. Obviously, I should have used my normal 55 drill for a 0.052-inch main jet air bleed. This carburetor is also fitted with a non S&S product—the Yost power tube and the supplied spacer.

The first thing we see is the over-lean condition from yanking the throttle wide open. The S&S accelerator pump is more generous than the Keihin pump, and some of this can be adjusted out. The accelerator pump on this carb is adjusted to work just right for normal steer use. So we will not change its setting; to do so will only cause the carburetor to waste fuel.

One of my design goals for this motor was for it to be very fuel efficient and not overly sensitive to 87-octane pump swill. That goal was, at least, met. It runs fine on 87-octane, although I prefer to use 90-octane when I can find it. The last time I checked the fuel mileage was on a 275-mile roundtrip to Anchorage and back. There was some city-traffic driving, but most of it was at highway speeds of 55 to 70 miles per hour. I would say that this mileage test also contained several wide-open throttle (WOT) bursts of 100-plus miles per hour to pass traffic and have some fun, but that would be highly illegal, so let's say that didn't happen.

Anyway, the motor produced exactly 50 miles per gallon. This was topped by my friend Alex, who was riding right next to me on my wife's fast little Sportster. It's running my 883-to-1200-cc motor recipe, and Alex did not take part in the illegal WOT episodes either (wink,wink, nod, nod). He averaged exactly 55 miles per gallon on the same run. As I stated earlier, a correctly built performance motor can, and often will, beat a stock motor in gas mileage.

The next point of interest is what happens at 3,200 rpm. Believe it or not, this is normal and common with all S&S Super E and G carburetors. Before we continue, let's take a look at a simulated fuel curve. It's important to understand the normal S&S fuel curve, because it's going to generate the problems we will encounter with my project bike's fuel curve. Note: I have taken liberties with the illustration to help simplify the explanation of the S&S carbs.

Between 2,000 and 3,000 rpm, the carb is running totally on the intermediate jet and all's happy. Between 3,000 and 3,500 rpm we see that the mixture gets considerably rich. This is the location of the transition point when the intermediate jet and the main jet overlap. The intermediate jet continues to deliver fuel until it reaches approximately 3,500 rpm, even though the main jet has begun delivering fuel at around 3,000 rpm. As both jets are dumping fuel into the mixture simultaneously, we see a big drop in the air fuel/ratio as the mixture becomes overly rich, causing a dip in torque and horsepower.

The way we correct this is by enlarging the main jet air bleed in steps until we tune most of this overlap out. But there's no free lunch here. By enlarging the main jet air bleed, we are adding more air into the main jet's emulsion tube, which will lean out the main jet circuit. If we add more air to the same amount of fuel, the mixture will get leaner. To correct for this, the main jet often needs to be enlarged to bring the air/fuel ratio back to the desired ratio. The bigger the air bleed, the larger the main jet has to be to get the same ratio.

After we pass around 3,500 rpm, the intermediate jet is out of the picture and the main jet takes over the control of the mixture. But the main jet on the S&S has a large rpm spread to deal with. In my case it's almost a 3,000-rpm spread. As the main jet is of a fixed size, it can't change the way it meters fuel. In the illustration, I have exaggerated its effect so you can see it better. As rpm increase, the main jet circuit leans out. If you set your air/fuel ratio to be optimum for the top end, the mixture will be too rich in the midrange. If you jet for optimum midrange, the top end will be too lean. This is the reason why ThunderJets are used. You use the main jet to control the mixture in the upper midrange and then a T-Jet to supplement the main jet on the top-end.

Now that we have reviewed how the S&S works, let's look again at my project bike's fuel curve and see why I say it's a mess, and I do mean more than what it looks like.

The first thing to fix is the transition point we see at 3,200 rpm, where the mixture is too rich at 11.5:1. The air bleed on this carburetor has already been enlarged from stock 0.042 to 0.0485 inch. If this were a normal situation, we would continue to enlarge the air bleed, but we can't! Look at the fuel mixture at 4,000 rpm; it's already too lean at 13.5:1. If you increase the main jet air bleed, the mixture at 4,000 rpm will get even leaner.

No problem you say, just install a larger main jet. Normally you would, but you can't in this situation because this S&S carb is not responding the way it should. As rpm increase, the fuel ratio should get leaner, right? But take a look at what's happening here; the faster the motor turns, the richer the mixture gets. The mixture at the top-end is already too rich at 11.8:1.

So what am I going to do? Fix it, of course, but how? That's going to take some thought. The first thing I'm going to do is install an air/fuel ratio meter so I don't have to spend (waste) any more of my hard-earned money on the dyno.

The first logical thing to do is try to remove the power tube and retest it. But I doubt the power tube has anything to do with what's going on here. I'm also smart enough to ask for help, and you should, too, when you need it. I will be contacting Bob Yost to see if he can explain this fishy fuel curve

First I removed the Allen plug from here.

I tapped this vent hole to the same thread size as the Allen plug I removed from the bottom of the carb. Note: No drilling is required to do this. Then I used blue Loctite and reinstalled the Allen plug into the newly threaded hole. Now the float bowl is vented to the outside air and is completely isolated from what's happening in the intake.

and how to correct it. I will also contact the great tech staff at S&S, but we both know what those guys are going say: it's not the carb. Why did you screw around with our main jet discharge tube and why did you alter our main jet air bleed?

But meeting challenges, solving problems, and dealing with compromises is often what building a performance street bike is all about. If it were easy, everyone would do it. Hopefully, after reading my book, you can share in the fun!

MYSTERY FUEL CURVE SOLVED

Nobody could explain exactly what was going on here, but after installing the RB Racing's air/fuel ratio meter kit, I was able to find and fix the problems.

First, I had to find out why the mixture was going uncontrollably rich on the top end. The cause turned out to be that the float bowl was going into a vacuum because the float bowl was not properly vented. So, I removed the Allen plug from the bottom of the float bowl vent passage. I then drilled and tapped the float bowl vent passage on the carb's face that was located inside the air cleaner. Next,

I installed the plug that I removed from the outside of the carb's body into the newly threaded hole. This completely disconnected and isolated the float bowl vent from anything within the air cleaner. What was happening was that at high rpm, the float bowl was being pulled into a vacuum. When this occured, the main jet circuit uncontrollably added too much fuel to the mixture at high rpm.

Next, I plugged the stock main jet air bleed and added an external adjustable main jet air bleed that enabled me to fix and completely tune out the over-rich condition that was happening at 3,200 rpm. Then, to test something completely different, I installed a Sifton Bombsight main jet discharge booster kit. I adjusted the main jet and main jet air bleed until I got the desired results on the air/fuel ratio meter. This fixed the lean condition that was happening at 4,000 rpm.

With the right combination of jets and air bleed, the air/fuel ratio stays perfectly flat from 2,000 to 5,000 rpm. It's so flat thanks to the air/fuel ratio meter it looks like fuel injection instead of a carburetor. Unfortunately, at 5,000 rpm the mixture starts to get a little lean, but it's

Here's a look at the Sifton main jet booster tube installed on an S&S G carburetor. The Sifton booster is very similar to the one sold by DaVinci. It's important to note that, if you are using an adjustable main jet air bleed with this type of main jet discharge tube, the correct size of the air bleed jet will be smaller than the air bleed jet you would use with the stock S&S main jet discharge tube. The correct jet size will be somewhere between 0.028 and 0.049 inch. The stock air bleed on S&S Super E and G carburetors is 0.042 inch.

still well within the safe range. The only way to fix this is with a ThunderJet, and that's my next move!

Will the motor make more power now? My guess is it has to, but only the dyno will tell how much. According to the seat of my pants, though, it sure feels a lot stronger.

You should have a better understanding of what your ultimate goal is when adjusting your air/fuel metering system now that you're at the end of the chapter on mixing air and fuel. Your goal is to supply the motor with the correct air/fuel ratio for maximum acceleration from 2,000 rpm to redline.

Is this goal easy to achieve? No, it's not. It will involve many hours and dollars to get right. The whole point of this book is to help you save money and still make your performance goals a reality. If you don't get your air/fuel ratio correct, you will never achieve your performance goals, much less know what your motor is capable of.

To help you save money, I'm going to ask you to spend some money. Buy a good quality air/fuel ratio meter, like the R B Racing meter I use, and use it to adjust and tune your air/fuel mixture. After that, if you make a change to your motor combination, like changing exhaust systems, the meters will show you if and where any changes to your air/fuel ratio need to be made.

Be sure to install the oxygen sensor as close as you can to the front cylinder head. You want to mount it on the front cylinder because of the Harley V-twin's offset 45-degree firing order, which makes the front cylinder run leaner. If you adjust the air/fuel mixture to the front cylinder, you'll know the back cylinder is safely running a bit richer.

When Harley mechanics see the air/fuel ratio and vacuum meters mounted on my project bike, they're a bit dismayed. And they should be, because they know I no longer need them to dial in my air/fuel mixture. I can use my meters and do it myself, and I can do it for free.

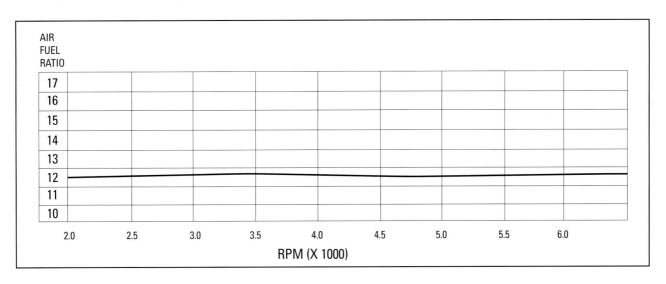

So, what should a perfect air/fuel ratio graph look like for a V-twin modified for acceleration? This is pretty close.

CHAPTER 5 GEARING

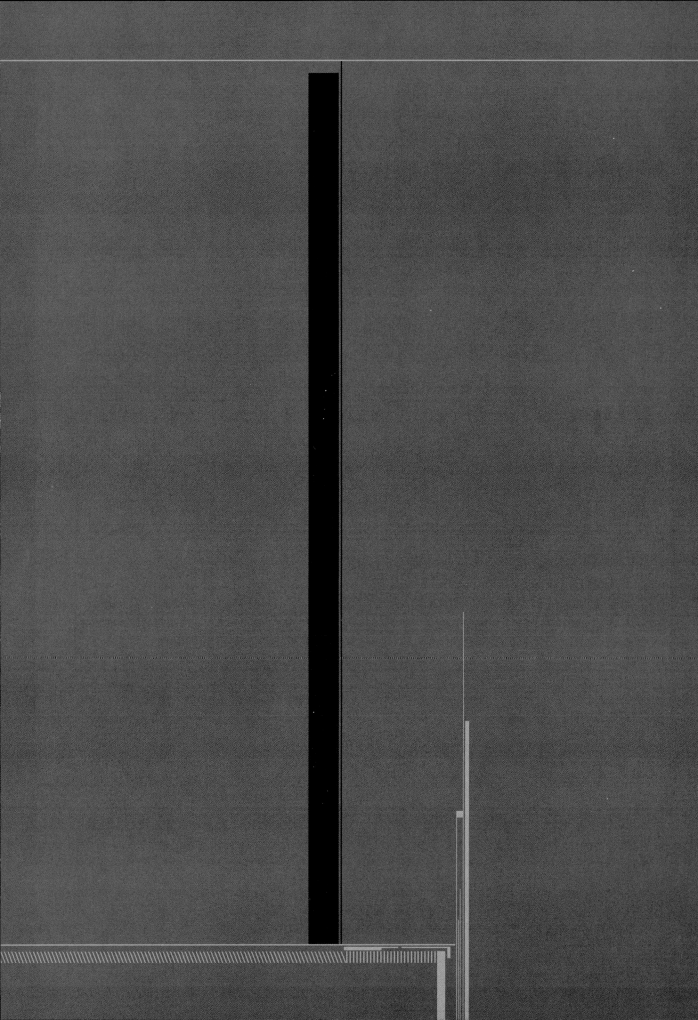

THE STOCK GEARING PROBLEM

One of the first issues you need to address for high-performance work is the Motor Company's stock overgearing problem. The factory has the bike set up for Joe, the average street rider, and Sally, the average highway cruiser. The factory doesn't set the bikes up for Bill, the hot rod nut.

Sadly, the stock gear ratios leave much to be desired for street performance and/or drag racing. First gear is set so low you could use it to tow a pickup truck out of a ditch, and the top gears are not much better. They are great for cruising at highway speeds with the motor barely chugging along above an idle. Of course, I like to cruise at highway speeds, too, but I don't want to waste more than about three seconds to get there. Once there, I'll cut the throttle back and smile. Well, sometimes I'll cut her back, but I always smile.

So first gear needs to be raised. Andrews makes a close ratio first gear set to fix this problem. Although it's labor intensive and expensive, for drag racing it's a must. Baker, JIMS, and others have six-speed transmissions that will fix this, but again, labor intensive and expensive.

So, what's a performance guy to do?

The easiest and simplest solution is a sprocket and/or transmission drive pulley change. The sprocket change will set you back about $100, but have you priced an Andrews trans pulley lately?

A NOTE FROM JERRY BRANCH

So how important is this gear problem? Let's see what the legendary Jerry Branch of Branch Flowmetrics has to say about it. The following is an excerpt from a letter that Jerry sent me back in February 2000:

Bill,

Harley has the motorcycle (Twin Cam) greatly over-geared and this is the most important thing that you can do to improve it. You need to drop the motor sprocket from a 25-tooth to a 24-tooth and change the trans pulley sprocket from a 32 tooth to a 30 tooth. Andrews makes the trans pulley and H-D makes the engine sprocket. The motorcycle will run 10 times better everywhere with this setup. If I had a choice of only one thing I could do to the motorcycle, I would take the gear change 10 to one, even if it were twice the price of the heads, cams, carb, and pipes. It's a must! Without it, you will only get 5 percent results out of all of this other stuff. Right now it's like having a trailer hooked onto the back of it. Get rid of the trailer and the motorcycle flies!

Sincerely,
Jerry Branch

Jerry clearly makes the point that the stock gearing is not much help in getting the power to the street, and this is an especially strong statement when coming from one of the most famous Harley head porters in the business. He indirectly says he would choose a gear change over a set of his own Branch heads! Ouch, that hurts!

Stock Dyna Gearing,	Model Year 2000
Engine sprocket	25 teeth
Clutch sprocket	36 teeth
Trans	32 teeth
Wheel	70 teeth

	Trans gears ratio	Overall ratio
First	3.21	10.111
Second	2.21	6.955
Third	1.57	4.945
Fourth	1.23	3.874
Fifth	1.00	3.153

The stock final gear ratio on the Twin Cam is 3.153:1. This means that in fifth gear, the motor will turn 3.153 times for each single turn of the back tire. If you think this is high, check out the gear ratio of an 80-inch Evo Softail. Would you believe it's 2.92:1! Being geared that high, it's amazing that the Fatboys or the Heritages can get out of their own way.

It's important to understand that the smaller the gear ratio between the motor and the rear wheel, the harder the engine has to work to turn the wheel at a given rate. If we increase this ratio, the motor will be able to turn more revolutions to turn the rear wheel at the same rate. What we are doing through gearing is mechanically increasing the amount of torque we can apply to the rear wheel. The more torque we apply, the faster we can accelerate.

Stock Twin Cam gearing: fifth gear at 2,200 rpm = 50 miles per hour

As with most things in the world of high-performance street Harleys, you have to compromise. If the overall gearing is too high, you won't accelerate worth spit. If you gear too low, you'll lose top-end miles per hour, and your engine will be racing and turning a lot faster that it needs to at highway speeds. Of course, the six-speed transmission with overdrive will fix all of this. Get the feeling I want one? Even I can dream!

Anyway, we're going to have to compromise on a street bike. Expert drag racers' lives revolve around going fast, and they will often recommend using a final ratio of 3.37:1 for a hot street Harley. Note that this is for the smaller displacement 80-inch Evo, so it should work well on the new larger Twin Cams. Again, stock on the Evo Sportster's was 2.92:1 and the Twin Cams are 3.15:1, so 3.37:1 is an improvement.

HOW TO DETERMINE YOUR GEAR RATIO

First, divide the number of teeth on your clutch sprocket by the number of teeth on your motor sprocket. This gives you your primary ratio.

Then divide the number of teeth on your wheel pulley by the number of teeth on your transmission drive pulley. This gives you the secondary ratio. Then multiply your primary ratio and secondary ratio together, and you get your overall gear ratio.

Reducing the size of your motor sprocket will increase the amount of torque (through gearing) that you can apply to your rear wheel. It will also improve your ability to accelerate and works just as well on a stock bike as on a modified bike. Switching to a larger motor sprocket will have the opposite effect. Either way, your speedometer will still read correctly.

Here's an example: stock Twin Cam, 25-tooth motor, 36-tooth clutch, 32-tooth trans pulley, and 70-tooth rear-wheel pulley.

Primary ratio
$36 \div 25 = 1.44$

Secondary ratio
$70 \div 32 = 2.1875$

Overall ratio
$1.44 \times 2.1875 = 3.15:1$

This, of course, does not take into account the transmission gearing.

Fifth gear on stock Harleys is 1:1, or direct drive, with no gear reduction. Note that the new Baker, JIMS, and Revtech six-speed transmissions are different, as their sixth gear is an overdrive. That means the transmission

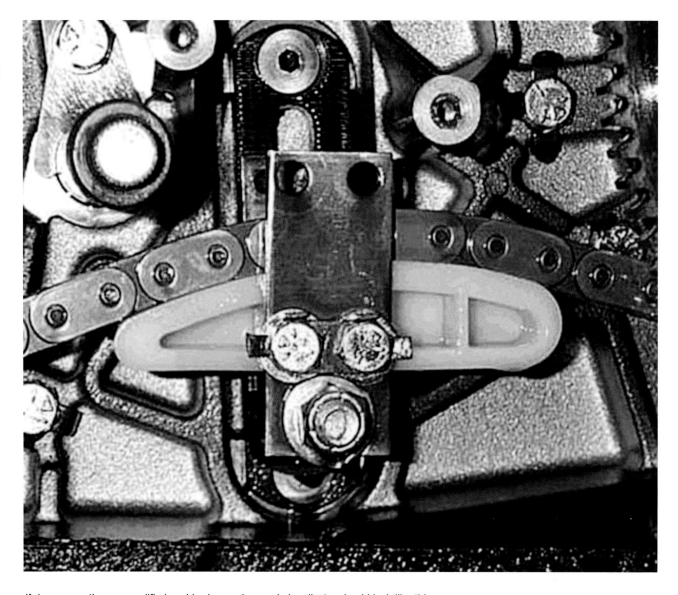

If done correctly, your modified upside-down primary-chain adjuster should look like this.

has a negative gear ratio.

But guess what lives right in the middle of your primary and secondary gear ratios? Yes, your transmission! So let's add that into the soup. Let's say that we want to find out what the final gear ratio would be if we were in third gear (its ratio is 1.57:1).

The basic idea is to multiply the primary ratio by the gear ratio, then multiply that product by the secondary ratio.

The math would look like this:

1.44 x 1.57 = 2.260
2.260 x 2.1875 = 4.945

So in third gear, your motor would turn 4.945 times to make the wheel turn once.

Gee, that was easy! Got any more formulas, Bill? Yeah . . . maybe later if you're good.

Let's get back to Mr. Jerry Branch. Jerry's recommendation was to get rid of that trailer I was pulling around. If I followed his advice, I would drop the motor sprocket from 25 teeth down to 24 teeth and drop the trans pulley from 32 teeth down to 30 teeth. This is the gear ratio he's recommending:

36 ÷ 24 = 1.50
70 ÷ 30 = 2.333
1.50 x 2.333 = 3.50:1

Jerry Branch is serious. He's recommending dropping from the stock 3.15:1 down to 3.5:1. This should get the rpm up and the back wheel spinning!

I don't doubt for a second that what Jerry Branch said is gospel. But remember that in the world of high-performance street Harleys, we deal in compromises. So I compromised with Jerry's recommendation and went for just the motor sprocket change, from the stock 25 tooth down to a 24 tooth. The advantage to this change is that it doesn't affect the speedometer's calibration.

So I'm now running a lower ratio of 3.285:1. Is it better that the stock tall 3.15:1? You bet! Cost? Motor sprocket, gasket, quart of primary lube, etc. will set you back close to $100. In addition to a torque wrench, you do need one other special tool, a sprocket-locking tool, to change out the motor sprocket. If you live in Seward, Alaska, you can borrow mine. If not, you can always shove the handle of a screwdriver between the sprocket and the primary chain and change it that way.

If you plan to use the smaller motor sprocket, you will need to modify your primary chain adjuster, because your primary chain will be too long with the smaller motor sprocket.

Here's how to modify your chain adjuster. First, remove and disassemble the primary chain adjuster and reposition the nylon/plastic shoe in it so it's upside down. Next, turn the whole adjuster unit upside down. Now the shoe is right side up, as it should be. Cool!

Now install the whole adjuster unit back in the motor in this upside down position, with the shoe's running surface pointing up in its normal position. Trust me, it will work!

Very important! Be sure to clean all of the oil out of the two threaded holes that hold the serrated fixed adjuster plate to the inter-primary housing. Clean and dry the two bolts that hold the adjuster plate in place. Install the clean and dry bolts with lots of 271 red Loctite. If you don't do this, the bolts will eventually come loose, and when they do, you will be extremely sorry.

On my Twin Cam, I went one step further and replaced both bolts with slightly longer stainless-steel tapered flathead Allen head bolts (you can see the top bolt in the picture). If I could back these bolts up with nuts, I'd do that, too!

LESSON LEARNED—
AUTOMATIC PRIMARY CHAIN ADJUSTERS

There are several makers of spring-loaded automatic primary chain tension adjusters. These adjusters are designed to regulate the tension on the stock primary chain to make shifting easier and eliminate future adjusting of your primary chain. They work well, but the problem is, if you go with the smaller 24-tooth motor sprocket, the length of your primary chain is no longer stock length. In the case of the Twin Cam, the stock chain is 82 links long. There is an 80-link chain available, but don't waste your money; it's too short and won't fit.

I recently tried to install one of these spring-loaded automatic chain adjusters on a Twin Cam running the smaller 24-tooth sprocket with the stock 82-link primary chain. I set the shims at 5/8 inch, as instructed, and buttoned the motor back up. As soon as the bike was started, I was greeted by the loud and disappointing sound of the primary chain trying to saw its way through the primary chain case. Needless to say, this was a bad thing and

not the desired result. I drained the oil and removed the primary chain case cover again.

Next, I tried to correct this by shimming the springs tighter to 1/2 inch and removing (grinding) some of the metal from the chain case where the chain was impacting it. This also resulted in failure. When the engine started, it produced a very loud whining noise. Then, at a certain rpm (out of gear), the springs caused a harmonic vibration in the chain that caused the top run to violently whip up and down. Both of these results were unacceptable.

Conclusion: The fancy automatic chain adjuster went back in its box and was later installed on an Electra Glide with a stock primary chain/sprocket combination. My upside-down chain adjuster (which cost nothing) went back in the motor, and the motor and I are both happy once again. If you decide to run the 24-tooth sprocket, remember this story. The cost of the automatic chain adjuster, chain case oil, and primary chain case gaskets (three in my case) can add up pretty fast, plus you waste a day of your life in the process. For me this was a clear case of some things work and some things just . . . well you know!

WHEN THE RUBBER MEETS THE ASPHALT

Now that we know how to calculate gear ratios, we can use the same formula (with one small addition) to calculate the amount of power you can put to the pavement. If you have had your bike on a rear-wheel dyno, you know how much rear-wheel torque your motor is putting out. But let's say that you want to know how much of that torque will be applied to the ground for acceleration.

Before we get to the formula, we need to look at torque again. Torque is measured in lb-ft. If your rear tire is 24 inches, the distance from your axle's center to the ground would be 12 inches, or 1 foot (remember lb-ft), from the axle's center to the street. If this were the case, all we would have to do is multiply the torque by total gear ratio, and we would know how much power we were theoretically applying to the ground.

But the average 16-inch rear tire has a diameter of about 26 inches, so it's 13 inches from the axle's center to the ground. You'll need to measure your own tire's diameter. Note that as you spin the tire, it will increase in size due to centrifugal force. Also, the weight of the bike is resting on the bottom of the tire and compressing it. Because of these reasonss, it would be better not to measure from the axle's center to the ground, but to some other location on the tire. If you measure the tire to any place except for the bottom you will get a more accurate measurement of the tire diameter. Pretty simple if you think about it.

So we need to convert the difference. Here's how to do that: divide the 13 inches by 12 inches (to get the foot in lb-ft); 13 ÷ 12 = 1.08. So 1.08 feet will be your correction factor if your tire is 26 inches.

A heavy-duty clutch spring from Barnett or H-D's Screamin' Eagle is often all that's required to make the stock clutch hold up in performance applications.

The last time I had my bike on the rear-wheel dyno in Anchorage, it peaked out at 104 lb-ft, so we will use those numbers.

How much theoretical peak torque could my bike apply to the ground when I accelerate off the starting line in first gear?

The primary ratio is 1.5:1 (Note: I took Jerry Branch's advice and changed the motor sprocket and trans pulley from stock 25/32 to 24/30—that's why the value is different from the 1.44 used in the previous example.)

The trans ratio for first gear is 3.21

The secondary ratio is 2.1875

The rear-wheel torque is 104 lb-ft

Tire correction factor is 1.08

1.5 x 3.21 = 4.815
4.815 x 2.1875 = 10.538
10.538 x 104 lb-ft = 1,095.4 lb-ft
1,094.4 lb-ft divided by our tire correction factor of 1.08 = 1,014.3 lb-ft

So at peak torque my Dyna (in first gear) could lay down a total of about 1,014 lb-ft of torque to the ground. Not bad, not bad at all.

As a comparison, in fifth gear at peak torque, I could only apply a total of about 316 lb-ft of power to the road. Fifth gear's 316 lb-ft is nowhere near the 1,014 lb-ft in first gear, but it's still plenty enough to make your speedo needle go in the right direction without having to downshift.

CLUTCH TIP

The stock clutch on Sportster, Evo Big Twin, and Twin Cam models is limited in the amount of torque it can handle. Clutch slippage can occur after performance modifications are made. If you allow your clutch to slip for any length of time, it will overheat and destroy the clutch plates. With a simple, inexpensive fix, you can make the stock clutch handle a considerable amount of torque.

Frequently all that is required is to change the stock clutch spring out for a heavier-pressure spring. These springs are available from both Barnett and Harley's Screamin' Eagle performance lines. With the heavy-duty clutch spring installed on a Big Twin or a Twin Cam, the clutch should be able to handle up to about 120 lb-ft of torque. Always try this before spending big money on a performance clutch kit that you may not need.

These springs will add about 20 percent more pressure to the clutch plates and about 3 pounds more pull to the required effort of operating the clutch lever. Warning: These springs will stiffen up the clutch lever operation, so they are not much fun to operate in, say, parades or heavy traffic.

The heavy-duty clutch spring to fit 1998 and later Big Twins and Twin Cams is available from Harley's Screamin' Eagle parts line. The only problem is that Harley doesn't list the part number for the spring as being sold separately in its catalog. To get the spring, Harley wants you to buy its entire Screamin' Eagle performance clutch kit at $230! To order just the heavy-duty clutch spring, order H-D 37951-98. Cost is around $25.

TIP ON BUYING PARTS FROM HARLEY

This practice of selling parts in kit form only, and not listing the parts individually, is common practice with Harley.

If you want to order a separate part from an item that is listed in kit form only, simply go to your dealer and ask it to pull up the instructions that come with the kit on its computer. The instructions will list a breakdown of the parts that are included in the kit, including the individual part numbers. With this information, you can finally now order just the part you need (in this case the stronger clutch spring).

STOCK SHOCKS

It has often been said that there are only two things wrong with the stock Harley shocks: the right shock and the left shock!

While adequate for some riders, the stock shocks leave much to be desired by performance nuts. Whoever chose the spring load on those shocks should be taken out and flogged, or at least forced to ride for eight hours on a bumpy road with a set installed. The springs are too stiff to absorb small bumps, and, should you encounter a pothole, the shocks will bottom out. Ouch! Then, they will rebound and attempt to throw you off the bike. No fun.

Harley knows this and offers better shocks now, but only on certain models. No matter what type of riding you do, upgrade the stock shocks to quality performance units. The only reason that most people don't do this is because good performance shocks are not cheap.

TIRE TIP

When it comes to rider safety, your tires and their condition are very important—as in your life depends on them. Also consider mileage when purchasing tires. Very sticky race tires work well on both the track and street, but one type of performance they won't give you is longevity. Nor are some of the stock tires noted for the amount of time they spend on your rims. And, of course, the faster your bike goes, the faster your rear tire goes away.

So when it's time to re-rubber again and you want to stick with the same brand, consider switching to Dunlop's K491 or other high-mileage tires. The K491s look and perform about the same as the D401 tires, except they can last 50 percent longer or more. You can now spend your tire budget on go-fast parts, like a new set of fork-tongued spark plugs. Only kidding!

ADJUSTING REAR DRIVE BELTS

Old timers like me grew up using chains to connect our transmissions to the rear wheels. When Harley first dropped the chains and switched to rear belt drives, I (and I'm sure many others) thought this was a bad idea. Surely these flimsy belts were not going to hold up and were going to be a source of all kinds of problems. Well I was wrong! These belts exceeded my expectations, as well as those of many others, including the Motor Company.

The belts last longer than anyone had expected; they rarely need adjusting; they cause less vibration; they don't require periodic oiling; they don't rust; and they keep the bike cleaner. More importantly, the belt weighs less than the chain it replaced, so it takes less energy to spin. That previously wasted energy can now be used to spin the rear wheel instead of the chain.

For maximum-effort bikes, like drag bikes, chains are still the only way to go, because they are considerably stronger than the belts. For most street performance applications, the belts will work fine.

Unlike chains, which must have some slack in them, belts are run under tension. Harley makes and sells a fancy tool to ensure that the belts are adjusted to the proper tension. I have the tool, and I'm sure it works as designed, but to date, I have never used it.

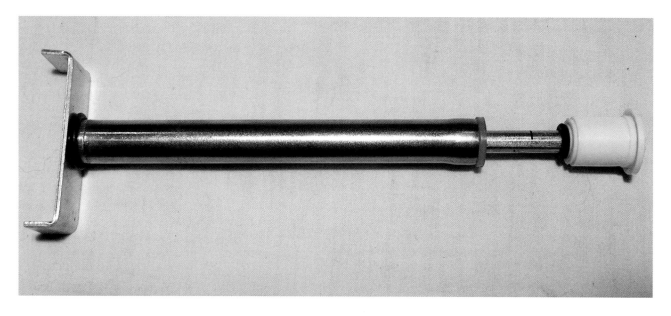

Harley sells this tool to check the tension of your rear drive belt.

There's an easier way to check belt adjustment than using the tool. I just have someone sit on the bike with their weight on the seat and the bike in an upright position. Then I grab the belt between my thumb and index finger and forcefully twist the belt to the right. If the belt is properly adjusted, I should be able to twist the belt almost one-quarter of a turn, but not all the way. If I can twist the belt to a full one-quarter turn or more, the belt is too loose and needs to be tightened. If I can't twist the belt to almost a one-quarter turn, the belt is too tight and needs to be loosened.

This sounds entirely too simple, but it works. After adjusting the belt, the rear wheel must always run true to the frame and not be cocked off to one side. There is a simple tool you can make to check wheel to frame alignment (I'll show it to you later).

REMEMBER THE OLD CHAIN RULE?

When you install a new chain, you should always replace both front and rear sprockets at the same time.

Unfortunately, the chain rule applies to belts as well. I used the word "unfortunately" because of the money involved. Compared to the cost of a chain and sprockets, the belt and belt sprockets (pulleys) are very expensive. For around $50 you can get a good chain, or for about $100 you can get a good O-ring chain. A set of front and rear chain sprockets will set you back about another $100. So for around 200 bucks, you could have a new set of sprockets and a good O-ring chain.

Looking in a big name aftermarket cycle catalog, a new stock-length Gates 1.125-inch belt for a newer Dyna or Softail will set you back about $250. That's two-and-one-half times the cost of a good O-ring chain. A stock OEM type set of pulleys (sprockets) will set you back another $400. It's a good thing the belts last longer than the chains, because the way I add it up, you're looking at about $650 just for parts. Now, if you want to run the fancy billet chrome rear pulleys, open your wallet a little wider because you could be looking at over a $1,000 for the set!

NOTES:

CHAPTER 6 **DYNAMOMETERS**

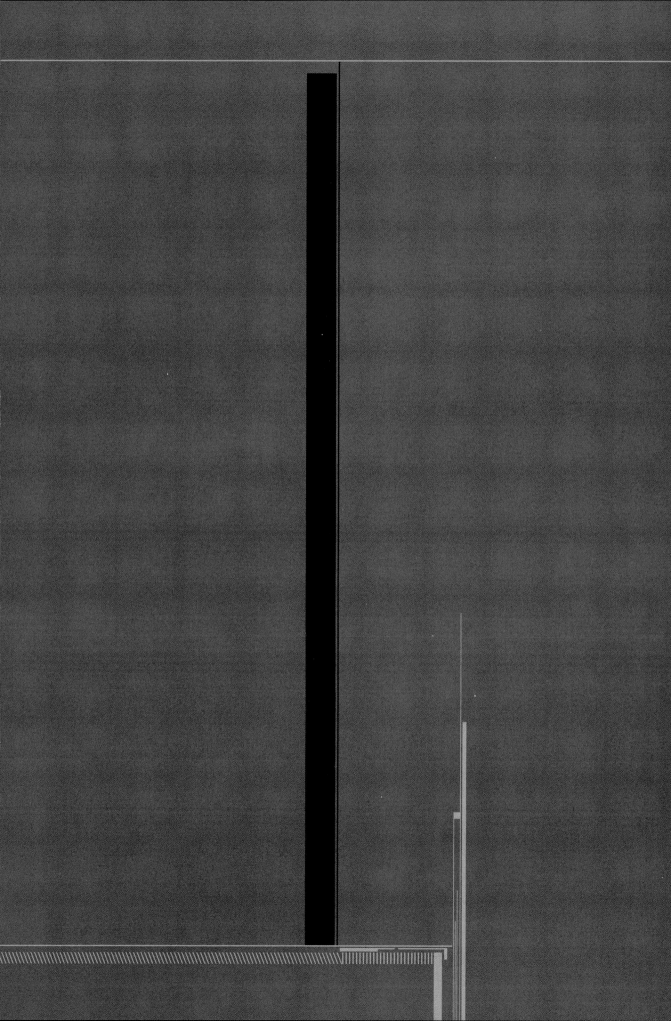

WHY YOU NEED THEM

The recent widespread use of dynamometers, commonly called dynos (mainly the rear-wheel type), has become a major asset for power tuning.

Not only will they let you know what works and what just costs you money, but they are also useful in silencing folk who like to stretch the truth a bit about their bike's power output. Most shops that have dynos will, for a small investment, perform a few pulls (usually three) and get an average baseline torque band and horsepower curve for you. The next time someone brags about his bike's power-making abilities, tell that person to put up (the dyno printout) or shut up. If he's telling the truth, he'll be more than happy to oblige, but if he comes up with an excuse, you can be assured he is stretching the truth a bit.

If you do your homework correctly, the dyno will back you up with a nice power chart. I laminate mine and post them on my shop's wall. It's easier to show people power than it is to try to convince them of its existence. I highly recommend that you utilize rear-wheel dynos for tuning carburetors, EFI systems, ignitions, and exhaust systems.

There are two basic types of dynamometers: absorption and inertia. I'll briefly explain both, but for our purposes, all you need to know is how they differ.

Absorption dynos are usually mechanically connected to the motor's crankshaft and sometimes to the transmission drive sprocket.

Inertia dynos usually involve the rear wheel of the motorcycle resting on a roller or drum. Of the two, the absorption dynos are better because you can vary the load resistance that the powerplant has to overcome.

Both types measure torque output to compute horsepower. The absorption dynos are better tools because you can do both steady-state and WOT testing. The simpler inertia dyno is more commonly used in bike shops because of the cost, lack of complexity, and speed of use.

ABSORPTION DYNOS

There are two main types of absorption dynos: water brake absorption and eddy current absorption.

The water brake absorption dyno, as its name implies, uses water (or sometimes oil) to measure power output. The motor is connected to a water brake device and must overcome the resistance of the water using vanes in an enclosed device (the brake). The amount of flow resistance applied by the water can be adjusted.

Power is then computed by the amount of pressure the motor can overcome, so this type of dyno is often just called a brake dyno.

The eddy current absorption dyno uses electricity to measure torque. In this case, the powerplant must overcome an electromagnetic field. The strength of that field can be regulated. Of the two, the eddy current dyno does a better job of measuring small power differences, but it's bulkier and more costly than a water brake dyno.

INERTIA DYNOS

These dynos use inertia—which is, for our purposes, the tendency of a body at rest to stay at rest (in other words, to resist acceleration)—to measure torque. I like to think of these as accelerometers, because they measure acceleration rates. Inertia dynos use the rear wheel of the motorcycle to rotate a heavy drum, or roller, of a known weight. Torque is then computed by measuring how fast (in time) the rear wheel accelerates the drum (in rpm). This type of dyno is usually just called a rear-wheel dyno.

Compared with the brake and eddy current dynos, the rear-wheel dyno is less complicated, easily maintained, cheaper, and much faster to use. Because of these reasons, it is the most common type of dyno in bike shops. The operator simply rolls the bike onto the dyno, adjusts the front wheel stop to position the rear wheel correctly on the roller, enters the correct environmental information, pushes a button to start the data recorder on the dyno, and opens up the throttle.

The downside to the rear-wheel dyno is the fact that you can't vary the dyno's load resistance, which means that these dynos are only good for measuring WOT performance. Some rear-wheel dynos can be converted to an inertia/eddy current hybrid by adding an eddy current absorption unit. This addition makes rear-wheel dynos much more versatile, but due to the increased cost, not many are converted. With an eddy current unit connected, though, a rear-wheel dyno is able to do steady-state measurements. The Dynojet 250 has this load-adding capability.

After the run is made, a computer connected to the dyno prints a graph showing the torque band curve and computed horsepower.

AVOIDING DYNO DISASTERS

If a dyno is maintained, calibrated, and operated correctly, it is very reliable and accurate. The two mechanical parts of the equation are usually not a problem.

Unfortunately, when dyno disasters occur, they can usually be traced to the human part of the equation: the operator.

Let's take a closer look at what information the dyno needs, and what the operator must do. We'll also discuss what you need to do before—and during—dyno runs. My goal is to help you avoid the dyno disasters I've encountered in the past.

DYNO TESTING

When a run is made on the dyno, raw data is collected. "Raw" just means that it has not been corrected for environmental conditions. For tuning purposes, using raw data will work because the data will still be relative. But, if there's a considerable environmental change between runs, the information will no longer be relative, so it won't produce an accurate comparison.

The dyno's computer software uses a correction factor (CF) to convert the raw data and produces a printout corrected to a standard. The common standard in the United States is the SEA CF standard, which corrects the dynos information to zero humidity, air temperature of 60 degrees Fahrenheit, and barometric pressure of 1,013 millibars, or 29.92 inches of mercury.

This way, data recorded on different days or in different locations will be relative and useful for power comparisons. But what happens if the operator enters incorrect environmental data? Well, if you put garbage in, you'll get garbage out.

TRICKS THEY MIGHT USE TO MANIPULATE THE NUMBERS

Some shops that carry out performance modifications offer (as either a bonus or a come-on) before-and-after dyno charts. If you're dealing with an honest shop that has a dyno operator who is both consistent and competent, this is great, because you get to see exactly what you bought.

But what happens if the shop is not quite honest? Could it manipulate the data in some way to make the modification look better that it actually is? You bet, and it's extremely easy to do. Here are a few ways they can juggle the numbers.

THE THROTTLE TRICK

The simplest way to juggle numbers is to alter the way the throttle is applied. This is also one of the hardest ones to catch, because it doesn't leave evidence behind. For this reason, you should always be present and watch the way the operator applies the throttle during the runs. If the shop won't let you watch, take your money elsewhere. Many dyno cells have had windows installed just for this purpose, so customers can safely watch their bikes being tested.

THE GEAR TRICK

Most runs on rear-wheel dynos are made with the bike in fourth gear, although some tuners like to use fifth gear to load the motor down for tuning purposes. If you use different gears between tests, you will get different results. If the "before" run is made in fourth gear and the "after" run is made in fifth gear, the fifth gear run will produce higher numbers, even if nothing had been changed on the bike. This is another good reason to witness the runs.

You can actually check for this on your power printout. On a Dynojet dyno printout, this information is on the bottom right side; look on your dyno printout for rpm/mph. If rpm/mph ratio numbers are different, so were the gear ratios between tests. If the numbers are in the low to mid 50s, this normally indicates a fourth gear run.

PLAYING GOD WITH THE WEATHER TRICK

Power output numbers can easily be manipulated by changing the weather data. Let's consider barometric pressure. If you entered 30.40 inches of mercury for the first run and then changed the pressure to 28.20 inches of mercury for the second run, the power figures will be higher on the second run even if nothing was changed on the bike. This is because the high pressure will get a negative correction value and the lower pressure will get a positive correction value. On the Dynojet printout, compare the weather data on the top line of the text for large discrepancies. Also look at the CF value for considerable changes.

You can use other environmental data to accomplish the same results.

In regard to CFs, I don't like to rely on data (even if inputted correctly) that has been computed using a CF lower than 0.95 or higher than 1.05. If you end up with a CF beyond these ranges, you are better off waiting to test on another day, when the weather conditions are more favorable for testing.

Now you know a few of the ways numbers can be manipulated. I am in no way implying that this is a common practice, but stuff happens, and I've been burned before—not on purpose, but by incompetence. My goal is to see that the same thing does not happen to you.

BEFORE DYNO TESTING

The first thing you have to do is find a dyno, and I don't mean that to be funny. As we have covered, there are several types of dynos. They also come with varying degrees of application parameters. For instance, a Dynojet 150 is limited to what it will do, the 200 is more advanced, and the 250 is even more so.

If your luck is better than mine, you may have access to more than one dyno in your area. Call around and find out which shop has what kind of dyno and get prices. If you can find one that has an exhaust gas analyzer, I highly recommend you use that one. It makes the job of tuning not only faster, but also more accurate. If you want spot-on carburetion, an exhaust gas analyzer is very helpful for dialing in your fuel curve. It also makes the tuning process faster, so you may even save some money. And that's a big part of what this book is all about.

The most important thing you should do before testing is to make sure that all aspects of your bike are ready. Here are a few things to check:

- Fill your fuel tank with fresh gas; never test with a low gas tank.

- Clean or replace your air filter and gas filter (if used).

- Check your carburetor for proper operation, ensuring that the throttle cables are operating correctly and fully opening your throttle plate.

- Check all lubricants—motor oil, transmission, and clutch case— and if they are not relatively new, change them (don't forget the oil filter).

- Check the condition of all electrical equipment; spark plug wires and battery connections; the state of charge in your battery and charge it if necessary; and your timing, if

This is often the only view people got to see of my 1984 XR-1000. The XR-1000 was an interesting mix, using the lower-end of a 1000-cc Sportster with shortened cylinders and the cylinder heads of a XR-750 factory racing bike.

The XR-1000 could be easily modified to produce over 90 horsepower by having Branch re-work the heads, installing a set of Harley's E cams, raising the compression, and opening up the exhaust system. (Note: Branch Flowmetrics did all the heads used on the XR-1000 engines.) Harley's racing division would even send you detailed instructions on how to make the modifications if you made the request. Unfortunately, due to their cost and lack of sales, Harley only produced 1,700 of these bikes in 1983–1984 before the XR-1000 project was dropped, yet many additional complete engines were assembled and crated. These engines were later sold, and many ended up on the street.
If you want to invest in an XR-1000, shoot for an original, documented production bike. In the past, Harley has been willing to confirm if a serial number is from a real production XR-1000 and could even tell you the day it was made. It was a sad day for me when I sold this piece of Harley history.

it's adjustable, and install new spark plugs, making sure they are gapped correctly (never test with old, dirty plugs).

- Check drivetrain parts, adjustment of the drive chain or drive belt, the primary chain adjustment, and air pressure in your tires.

- Check to see that all fasteners are tight—motor mounts, axles, shocks, etc. (The last time I witnessed a bike being tested, a part fell off in the middle of a run, surely embarrassing its owner in the process).

- Check adjustment of engine and drive components—pushrods, clutch, etc.

- Check everything else that I may have forgotten!

THINGS TO DO AT THE DYNO

Before putting your bike on the dyno and your money in the operator's hand, go to the shop, talk to the operator, and ask him to show you the equipment. Ask some general questions about the dyno: What type is it? How long has the shop had it? How long has the operator been operating dynos? When was the dyno last calibrated? What kind of options does it have? Will you be able to watch the runs? What kind of ventilation does the cell have? Finally, ask if the dyno is set up to display rpm or miles per hour. You want the readouts in rpm.

If the operator puts up with you and gives you straight answers, you've probably found a good shop to work with. If the operator is evasive or punches you in the nose for being a pain in the butt, you're better off taking your business—and your nose—somewhere else.

Shortly before going to the dyno shop, you should try to record accurate weather information yourself. Bring this information, and something to write with, to the dyno shop. Once there, ask the operator what the barometric pressure, humidity, and temperature is at the time, as well as the elevation of the cell above sea level. Write that information down and see how it compares to yours. By doing this, hopefully the operator will remember to enter all of the right information into the dyno's computer and will figure that you know what you're

doing and are going to be checking and comparing that information against the dyno printout. Don't forget to check that the dyno information is in rpm, not miles per hour.

THINGS TO CHECK AT THE TIME OF THE RUN

Again before starting, talk with the dyno operator and explain why you are there and what you are trying to accomplish with the dyno session. Are you going to be tuning something or just making a power run? At what rpm will the run start and stop? Ask the operator for advice on how to accomplish your goals. If the operator has been doing this for a while, his knowledge and expertise will be extremely valuable to you. Remember the bottom line: you're paying to be there.

Make sure that your motor and its oil are at normal operating temperature before testing starts. Confer with the operator about how this will be done.

Make sure the ventilation system for the cell is in operation. Never allow your bike to be tested in a cell without a constant fresh air exchange. You can't make power without lots of oxygen.

I once witnessed an operator in Anchorage make several runs in an enclosed dyno cell without the ventilation system running. When he looked like he was about to be asphyxiated, he finally opened a door to let some outside air into the cell, and then went back to testing, still minus a ventilation system.

Pay attention while the operator is making the runs. How is the bike positioned on the roller? How is the throttle being applied? What speed are the runs starting at? Watch the gear shifting and note which gear the bike is in during the run.

SUMMARY

Hopefully, I didn't make the dyno experience sound like a nightmare, because it's not. I always look forward to, and enjoy, taking on the machine!

After your first time around, this stuff will become second nature. The dyno is a valuable tool, and if you have a good operator, it can be an enjoyable and enlightening experience. Remember that in order to build a high-performance motor, you must plan and execute everything correctly to achieve your desired results. The same thing holds true for dyno testing and tuning.

CHAPTER 7 **COMPRESSION 101**

SQUEEZING AIR AND FUEL TOGETHER

Question: What's your compression ratio?

Answer: Which one do you want to know?

I recently had a conversation with a newbie. My definition of a "newbie" is someone who has recently (within the last few years) purchased a Harley. The newbie had read some bike magazines and became a self-appointed expert in the field of high-performance Harleys.

Anyway, the newbie asks me what compression I'm running. I tell him it's only 9.6:1 in this bike right now, but I need to raise it to 10:1. Newbie says: "You don't want to do that, man; 9.5:1 is as high as you want to go on a street bike!"

I just smiled and said to myself that the damn fool doesn't have a clue what he's talking about. That got me to thinking: since compression is so important when designing a performance motor, maybe I should collect my insights on the subject and share them with you. If your compression is too low, you will go slow, and if your compression is too high, your motor will die.

If you ask today's average novice weekend Harley or alterative V-twin riders what their bike's compression ratio is, perhaps 10 percent of them would be able to give you a number. The next question would be what type of compression it is—dynamic, corrected, mechanical, effective, cranking, or static?

If you're lucky, maybe 10 percent of the 10 percent would know and say it's mechanical, because it's the mechanical compression figure that is most commonly used. So if my take on this is anywhere close to reality, only 1 percent of all average novice riders know what their compression ratio is and that the value is describing mechanical compression.

So, since mechanical compression is the most commonly expressed type of engine compression, does that mean it is the most important one you need to know? My response is no!

What's important about these other types of compression—static, effective, dynamic, cranking, and corrected?

I will now try to answer that question by explaining the different types of compression and how they relate to making Harleys go fast—hopefully without blowing up in the process! I'll also share some compression recommendations, but keep in mind that every motor combination is different. You can go from mild to wild, and the ballpark figures I'll give you are what I consider to be safe for a happy high-performance street motor that is running on pump gas with torque in the middle and horsepower on the top.

MECHANICAL COMPRESSION

This is the way compression is most often referred to. Think of mechanical compression as uncorrected compression, or as a reference number to use in figuring out what is really going on inside of your cylinders.

Another way to think of mechanical compression is the total compression you could mechanically create with the parts assembled. Mechanical compression is computed by measuring the head's combustion chamber volume, then adding that figure to the deck height (the volume occupied by the head gasket). That number, usually in cubic centimeters, is then divided by the piston's sweep area, also in cubic centimeters (bore and stroke). That will give you a baseline mechanical compression to start from.

Why did I say that mechanical compression is not the most important thing to know?

Because mechanical compression assumes the intake valve closes at bottom dead center (BDC) just as the piston starts its way up the cylinder, but this is almost never the case.

In reality, the intake valve closes sometime after the piston is on its way up the cylinder. If the intake valve did close at BDC, the motor would lose potential power because it would not be taking advantage of the inertial velocity of the incoming air. Physically, the motor cannot start making compression until the intake valve closes, so if the intake valve never closed, you would have zero compression. Do you see my point? Mechanical compression is a starting point, but on its own it is not very important.

CORRECTED COMPRESSION

In my opinion, this is the most important type of compression you should be concerned about in motor design.

A better way to describe corrected compression is to call it corrected mechanical compression. Corrected compression is controlled by your cam's timing and when the intake valve closes. That's why our newbie's 9.5:1 (one size fits all) maximum compression ratio is total B.S.

Here's an example: In this case, the test bike is a 95-inch Twin Cam with the newbie's magic 9.5:1 mechanical compression ratio. Say you want to run the Andrews TW60 cam. The TW60 closes the intake valve at 56 ABDC, so with that cam timing the corrected compression on this motor would now be 8.01:1.

Will a naturally aspirated motor with an 8:1 corrected compression ratio be very powerful? Of course not! By the way, this is the same corrected compression ratio that the stock Twin Cam has.

In my opinion, a motor with a well-designed cylinder head and good cylinder mixture turbulence on 92-octane pump gas can safely handle up to a maximum of 9.2:1 corrected compression. Pushing it past that ratio can lead to detonation and other bad things.

I would not recommend running this 9.2:1 corrected compression ratio in Alaska where 87-octane gas is often the only thing that's available and 90-octane is an occasional option.

To stay on the safe side, I'd keep the corrected compression at or just below 9:1. I've had good, safe results up here with 8.8 to 9.0:1 corrected.

To get our example bike's corrected compression to 9:1, you would have to increase the mechanical compression ratio to 10.7:1. If I were designing this motor, I'd go with a mechanical compression of 10.5:1, which would yield a safe 8.8:1 corrected compression and the motor shouldn't complain too much if it has to drink 87-octane gas every now and then.

So how do I figure out my corrected compression ratio?

Here's the old hard way. Remove the heads, install a degree wheel, rotate motor to the timing position ABDC when the intake valve closes, measure sweep area left in the cylinder, and then use the mechanical compression formula.

And here's the easy way: Do what I do, and use a computer software program like Accelerator Pro III or Desktop Dyno 2000.

The importance of correct compression is critical to designing and building a successful street performance engine. I am extremely disappointed that other writers throw compression ratio numbers around without clearly addressing what they mean, or explaining the importance of corrected compression. If you get corrected compression wrong, you will end up with a detonation-prone engine that won't last very long, or an engine that is extremely low on power.

STATIC COMPRESSION

The best way to describe static compression is just to think of it as the average real-time operating compression (pressure) that happens in your cylinders as you accelerate down the road. Peak static compression will occur at or near the location of your motor's peak volumetric efficiency. Static compression is important because it will give you an idea of the potential power output your combination could create. It can also warn you of the possibilities of detonation when you go too far.

High static compression can cause hard starting and a motor that will run hot. I don't recommend going over a computed 160-psi static compression, but I'm Mr. Safe. H-D, as in the factory, likes to keep its bikes at or below 140 psi.

EFFECTIVE COMPRESSION

Effective compression can be described as hypothetical operational compression, or possible total effective compression in real time when operating at higher rpm.

It is computed and controlled by your cam's timing, i.e., when the valves open and close and the cams overlap at TDC.

The efficiency of your induction system is very important when computing effective compression, because effective compression relies heavily on the velocity of the air/fuel mixture and the ram air effect of the moving mixture. The whole purpose of big carbs, ported heads, performance cams, etc. is to pack the most air and fuel you possibly can into the cylinders before the intake

valve closes. Effective compression and camshaft percentage go hand-in-hand in letting you know what your combination may do.

Here's an example of effective compression as compared to other types of compression. In this example, the motor has a mechanical compression of 10:1. Because of the cam's timing (when the intake valve closes), it has a corrected compression of only 9:1.

The efficient ram air effect of scavenging, caused by inertia from the cam's overlap and the velocity of the air/fuel mixture in the intake tract, means the cylinder is being filled with air and fuel to a greater capacity than would happen if the mixture were not moving. In this case, we'll say that the efficient ram air effect we are getting is producing an effective compression ratio of 11:1.

As a rule, effective compression only comes into play at higher rpm, when the induction system can take full advantage of valve overlap and the ram air effect of inertia.

To review, our mechanical compression ratio is 10:1, our corrected compression ratio due to when the intake valve closes is 9:1, and our total effective compression ratio at high rpm due to efficient inertia scavenging is 11:1.

Effective compression and camshaft percentages are useful in comparing different cam characteristics. Insufficient effective compression can cause a motor to be down in power in the mid to top range.

WHAT IS CAMSHAFT PERCENTAGE?

Camshaft percentage is an accurate way to evaluate cam durations and characteristics when comparing one cam to another. It is also useful for estimating the possible engine efficiency of one cam grind compared to another. Basically, it is an index of how long the intake valve is open and occupying the cylinder, and it is controlled by the duration of the camshaft. It is calculated from when the intake valve opens at BTDC, to when it closes at ABDC. Camshaft percentage is one of the factors used to compare camshafts with computerized engine simulators and modeling software.

As an example, the stock cam in the Twin Cam has a value of 107 percent and is relatively mild when compared to the more aggressive stock Evo Sportster cam's percentage of 109.3 percent.

Equally, a camshaft with percentages of more than 120 percent will probably shine at the top end, but it won't do much in the low to mid ranges. A camshaft with a smaller percentage of 110 percent or less can cause a power loss at the top end, but will produce good torque down low. For a street bike, I like to shoot for a camshaft percentage around 115–120 percent, but no greater than 120 percent for a hot street bike.

If you just want to make power on the top end, to run on the drag strip, or turn big horsepower numbers on a dyno, you'll want a cam with value of 120 percent or greater.

Knowing that too much camshaft duration can be a

bad thing for a street motor, I went with a milder cam grind with only 111 percent the first time around on my recent Twin Cam project bike. This was the best choice among the few cam grinds that were available back then.

The goals I had for my new street performance project bike then were simple: 95 = 100 + 100 on 87. Translation: the Twin Cam motor would be limited to the easily obtainable 95-inch displacement. The motor must produce an extremely flat broad torque band with a targeted goal of 100 lb-ft, and it will be limited to a 6,200 rpm redline. The targeted horsepower output will be 100 at or before redline. Finally, the motor must be able to accomplish all of this while running on low 87-octane pump gas.

I've included a dyno chart of my early test results running a camshaft with only 111 percent.

The Dynojet Model 200 rear-wheel dyno showed that I was very close to achieving my targeted goals, but I wasn't going to get there with this camshaft.

The conservative 111 percent camshaft was causing the motor to run out of airflow on the top-end. Notice how the horsepower flat-lines from 5,400 rpm to redline. With the assembled parts, this cam may have been adequate for an 88-inch motor, but it wasn't going to cut it on a 95-inch motor.

Interestingly, by entering the correct information and Branch's flow data, the Accelerator Pro software predicted that this cam would cause the motor to run out of airflow within 100 rpm of where it happened on the rear-wheel

dyno, and the horsepower prediction was within 1/2 horsepower.

This is a good example of how useful these programs can be, if used correctly. What about peak torque? The Accelerator Pro program didn't even come close, but Desktop Dyno 2000 did. As I said, these are tools for comparing combinations, but their numbers are not to be taken as gospel.

To accomplish my goals back then, I had to wait six months for the right camshaft to become available. All that was required was a cam with a little more lift and 116 percent of duration.

The compression was also raised 1/4 point to match the new intake valve-closing event, and I tossed in a set JIMS roller rocker arms and big axle Powerglide lifters for good measure. Even with these changes, the motor still runs out of air at 6,000 rpm, but this is about the best I can do while still producing my required and important torque band.

CRANKING COMPRESSION

Cranking compression is a diagnostic tool and has little to do with what's happening when the engine is running.

Would you freak out if you checked your compression and measured 205-psi cranking pressure in your cylinders? Remember that approximately 140 psi is stock static compression. Well, 205 psi is exactly what I had in the 95-inch Twin Cam when I was running the TW-37B

Here we see the rear-wheel dyno graph from the first cam I tried in my 95-inch Dyna Twin Cam project bike. Although 104 lb-ft of torque and 93.5 horsepower is respectable, I designed this motor to do better. The peak torque is good, but the torque band should have been broader and should have peaked about 300 to 400 rpm higher. Also, the horsepower should have continued rising to 6,000 rpm. Obviously, the cam was causing the motor to run out of air; a simple cam change and compression correction should solve this problem so my targeted design goal can be achieved. Note: An exhaust gas analyzer was not available on this dyno at the time this run was conducted.

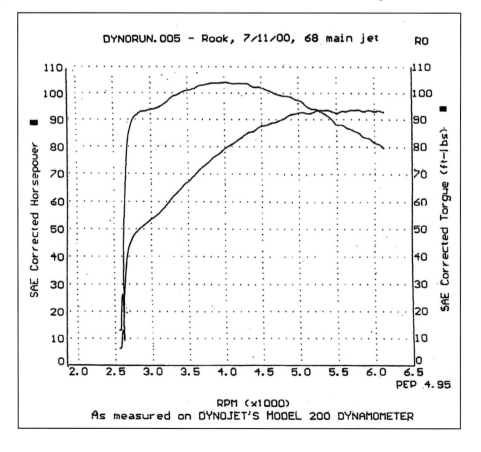

cam. The motor pulled really hard down low and, due to the combustion chamber shapes, it ran fine on pump gas.

Cranking compression is measured statically by inserting a compression gauge into the spark plug hole when the motor is warm, opening the carb wide open, and cranking the motor over until the needle on the gauge stops moving up.

By checking and comparing cranking compression as time goes by, you can monitor how well your pump is sealing, and it will let you know if you are beginning to have ring or valve-seat sealing problems. Over time, your compression could actually increase if the rings and valves are still doing their jobs, and at the same time, carbon builds up in the cylinder heads and/or piston crowns.

Here's an example of cranking compression compared to the real world. As measured with the TW-37B cam, I had 205 psi of cranking pressure in my cylinders on the Twin Cam. By itself, 205 psi sounds scary, like a motor that will need 110-octane fuel to stop it from detonating. But in the grand scheme of things it means little, other than the fact that I had a pump that was sealing very well. When running at idle with a compression gauge inserted into one of the cylinders, the motor had a real-time operating pressure of only 75 psi, and its computed static compression, accelerating down the road under load, was only 154 psi.

In other words, the only time I have to worry about the 205 psi is when I'm checking the cranking compression. With today's efficient combustion chamber designs that maximize turbulence through the use of squish bands, cranking compression numbers are moving up. Today, 190 to 200 psi of cranking compression is not uncommon on a properly set-up street motor.

DYNAMIC COMPRESSION

Dynamic compression, like cranking compression, is another diagnostic tool. About the only thing I have found it good for is monitoring your motor's sealing ability, as in the rings and valves. If there's another use for it, I can't find one!

To determine your dynamic compression ratio, take the pressure of 1 atmosphere (which is 14.7 psi) and add that to your cranking compression, and then divide the total by 14.7 psi. Do a dynamic compression check to baseline your motor shortly after a top-end overhaul. If your dynamic compression drops by one atmosphere, it's time to start thinking about freshening up the top end.

Back when I was running the TW-37B cam, I had 205 psi of cranking pressure, so my computed dynamic compression was 14.9:1! After I changed to the TW-55 cam, I was down to 185 psi, or 13.6:1 dynamic.

So the next time a newbie wants to know your compression ratio, just rattle off your dynamic compression numbers, and you'll be telling the truth. He'll be most impressed, although somewhat confused. The newbie's discomfort is not your fault; after all, he's the expert, not you. See ... knowledge can be fun sometimes.

LEAKDOWN TESTER

As long as we're discussing diagnostic tools, let's look at the leakdown tester, as it's very useful for diagnostic compression monitoring.

To use a leakdown tester, you must lock the piston in the cylinder to be tested at, or near, TDC on the compression stroke with both valves closed. Screw the leakdown tester into the spark plug hole of the cylinder you are testing. Apply air pressure from an external source to the cylinder through the leakdown tester. You should typically use 100 psi to simplify calculating leakdown percentages.

Leakdown testers have two gauges. Compare the applied pressure gauge (100 psi) to the cylinder side gauge—for this example, we'll say it reads 96 psi. That means the cylinder has a leakdown rate of 4 percent. Zero percent is perfect, but it is almost impossible to obtain. Racers try for no more than a 2 percent leakdown, and leakdown rates of 3 to 5 percent is considered decent.

It is not unusual to see new factory motors being shipped with up to 7 or 8 percent leakdown. After the rings seat, hopefully this percentage will go down, because much over 7 percent is not very good for making power. If you are seeing a rate this high, it's time to

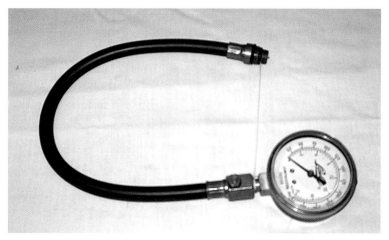

Compression gauges are used to measure the cranking compression of a cylinder.

start budgeting for parts, because it means your rings and/or valve seats are in need of repair.

With the leakdown tester, you can often pinpoint a top-end problem. First, remove carb and intake manifold and the exhaust system. Next, inject some motor oil into the cylinder and then move the piston up and down the cylinder a few times to coat the piston rings. If the leakdown percentage decreases, it could mean the rings are bad.

To check valve seats for sealing, apply air pressure and listen for escaping air from the ports, or inject a small amount of soapy water around the valve seats and look for bubbles. As the leakdown percentage increases, your pump's sealing ability and performance will decrease. If the rings are allowing combustion gas blow-by to pressurize your engine cases, bad things can happen.

Leakdown testers usually run over $100, but I made one for about $30 using old parts, and I'll tell you how to make one in Chapter 12, Tools. The hardest part of using the leakdown tester by yourself is trying to figure out a way to lock the piston in position with the rear brake, so the piston won't move during the testing process.

COMPRESSION REVIEW

Mechanical compression: This is the baseline. On its own, it doesn't give you enough information on real operating compression, because mechanical compression doesn't consider when the intake valve closes on the power stroke. And if the door's still open, you're not compressing anything.

Corrected compression: This is a more realistic way to look at compression, because corrected compression considers when the intake valve does close. I consider this—hands down—to be the most important compression the motor designer and builder needs to know. Corrected compression does not take into consideration the ram air effect of inertia gained from airflow velocity.

Static compression: This is the average compression you should be generating in the cylinder when the motor is operating at a high volumetric efficiency (VE). It is controlled by cam timing, overlap, and intake tract efficiency.

Effective compression: This takes into consideration the ram air effect of inertia gained from airflow velocity. It looks at cam timing, cam overlap, and intake tract flow capabilities. Head flow data and induction system capabilities are important in effective compression.

Cranking compression: A diagnostic tool for monitoring rings and valve seats.

Dynamic compression: A diagnostic tool for monitoring rings and valve seats, and a very useful tool for impressing newbies.

Camshaft percentage: This is the percentage that the intake valve occupies in the cylinder when it is opened. Stock camshafts usually run below 110 percent. Strong torque cams and mild horsepower cams usually run in the 110 to 120 percent range. Camshafts with percentages above 120 percent are usually designed for high-rpm top-end horsepower. Low to midrange power with cams of 120-plus percent may be soft, and slow-speed tuning may be more difficult. Increasing compression with these cams may help recover some of the lost midrange power; or you can just stay below 120 percent.

AS A SIDE NOTE

To confuse and complicate compression matters even more, the terms (even by very knowledgeable engine builders) are consistently interchanged and/or misused.

Here are two of the most prevalent examples: Static compression is often used when referring to mechanical compression, and dynamic compression is often used when referring to effective compression.

Even the experts get this mixed up, so don't feel so bad if you do, too.

I've tried to present my thoughts on compression in a way that will help you understand and make good use of computer-based engine building software programs like Accelerator Pro III.

COMPRESSION, CAMS, AND REVERSION

Now that we have a better understanding of compression, we can deal with cams and intake tract reversion. When a V-twin is modified, it is generally done to increase performance, not decrease it.

The first logical improvements deal with correcting the carburetor's air/fuel mixture and unrestricting the intake and exhaust tract flow abilities. After that, you're looking at increasing the amount of air and fuel you can flow through the motor, and the easiest way to do this is with a cam change. But which cam should you use? Choosing the wrong cam for a particular application is very common. Thanks to engine-building software programs like Accelerator Pro III and Desktop Dyno 2000, this doesn't have to be as tough as it used to be, but you must still come face to face with what you want your motor to do.

There's an old saying that a light bike can handle more cam than a heavy bike. But if both bikes have the same V-twin motor, how does this apply? The underlying concept has to do with vehicle weight and reversion.

Given the importance of corrected compression when designing a motor combination, we know we have to pay close attention to cam timing, especially the point at which the intake valve closes. As a rule, performance cams' intake valves will close later than those of stock cams.

Therefore, we will most likely need to increase the mechanical compression to achieve the proper corrected compression ratio. Mechanical compression can be increased several ways: milling the heads; using a smaller head gasket; using a domed piston; increasing bore size; or by a combination of these methods. But there's more to deal with here than just fixing the corrected compression ratio. Now we have to worry about intake tract reversion.

SAY WHAT?

In the cam section, remember when I said that to select the right cam, first you have to be honest about the results you want. You can't make a motor with stump pulling low-end torque and high-rpm horsepower with a cam change alone!

INTAKE REVERSION DEFINED

Have you ever heard people say "my bike gets on the cam at xxxx rpm" or "my bike really comes on strong at xxxx rpm" or "my cam really hits hard at xxxx rpm and pulls to redline"? Sure you have. Although they may not know it, what they are describing is intake reversion, or more specifically, the point at which intake reversion stops screwing things up.

We now understand that the intake valve does not close at BDC, but somewhere ABDC. We also know that you can't compress anything if the door is still open, and in our case the door is the intake valve.

Reversion, sometimes referred to as fuel standoff, is caused by the distance the piston travels up the cylinder, and the volume of air it displaces while doing so before the intake valve closes. Engine speed plays a big part here. If the motor is not turning fast enough when the piston is moving up the cylinder while the intake valve is still open, some of the air/fuel mixture will be forced back out. It can then travel as far as, or even beyond, the carburetor. Reversion, therefore, robs lots of power from the low end, and also makes it very hard to adjust the idle and low-speed jetting circuits on your carburetor.

Have you ever head someone complain that his bike's carb drips gas out of the air cleaner and onto the motor? It's either coming from the crankcase breather or it's a byproduct of intake reversion. Different cams are designed to do different things in different applications, and at some point every engine will reach a high enough rpm that reversion for its cam will stop, and its power will increase. This is what people are talking about when they say their bike "gets on the cam at xxxx rpm." The later the intake valve closes, the faster the motor must turn to overcome its reversion point.

(As noted earlier, in addition to gas dripping out of the air cleaner, the poor design of the stock breathers on the Evo Big Twins can also cause oil to drip from the air cleaner. Modifying the crankcase breather in the cam chest and using efficiently sealing piston rings can help alleviate some of that problem.)

In conclusion, a heavy bike requires a different cam than a light bike for two main reasons. Heavy bikes are just that, and they require more low-end torque to accel-

erate at the same rate as a light bike. Heavy bikes are used for touring work, and their rpm stay in lower ranges than lighter sportbikes. To make matters worse, heavy touring bikes are often geared higher to reduce rpm at cruising speeds. To choose a cam for a heavy bike, we would look for a low-rpm torque cam.

A cam with an early closing intake valve event will help stop reversion at lower rpm and will make lots of power where a heavy bike's motor lives—below 4,000 rpm. If you install a cam with a late intake valve closing event or one with too much overlap in a heavy bike's engine, it will make less power than the stock cam. You lose all the way around, your power and your money.

Reversion is the same on a lighter bike, but a lighter bike can deal with the power loss at low rpm since it does not require as much low-end torque to accelerate at the same rate as the heavier bike. Even though the low-speed reversion still happens, it's not as big a problem on the lighter bike.

REVERSION PROS AND CONS FOR HEAVY AND LIGHT BIKES

A heavy bike needs a cam that closes the intake valve sooner than a light bike.

A heavy bike needs a cam that will let it pull hard off the line and at highway speed, even when heavily loaded. Maximum torque will need to be in the range where this bike lives—2,500 to 3,500 rpm.

However, this type of cam will not be able to supply enough air to feed the motor at high rpm, above 5,000 rpm, so don't expect much in the way of extreme top-end speed or horsepower.

A lighter bike can handle a cam that closes the intake valve later, which will produce better cylinder refill at higher rpm. And more cylinder refill equals more power!

A lighter bike can have a torque curve that peaks much higher in the power band and produces more horsepower at higher rpm levels. It can use a cam that makes more power at higher rpm levels because it supplies more air to the motor at high rpm.

But too much reversion will cost you low-rpm power or low-end torque. Although this loss may not feel as dramatic on a light bike as it does on a heavy bike, either bike's engine will need to be revved higher to reach its sweet spot when using a cam that closes the intake valve later. You may want to consider lower gear ratios with this type of cam combination to keep the motor in its power band.

Here are some numbers to give you an idea of what to expect from cam-caused reversion:

Intake valve closes	Reversion stops at about
30 degrees ABDC	2,400 rpm
35 degrees ABDC	2,900 rpm
40 degrees ABDC	3,400 rpm
45 degrees ABDC	3,750 rpm
50 degrees ABDC	3,900 rpm

The above information is based on data from Joe Minton, a longtime technical high-performance Harley guru. When you compare this chart to available performance cams, you'll quickly see how the effects of reversion influence a bike. From seat-of-the-pants riding experience, these numbers look a little on the high side, but I'm not going to dispute Joe Minton on this.

So there you have it: My take on engine design, compression, cams, reversion, carburetors, gearing, and a whole bunch of other stuff.

Hopefully this will help you make the right choices when you pull out your wallet. The most important thing to remember when modifying your motorcycle is that you must be honest with yourself. What is really best for you and your riding style? How do you normally ride and what do you want your bike to do?

COMPUTER-BASED SIMULATOR PROGRAMS

Modern engine-building software has come a long way and, providing you understand how to use it and know its limitations, can greatly assist you in comparing motor combinations so you can get it right the first time around. Many old-time performance motor builders scoff at these computer programs; I don't, because they have saved me a lot of time and money.

They are excellent tools for making comparisons, like torque bands produced by different cam grinds, and are very handy at computing things, like mechanical and corrected compression ratios.

Believe it or not, if you input accurate flow data from, say, Branch Flowmetrics, the horsepower number can be unbelievably close. Compared with Branch's flow numbers, though, most head flow numbers are on the high side. This will cause the programs to compute a higher horsepower number than what you'll get on the rear-wheel dyno. So when using these programs, remember that they are designed for comparison purposes only and have their limitations. Be honest when you're putting information into these programs, because if you put garbage in, you'll get garbage back out.

AIRFLOW REQUIREMENTS

Airflow requirements are probably the most important calculations I've learned from hours spent on these engine simulation programs. Satisfying the needs of a 74- or 80-inch motor is one thing, but when the displacement grows

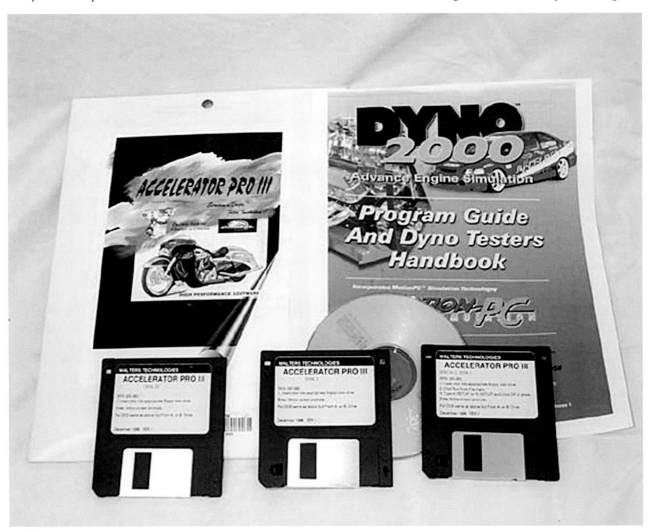

How fast can an old Ironhead Sportster go? It all depends on who put it together and what parts were used.

In the mid-1970s I went through my chopper phase. I'm the tall guy; the shorter guy is my brother, Gary, who is still a dedicated Ironhead Sportster fan. These photos of choppers in the development stage will give you an idea of what I was doing back then. Most chopper builders concentrated on looks. I liked looks, too, but power was just as important to me. To achieve this, the bikes were kept light and powered by modified XLCH magneto-equipped Sportster motors. By the way, did you notice the American Machine and Foundry Company (AMF) t-shirts? This was the decade that AMF ruled H-D.

to 95, 100, or even 120 inches, flowing enough air to keep these monsters breathing to 6,000 rpm becomes a challenge that is not easily met. If you want them to work to 7,000 rpm, it takes even more planning, work, and money.

It's always easier to design and build a really good small high-output motor than it is to build a large one. The big-inch motor requires you to look long and hard at head flow rates, cam timing and induction and exhaust tracts, because these things will make or break big-inch motors!

If you spend all of your time addressing airflow requirements at 6,000-plus rpm, you'll end up with heads that will have next to zero port velocity at low rpm. If that happens, the motor won't run worth spit on the street. Designing a happy motor is a balancing act, because the sum of its assembled parts must

work together in harmony to achieve your desired result.

To satisfy the airflow requirements on a Twin Cam motor with the 95-inch kit installed, the heads and intake system must flow approximately 175 cfm at 10 inches of H_2O to get up to 7,000 rpm. The stock heads will only flow about 118 cfm, so they could only meet the flow requirements of about 5,000 rpm on a 95-inch T-C motor.

It will take some serious work to get a set of heads to flow at 175 cfm and still have good port velocity at lower rpm.

Don't go whole hog with your Hog! Once you get a handle on designing and building a performance street motor, it's very easy and oh-so-tempting to get carried away and assemble a maximum-effort engine. Unless you have another bike that you plan to use as your daily rider, do yourself a favor and don't go down this route! If you do, you may want to pick up a "for sale" sign, because you'll need it soon enough.

Make a list of your required performance goals before you start and then stick to them!

Considering the investment I made in building my most recent happy street performance motor, I could have easily built a 120-plus-horsepower beast with a different combination of parts. That sucker could have melted the rubber off of the rear tire, turned great numbers in the quarter mile, impressed the hell out of the guy running the dyno machine, and would have been totally worthless as a street bike.

The guys at the airport would soon get tired of seeing me and my jerry can trying to score some AV100 fuel. The lesson here is to be careful what you wish for, because what you end up with may not be what you really want at all, much less what you really need!

NOTES:

_____

_____

_____

_____

_____

_____

_____

_____

_____

_____

_____

_____

_____

_____

_____

_____

_____

CHAPTER 8 **DO IT YOURSELF AT HOME HEAD FIX**

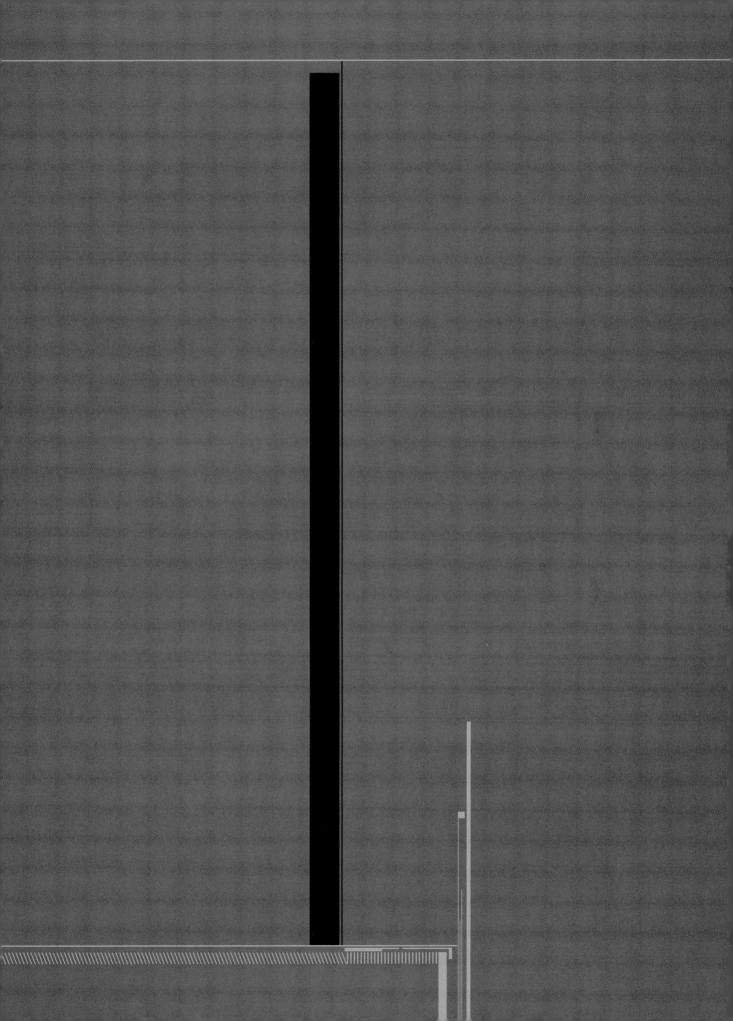

Sooner or later almost every Harley owner will modify his or her bike. The modifications are often done in an attempt to increase performance. Unfortunately, performance modifications are often poorly planned and expensively performed. Some things work, and some things just cost you money!

I've seen the installation of a performance cam in a mostly stock bike many times. The cam changes will often net the owners of these bikes less power where they need it, and a little more power where they never get to. Drag pipes accomplish just about the same thing, but they at least make the bike sound faster.

Another example of this is installing an outrageously large carb on a mostly stock bike for a gigantic 2- or 3-horsepower gain on the top end, and poor low-speed drivability where the motor spends most of its time. The list goes on and on. For real performance gains, the entire motor combination has to be addressed, not just one or two parts.

If you believed everything you read in magazines, then you would figure power is really easy to make or—should I say—buy.

To have some fun, I've created a few parodies of performance magazine advertising. What is depressing about these phony ads of mine is that every one of them is based on a real ad. Some of these products do work, and some . . . well, you know. Can you figure out which ones do work? How many of these things do you have on your bike right now?

- Install our new "Hurricane" four-throated super sucker carburetor (patent pending) and get 10 more horsepower.

- Install our one-of-a-kind mega-noise super-double-inverted reverse-cone exhaust system and get a 20 percent increase in power.

- Install our pass-a-speeding-bullet cam set and get a 10-horsepower increase.

- Install our unique, super, one-of-a-con carb gismo and get 5 more horsepower—you'll need a new clutch after you put on this sucker!

- Install our revolutionary new computer-controlled and programmed-from-the-internet quadruple-fire ignition system and get 10 more horsepower instantly! (Lap-top computer sold separately.)

- Install our color-coordinated super-duper-hyper-hype ram air cleaner (batteries not included) and get 8 more horsepower.

- Install our slick new fork-tongued triple-plutonium-plated sparkplugs and get 5 more horsepower—now you and the spark plugs can both glow in the dark!

- Install our new revolutionary "Lightning Rod" spark plug wires, color coordinated to match your paint scheme, and you'll be shocked by the increased power output.

- Install our new state-of-the-art Blow Hard crankcase vent (two required) now available in billet, super billet, and mega billet and get 5 more horsepower; triple chrome plating adds 2 additional horsepower!

- Toss a couple of our tech-no-tech pellets (made from real space meteors) in your gas tank, and you may have to install seatbelts! (Note: asteroids may be substituted for meteors without prior advance notice.)

And the list goes on and on. If you buy into this stuff—and "buy" is the key word, because it's your money that they want—a 100 horsepower motor can be easily acquired by bolting on a few fancy doodads. But as P. T. Barnum used to say, "There's a sucker born every minute"!

So if you really want increased performance, use your head and spare your wallet. Remember, when in search of performance and power, some wallet is always required, because the best things in life are rarely free.

There are two important things that should be done to every Harley with a carburetor.

First is to fix or replace exhaust system with a less restrictive system. I like fixing the exhaust system, because it's free!

You can run out and buy a $500 exhaust system, maybe even a $750 one, or how about $1,000 for set of drag pipes, or you can spend nothing and fix the stock mufflers. After all, they're paid for already.

There are several ways to do this. The crude way is to take a long steel rod about 2 feet long and grind a point on one end. Insert the pointed end of the rod into the muffler, and bash out the baffle plate using a large hammer.

Another way is to use a long electrician's drill bit and drill a hole through the baffle plate. Even a hole as small as 1/2 inch will yield a performance gain over the stock baffles.

Here' the way I fix the stock mufflers. First, remove the mufflers. Get a 1 3/4-inch hole saw and cut the weld just inside of the outboard end of the muffler. Work slowly and be careful to stop as soon as you get through the weld. Take a rod, broomstick, or whatever, and drive the entire super-restrictive baffle out of the muffler from the opposite side. You now have an open glass-packed muffler with almost no restriction, and it even has a built-in reversion cone at the front to boot. You'll have a Harley that sounds like a Harley without being overly offensive. This system won't do much for you power wise at low rpm, but it will work decently at higher rpm, and it's free!

The second thing to do to every Harley is to remove the stock air cleaner and either fix it or use it as a paperweight. Although it can be fixed to some degree, I recommend replacing it with a free-flowing unit. If it doesn't already

Cut this weld, and the super-restrictive baffle will come out of the muffler from this end. Remember: To remove the baffle, you must remove the muffler from the exhaust header pipe. In this picture, the baffle has already been removed, and you can see the glass pack.

105

come with one, install a K&N style filter. Finally, fix the stock EPA-jetted carburetor by re-jetting or installing a recalibration kit. That's it. You're done!

Fuel injected Harleys will benefit from the same modifications, but you will need to have your chip flashed to a stage-one configuration. If you don't, you will end up with a dangerously lean fuel mixture.

If you want to spend a few more dollars, you should improve your Harley's the ignition system.

It's always a good idea to replace the stock coil with a high output coil, and replace the stock spark plugs and wires with performance ones. I like Taylor Spiro-Pro wires for bikes with electronic ignitions. They have very low resistance and have always worked well for me. (More on that in Chapter 9, Low-Tech, Bare-Bones 883 Sportster Fix.) The same goes for Autolite's no-hype Platinum fine-wire sparkplugs.

Unless you have deep pockets, be happy and stop here. Your bike will now run as God and the Motor Company intended, before the pollution police got involved.

LOW-BUDGET MOTOR RECIPES FOR THE 883 SPORTSTER AND THE TWIN CAM 88

The two recipes I am going to present in this book are low-budget (read bare-bones), real-world performance modifications. No B.S., just horsepower and a broad strong torque band in the low end and midrange—where you want it!

Since the easiest way to accomplish more power is with more inches, we will be adding inches to both of these motors. Interestingly, Harley designed both of these engines to be bigger than what it's selling. Harley designed the 883 to be a 1200, and the Twin Cam to be 95 inches.

I've included projected horsepower numbers. At first glance you may consider it to be a lot of work for a relatively slight horsepower increase. But, if you have read this far, you have learned that there are more important factors to consider than horsepower. If all you want is horsepower and not torque, buy a Japanese sportbike.

Remember, torque is the twisting force that accelerates you down the road, and it is the only force that we can easily measure.

Horsepower is derived from this formula: (torque x rpm) divided by 5252 = horsepower.

As we can see by looking at the formula, to make high horsepower numbers you not only need plenty of torque, but you need that torque at high rpm!

If you only produced a small amount of torque at very high rpm, you would have impressive horsepower, but you would lack the ability to accelerate except at the very top end of the rpm range.

Once again, you can't have power both ways. To get high horsepower, you must move your peak torque location higher in the rpm band. When you do this, you will

remove torque from the low to midrange of the rpm band, where Harleys (and you) want and need it.

Having ridden V-twins with both types of power bands, all I can say is that a bike with strong torque at 2,500 rpm is a lot more fun to ride than one with a torque band that peaks at 5,000-plus rpm. Be honest with yourself: How many hours do you spend riding at 5,000-plus rpm?

My 883 and TC-88 low-budget fixes will produce a strong torque band that's just where you need it—in the low and midrange of the rpm band.

Because of the stock cylinder heads' airflow limitations, these motors will run out of airflow at high rpm, before they could produce hypothetical high horsepower numbers.

STOCK HEAD RESTRICTIONS

The stock cylinder heads are without a doubt the biggest obstacle that the performance engine builder has to overcome. Generally, modern Harley heads have small ports and valves when compared to their displacement. This is done for two reasons.

1. To keep our friends at the EPA happy.

2. To produce that strong low-end torque that makes Harleys famous.

Let's look at the horsepower formula again. If we can't enter a high rpm number, our horsepower figure will not be very high, even though our new motor has gobs of stump-pulling torque for roll-on acceleration.

Here's what's going on. The cylinder head works by two principles: port velocity and port volume. For a head to reach its peak potential, both velocity and volume must be matched to the airflow requirements of a particular engine combination. Too much or too little of either will cost you power! A large port that can flow huge volumes of air without good velocity will not work well at low rpm, and a small port with high air velocity and insufficient volume will be useless at high rpm.

Stock 883 and TC-88 heads generally have small ports and valves when compared to the engine's displacement. These small ports will produce a high port velocity that will produce strong low-end power, via good cylinder filling qualities, at lower rpm.

This port velocity is the reason an 883-converted-to-1200-cc Sportster will always beat a stock 1200 Sportster in a roll-on acceleration race from 2,000 to 5,500 rpm. Above 5,500 rpm, the factory 1200-cc bike, with its larger ports and valves, will have the advantage and will pull away from the modified 1200-cc bike with its smaller 883 heads. But at 5,500 rpm, the converted 883 will be going 115 miles per hour—time for most people to slow down anyway!

We are going to use the stock flow-restricted heads on

these motors, as well as enlarge the displacement. The motors will not give you bragging rights at the dyno by producing big horsepower numbers. But they will be a lot more fun to ride than a stock bike!

Before we get to the motor recipes, let's look at cylinder heads a bit more. To make real power we need to do something with the stock heads. There are several ways to modify your stock heads. You can send them to a professional head porter, buy aftermarket performance heads, or go all out by buying aftermarket high-performance heads and sending them to a professional head porter. Of course, money is the concern here, because either way you go, it's going to be expensive!

HERE'S SOME HEAD TRIVIA.
Correctly modified stock parts yield extra power. If you're into Sportsters, you've probably heard of the famous Buell S1 Lightning heads. Guess what? These heads started life as a set of stock 883 heads before being modified to Buell specs.

HEMIS AND HEMISPHERICAL-SHAPED COMBUSTION CHAMBERS
Let's take a look at the old hemi-shaped combustion chamber. The hemi-shaped combustion chambers have been around for a long time; they were used as early as World War I in aircraft engines. During World War II, they become commonplace in aircraft engines, which required high power output. The thought back then was, if you inclined the valves on a 45-degree angle, you could use the largest possible valve sizes in the combustion chambers. The bigger the valves, the more air could flow through the motor.

Engine technology back then was not what it is today. Compared with other chamber designs of the time—like the side-valve flathead—the hemispherical-shaped combustion chamber did improve power output in the aircraft engines. Of course, these engines were running at high rpm, so the lack of flow velocity at low rpm was not a problem.

Back in the hot rod days of the 1950s and 1960s, the same theory was applied. People believed the bigger valves in the hemis would flow more air volume than heads with smaller valves. The theory then was, as it is now, that the more air you could flow through the motor, the more power you could make. By using a 45-degree inclined valve angle in the heads, you could use the largest possible valves.

In theory all of this is true, but on the flow bench it doesn't pan out that way. Big valves are only good if you can maintain good flow velocity through the heads. Flow velocity is every bit as important as valve size. The same thing holds true for port size. A giant port can flow cubic yards of air, but this volume is useless without good port velocity.

Here's another drawback: What do you do with that big, empty space in the top of the cylinder head? After all, you have to compress the air/fuel mixture before you ignite it. Back in the day, the answer was to run tall, domed pistons. Although they looked really cool, they were extremely inefficient when compared to flat-top pistons and small, compact, efficient combustion chambers.

Looking back at the hemi-shaped combustion chamber, it had so many issues working against it that it's amazing it was used for as long as it was. Let's look at some of the many drawbacks of the old hemi-head.

We know that to maximize power the combustion chamber must be designed to flow the most possible air/fuel mixture into the cylinder. Once in the cylinder, the mixture needs to be homogenized by turbulence, usually created by compression and by squish bands. The homogenized mixture then needs to be packed into a small, compact, unobstructed combustion chamber that provides an even flame front with little surface area that could absorb (rob) heat from the combustion process.

THE HEMI'S PROBLEMS
We have just covered its first problem. The large valves could flow huge volumes of air, but they lack velocity. Without flow velocity you will get poor cylinder refill. Once the mixture does make it into the hemi's combustion chamber, it faces a whole host of other problems that will reduce its efficiency and its ability to make power. Let's take a look at the hemi-headed Sportster.

Ideally in a hemi head, the spark plug should be located centrally, in the top of the cylinder head between the two valves. Yet, the Sportster's hemi heads have the spark plug located down on one side and they also use that tall dome piston. At TDC the piston dome masks the spark plug and severely interferes with flame propagation. This is why early Sportsters needed the excessive 45-degree advance timing.

To homogenize the mixture, we create turbulence by compacting and squeezing the mixture in the combustion chamber with squish bands. The hemi has no squish band, so the mixture is not well mixed and therefore a larger amount of fuel molecules will not burn during the combustion process. Less burn equals less heat, and less heat equals less power.

The tall piston dome has a large amount of surface area, which absorbs a lot of combustion heat. Remember, the two things that reduce power are heat absorption and friction. The more heat the piston absorbs, the less heat we have left to force the piston down the cylinder and make power.

The hemi head has just about everything that could work against an efficient combustion chamber design.

So why were they used for so many years on dragsters? The answer is simple. When you're using a blower, the flow velocity is not that important because you are forcing the mixture into the cylinders under pressure. Due to this, volume is more important than velocity. When running a blower, lower compression is required and flat top pistons are usually used. They're also often running extremely volatile fuels, like nitromethane. So if you're tossing hand grenades into the cylinders, chamber shape becomes less important. Yes, I know hemis are still being run on the drag strip and in other applications. But the new hemi motors are considerably different than the old hemi motor we have been talking about here.

HEAD CONSIDERATIONS

You can purchase a complete set of performance heads form Harley's Screamin' Eagle line for less money than most real professional head porters will charge to modify your stock heads. If you go this route, you save a few bucks and still have your stock heads. On the downside, these heads won't flow anything like a set of professionally ported heads from, say, Branch Flowmetrics, Carl's Speed Shop, Head Quarters, Baisley Hi-Performance, Zipper's Performance Products, etc. In addition to Harley's Screamin' Eagle heads, there are many other good quality performance heads to choose from, like S&S and STD to name a couple. Although I have never used Edelbrock performance heads, they are definitely worth considering.

On the other hand, the professional head porter has the advantage of custom modifying a set of heads to match a particular engine combination.

A set of quality aftermarket performance heads designed for use on an 80-inch Evo will not work very well on a 120-inch motor, as a bigger motor will require larger valves and ports than the smaller one.

LOW-BUDGET HOME HEAD MODIFICATION 101

Is there anything you can do by yourself to help your stock heads work better? If you have the right tools, know how to use them, and have $5 for a new set of valve guide seals, the answer is yes!

We will be removing casting flaws from the port walls, and pocket porting the bowl area of the head. We will not change the size or shape of the ports. This low-budget head fix will help all stock V-twin heads.

As mentioned in Chapter 1, the most important area of the cylinder head is the valve bowl area—the area from the valve seat to the short-side radius of the port. This is where we will work.

I take the tools required to do this for granted because I have all of them and do this kind of modification to just about every set of Harley heads I disassemble. My motto has always been: if it's stock, I can make it better!

You, on the other hand, may not have all of the tools required to do the job. Because this is a low-tech, low-budget job, we'll try to keep the tools low tech and low budget, too.

REQUIRED TOOLS

The Harley shop manual for your year and model bike is always the most important tool you'll own! Here are some other necessary tools:

- Valve spring compressing tool and a valve seal installation tool
- Hand electric drill (a battery-powered drill works great) with several sizes of paddle-type sanding wheels that fit in the ports
- Dremel tool (preferably one with the wand attachment) and several small sanding wheels and burrs
- Small, beveled, flat file
- Small screwdriver
- Valve lapping tool
- Coarse and fine-valve lapping compound
- A flat piece of glass
- Wet/dry sandpaper
- A small bottlebrush that will fit into the valve guides, or something for cleaning the insides of the guides
- Air compressor
- Brake cleaner and WD-40 for removing grinding materials and protecting parts
- Assembly lube (preferably) or motor oil to lubricate the valve stems when you reassemble them
- Access to a glass beader and a drill press is also nice, but not mandatory

HERE'S HOW TO DO IT

Disassemble the valve springs and clean the heads. Mark and label all small parts, or use small zip-lock bags to separate the valve components, so they go back in the same port they came from. As you disassemble the heads, inspect all components for damage.

As a general performance rule, if the valve springs have many miles on them, you should automatically replace them. My personal rule is if the valve springs have more than 25,000 or five years of use on them, I replace them. If you can't afford to replace them, the old stock valve springs may still be okay when following my low-budget hop-up recipes. This is due to the fact that the cams in both of these motors are mild, and the motors will run out

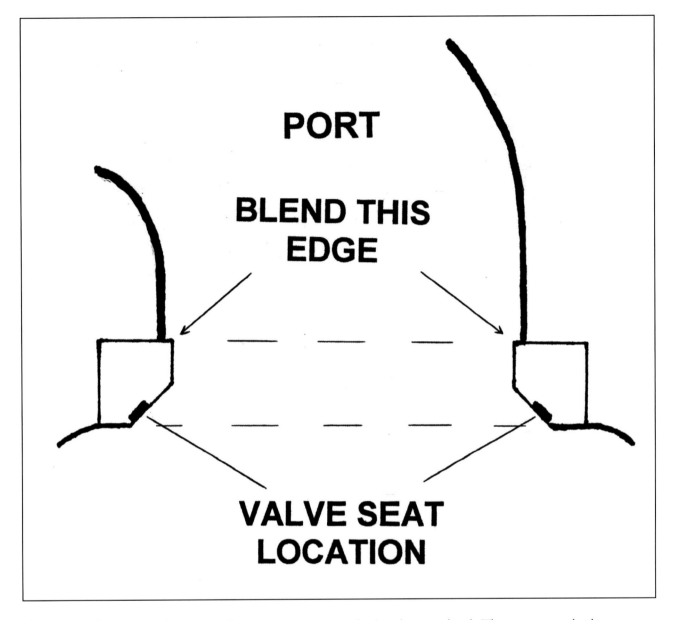

PORT

BLEND THIS
EDGE

VALVE SEAT
LOCATION

of air long before they reach the valve-float rpm range.

When you go beyond this stage or use a different cam, you will want to replace the valve springs . . . period!

If you have access to a glass beader, remove the valve springs and collars, but leave the valves and seals in place.

Then lightly blast the combustion chamber and valve faces. Do not damage the valve seat area on the head! If you don't have access to a beader, use whatever will work to clean the combustion chamber and ports. Worst-case scenario, you can use a small screwdriver and slowly scrape away the carbon buildup, but be very careful not to put any gouges in the combustion chamber. If you do, you will want to sand them out.

Ideally, you'd like the inside of the combustion chamber to be as smooth as possible. If you have Branch Flowmetrics do your heads, when you get them back the combustion chambers will be so polished they'll look like

they're chrome plated. There are several advantages to having a highly polished combustion chamber.

It does not expose as much surface area to the flame front, so it absorbs less heat. Less heat absorption by the cylinder head means more heat is available to force the piston down the cylinder.

It also does not build up carbon as fast as a porous chamber finish. Carbon buildup can cause hot spots in the combustion chamber that could pre-ignite the mixture and/or interfere with an even flame front.

Anything you can do to smooth the chamber's finish is ideal.

Next, blow off any beading material from the valve stem and then remove the valves. From the intake port side of the head, lightly blast it to remove crud, and repeat on the exhaust side of the port. Again, be careful and don't damage the valve seat area while doing this.

Now that the heads are clean, you can start fixing them.

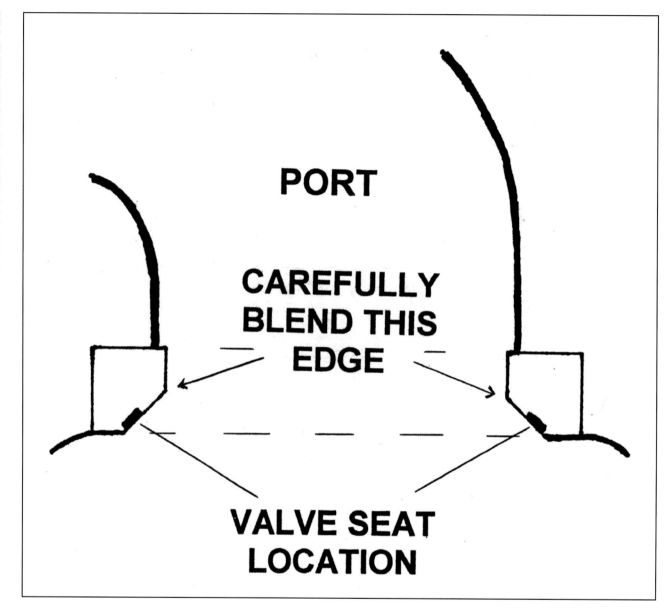

PORT

CAREFULLY
BLEND THIS
EDGE

VALVE SEAT
LOCATION

You must be very careful when attempting to radius this edge. Unless you are confident you can perform this modification without damaging the seating surface, you may not want to attempt it.

First, you will attack the highly important valve bowl area.

Examine the bowl area of the head on the inside, just above the valve seat. You can see where the aluminum head was milled out so the steel valve seat could be pressed in. Also examine the steel seat itself. Chances are you will find a sloppy ledge where the valve seat meets the port. This has to be fixed.

Remember, rule number one is to do no harm, so be extremely careful around the valve seat. With the Dremel tool and a small sanding wheel, delicately remove only the amount of material needed to smoothly blend the steel seat to the aluminum port. The softer aluminum will grind away faster than hard steel, so again, be very careful.

Next, clean off any grinding material dust. Check the head where the valve seat is to determine if you can see where the valve seals against the valve seat. If not, use your valve lapping tool and lapping compound to highlight where the valve contacts the seat.

Now gently radius the area from just above the seat into the bowl of the port. We're looking for a rounded finish, not a straight finish.

You've heard of the three-angle valve job and the better five- or seven-angle valve jobs, right? The valve seat itself uses only one of these angles, and the extra angles are used to blend the area around the true valve seat, so air flows better in this area. A fully radiused area around the seat would be even better than a bunch of different angles. This would make the transition flow smoother

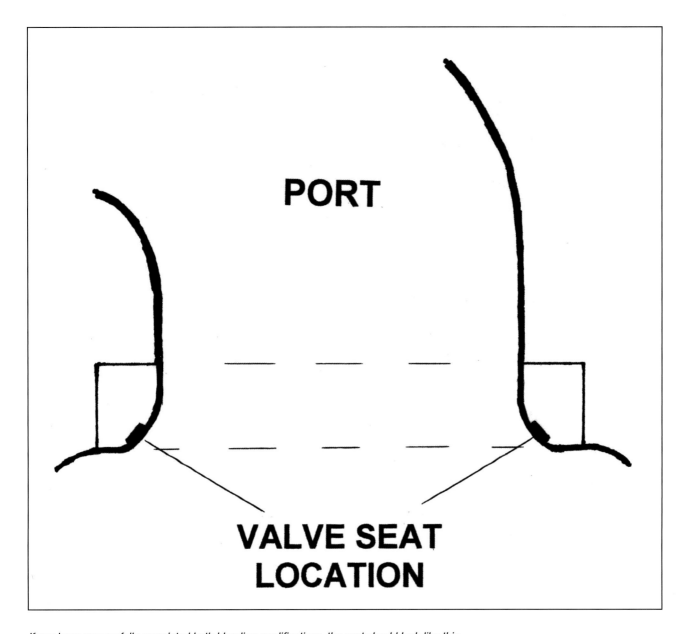

If you have successfully completed both blending modifications, the seat should look like this.

around the seat. We will attempt to do that next.

With a small, beveled flat file, gently radius the area above the seat into the head. You can also use the small sanding wheel on the Dremel tool. Just remember that the Dremel tool will remove metal at a faster rate than a small hand file, which means you can do more damage more quickly with the Dremel tool. The area above the valve seat should be blended in a round shape, not flattened out to the valve seat. If you feel the least bit uncomfortable about your ability to do this without damaging the valve seat, don't try it! If you damage the seat, a new valve seat will have to be cut preferably on an expensive Serdi valve-milling machine or by hand with a Neway valve seat-cutting tool. If you really damage it, the whole seat may need to be replaced. So work carefully.

Next, remove casting flaws from the ports. A small sanding wheel on the Dremel tool wand works well for this. Remember, we're not Jerry Branch. We're just trying to remove inconsistencies and smooth out the walls of the existing ports. We're not reshaping them!

Paddle-type sanding wheels on an electric drill can also be put in use here. The valve guide extends into the port and interferes with getting to the port's entire surface area, so just clean up the areas you can reach. Something is better than nothing, and a polished mirror finish is not required here.

I like to improve the shape of the short-side radius of the intake port. In other words, when looking into the port from the intake manifold side, the intake port should have a flattened shape on the short-side radius. The port should take on the look of the letter "D," with the flat side of the D on the bottom. Unless you really know what you're doing, don't try this at home! If done incorrectly, it will reduce flow and performance.

Next we will install the intake manifold, positioned properly, to the bare head's intake port. What we're looking for here is the transition point where the intake manifold ends and meets the head. If it's fairly smooth, you're okay. If the head forms a pronounced ledge, you'll need to fix this, because as the mixture flows through the intake manifold and hits this ledge at the head, it will cause an eddy that will disturb orderly airflow.

Use a scribe or marking pen to mark the area on the head that is creating the ledge. Remove the intake manifold and remove the ledge with a beveled hand file or grinding wheel on the Dremel tool.

Remove only the material required to smooth the protruding ledge. You'll want to blend this area into the port. If done correctly, you won't be able to notice that a small amount of material has been removed from the head.

As long as you have the intake manifold in hand, give the inside a once over with a 60 or 80 grit sanding paddle wheel. You don't need a mirror finish here, just smooth out the lumps, bumps and casting flaws.

Next, we'll clean the valves; the low-budget way, of course.

Mount the valve on a drill press or on a hand drill that's clamped in a vise. You want the whole valve stem and face to be accessible. We don't want to damage the valve stem in any way!

Put only the very end of the valve stem—the part above the groove, where the keeper goes—in the drill chuck. Make sure the valve is straight and the drill chuck is tight! The last thing we want is for the valve to go flying across the shop.

Turn on the drill. I use a small flat-bladed screwdriver as a lathe-cutting tool to remove hard carbon buildup. This works really well, but be very careful and stay away from the valve seat area of the valve. After the heavy stuff is removed, you can polish the valve and the valve stem with fine 600- or 400-grit wet/dry sandpaper. Again, stay clear of the valve's seating area.

HERE'S A VALVE PERFORMANCE TIP: BACK CUTTING THE VALVE FACE

Back cutting valves is a trick automotive racers have been using for many years.

Let's look at airflow around the valve. Air flows through the port until it reaches the valve head. Then it must turn a corner, and when it does, the airflow is directed at right angles from the flow of the intake port.

Ideally, we want airflow to take on the shape of a cone after it passes the valve head. Generally, as the air flows through the port and hits the valve head, it flows off to the sides. What we want to do is change its flow direction and get it flowing into the cylinder, perpendicular to the valve stem for greater cylinder fill. One way to

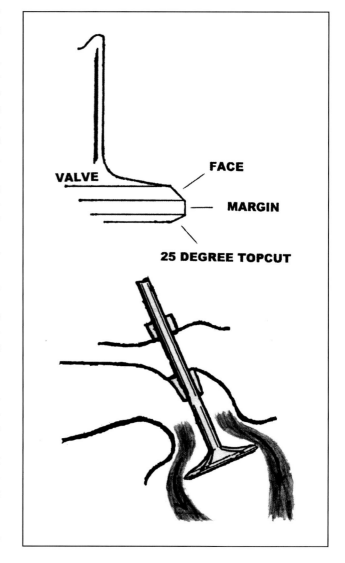

achieve this is by back cutting the valve face.

As you follow the valve stem down, you will come to the underside of the valve face. This leads to the valve seating area, usually always cut at 45 degrees. Next you reach the valve margin area that is perpendicular to the valve stem. After that you have the valve face in the combustion chamber. (See the illustration.)

Some automotive racers back cut the area between the vertical margin and the valve face, and they back cut the face of the valve at a 25-degree angle. So if you were to look at the valve, you would now have the valve seat, the side margin, the 25-degree back-cut and the valve face in the combustion chamber.

What this does is create a low-pressure area at the bottom of the margin that directs the airflow back under the valve face, producing that desired cone shape.

The edges of the valve seat, the margin, and back-cut should be left sharp. Do not round these edges off! This trick not only helps the flow on the intake valve, but also improves the flow characteristics of the exhaust valve.

Next we will lap the valve seats.

Clean and lubricate the valve stem. Lap the valve with coarse lapping compound first, then finish with fine lapping compound. Remove all lapping compound from valves and heads before assembly. Clean everything!

Lubricate valve guides and valve stems with assembly lube or motor oil, and assemble heads. Note that some heads use different-diameter valve stems and seals, so be sure to match the seals to the correct valve stems before installing them.

Be sure to install the valve guide seals correctly. If not done properly, the sharp edge where the valve keeper goes can easily ruin the seal. If you don't have the little plastic cap-seal-protector tool to do this, just use a wrap of scotch tape over the area where the keeper goes to protect the seal. It works fine and is in keeping with the low-tech theme. Note that the valve must be inserted in the guide before you apply the tape.

Now that the head is assembled, we are going to lap the head's deck to make sure it's flat.

We will need a piece of glass about one foot by one foot square, or a little bigger than a full sheet of sandpaper. I have a piece of 1/2-inch glass that works well because it doesn't flex.

Lightly clamp the glass to your workbench (or whatever) to keep it in place. Tightly tape a piece of sandpaper to the glass using—you guessed it—duct tape.

If the head is in good condition, 320 wet/dry may be a good choice. If the head is considerably out of flat, you'll want to start with a coarser sandpaper. Rub back and forth on the head's deck where the head gasket goes. Occasionally stop and turn the head over to check your progress. You are done when the sandpaper has polished every part of the head's deck area and you can't see any light between the head and the glass. The head's deck is now as flat as it's going to get and it's ready to be installed.

You can also use this trick on the tops of used cylinders before re-installing them, although the steel cylinder liner does make this a little harder to accomplish.

If done correctly, you have made a significant improvement to your stock heads for $5 and a few hours of work. These heads are not ported and polished; they are what I call cleaned up or fixed. Harley would do this to the heads, but production costs would be prohibitive.

I have deliberately kept the methods very low tech to accomplish your desired modification goals.

At the beginning, the question was if there was anything you can do to increase the performance of your stock head. After all, you are not concerned with how much money you didn't spend by doing the work this way. All you're concerned about is the results, and that you did the work yourself and got to use duct tape at least once!

What you have accomplished here is the smoothing and radiusing of the inside of the ports. You have removed what obstacles we could that would interfere with smooth and orderly progression of airflow through the ports.

You have radiused the area around the valve seat, which has been the most important improvement to the cylinder head.

You have also hand-lapped the valve seats, which should now seal better. You have new valve seals to prevent oil from entering the combustion chamber and contaminating our air/fuel mixture.

You have also inspected the condition of all the parts, in the event that there is something obvious that requires replacing that's above our or our equipment's ability.

A QUICK NOTE ON INSPECTING PARTS

When you disassemble any part on your motor, closely inspect every part for damage, hairline cracks, etc. It's always cheaper to replace a bad part now than deal with what's left of your motor after it lets go under operation.

Until you open it up and look, you'll never know what you'll find. Case in point: A guy brought me his bike to replace a leaky gasket. When I pulled off his rocker boxes, one of his valve springs was broken in half. When I showed it to the owner, he was surprised and said that his bike was running normally. He had no idea he was riding around with a busted valve spring.

CHAPTER 9 **LOW-TECH, BARE-BONES 883 SPORTSTER FIX**

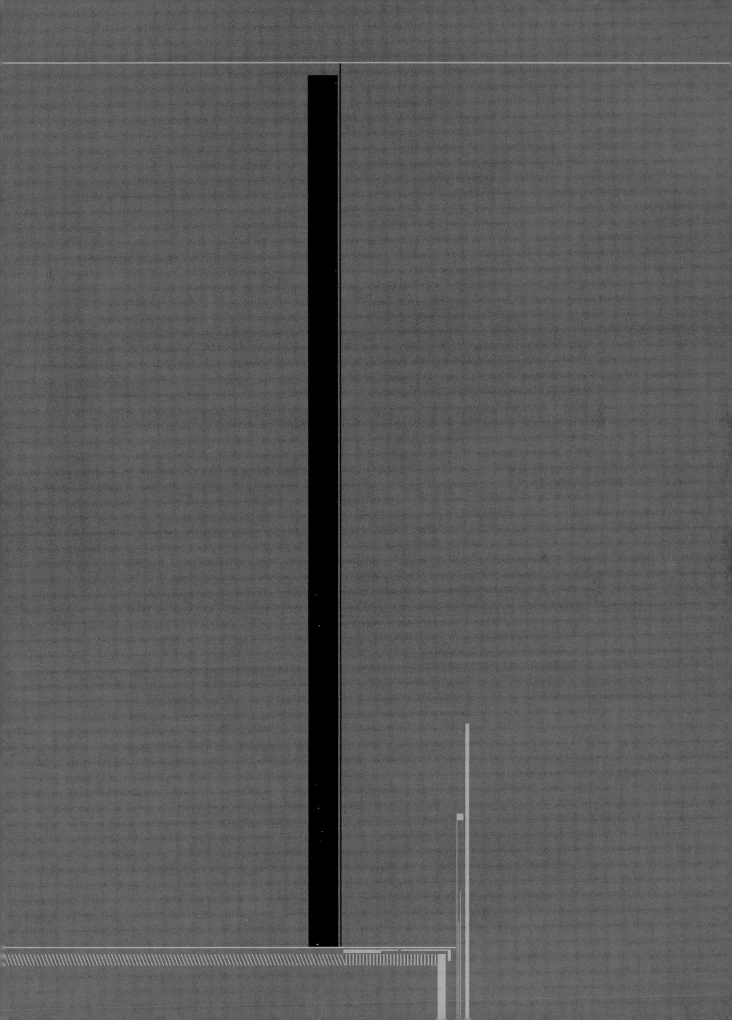

QUICK AND CHEAP

This is my proven 883-to-1204-cc Sportster recipe. I have built and ridden this motor many times.

It has lots of torque and is a lot of fun to ride. It pulls hard from 3,000 to 5,500 rpm. It's like night and day compared to an all-stock 883. I like this combination so much my wife's XLH now has this exact setup. There are very few Harleys in our town that she can't keep up with or put away.

In full riding regalia, I tip the scales at 200 pounds, and even with me on it, this bike quickly and smoothly accelerates to 115 miles per hour at 5,500 rpm. I shut her down at that point because I know the 883 cylinder heads will start running out of air at this rpm and there's little to gain by flogging a dying horse. To make good power over 5,500 rpm, the bike would require larger valves and ports.

I'm deliberately sticking to the keep-it-simple-stupid (KISS) concept for assembling this engine.

That means we won't be boring cylinders or using programmable ignition systems, exotic carburetors, or fancy exhaust systems.

We will use only cost-efficient (that means the cheapest) quality parts that are both available and easy to install. Whenever possible we will fix and use stock parts instead of purchasing new parts.

Other than a torque wrench, you will only need normal tools you should already have on hand—a socket wrench set, an open-end wrench set, an Allen wrench set, screwdrivers, etc. The only book (besides mine) you will require is the stock Harley shop manual for your bike. Just follow the shop manual's clear instructions on top-end disassembly and reassembly. You can do all the work yourself!

I only deviate from the shop manual on the final torque value on the head bolts. I use a torque wrench set at 40 lb-ft. It works for me, but you may just want to use the manual's recommended one-quarter turn after reaching the second torque value.

The required parts list I've assembled assumes that your bike is still 100 percent stock. But truthfully, I think the only place where you'll find a 100 percent stock bike is on the showroom floor. You may have already done some of the required modifications; if so, you're ahead of the game.

The parts required to do this modification are available from many distributors. For simplicity (to make it easy on me), I will list the suggested retail (year 2001) prices from Harley-Davidson or from one aftermarket supplier, Tedd Cycle aka V-Twin Manufacturing. Remember always to shop around for the best prices.

You should be able to find these parts at dealers that sell below suggested retail. I will not only list each part, but also explain why each part should be used. So if you're ready, let's build a low-tech, torque monster Sportster.

THE PARTS LIST

- An 883-to-1204-cc Wiseco piston and cylinder set

- Genuine James Gaskets top-end gasket set

- One 0.040-inch head quality gasket set (note: my favorite is Cometic EST gaskets, but any good quality head gasket will work as long as it has a thickness of 0.040 inch)

- Kinetic-Karb Keihin CV recalibration kit

- One 46 and one 48 slow jet

- High-flow chrome teardrop air cleaner kit

- K&N high-flow air filter element

- V-Twin Manufacturing chrome breather kit

- V-Twin Manufacturing chrome gas petcock

- Screamin' Eagle 1200-cc performance ignition module

- Blue Streak 40,000-volt ignition coil

- One set of Taylor Spiro-Pro spark plug wires

- Autolite MP4146 Platinum fine-wire center electrode spark plugs

TOP-END PARTS BREAKDOWN
An 883-to-1204-cc Wiseco piston and cylinder set
Cost: $460
Source: V-Twin Manufacturing
This kit comes with the following: one set of bored and honed, ready to install 1204-cc cylinders; one set of Wiseco -11.2-cc reverse-dome forged pistons (note: Wiseco also sells pistons with a 8.5-cc reverse dome. You don't want to run these pistons with the stock cams!), rings, wrist pins, etc; and one complete top-end gasket set. This is a nice big-bore kit that comes with new, straight cylinders, which will save you the cost and hassle of boring your old cylinders. By going this route, you'll still have everything you'd need to return the bike to 883 cc—though for the life of me, I don't know why anyone would want to do that.

This kit comes with a complete gasket set, but we are not going to use it; instead, we will save it as a spare. What we will be using is a better quality gasket set from Genuine James Gaskets. It's no fun having to pull the top end off in 500 to 1,000 miles to replace leaking base gaskets. Been there, done that, won't ever make that mistake again.

Genuine James Gaskets brand top-end gasket set

Cost: $66

Source: V-Twin Manufacturing

Genuine James brand gaskets are high quality and come with rubber-coated metal cylinder base gaskets. Never ever use the stock-style paper cylinder base gaskets! Always use rubber-coated metal base gaskets. Even with the Genuine James base gaskets, I always apply a small amount of Hylomar or silicone gasket sealant at assembly time.

Just like on the Big Twins, base-gasket oil leaks on Sportsters are the norm if you install the stock-style paper gaskets. When you start to see the paper-style gaskets protruding out from between the case and cylinders, prepare yourself to pull the top end off, because after the paper comes the oil!

One set of 0.040-inch quality head gaskets (Cometic, HES, James, etc.)

Cost: $38

Source: V-Twin Manufacturing

Using the smaller (3-inch bore) 883 heads with the large (3.5-inch bore) 1200-cc pistons, we have a very nice squish band to take advantage of, and remember what we know about squish bands. Squish bands create cylinder turbulence for improved power and gas mileage from better combustion efficiency. The maximum height for a squish band to be useful is 0.040-inch cold. Of course, 0.030-inch cold works a lot better than 0.040-inch cold, but I have chosen the latter for two reasons.

First, to keep the corrected compression down. This motor already has a high corrected compression ratio, and running a thinner 0.030-inch head gasket would

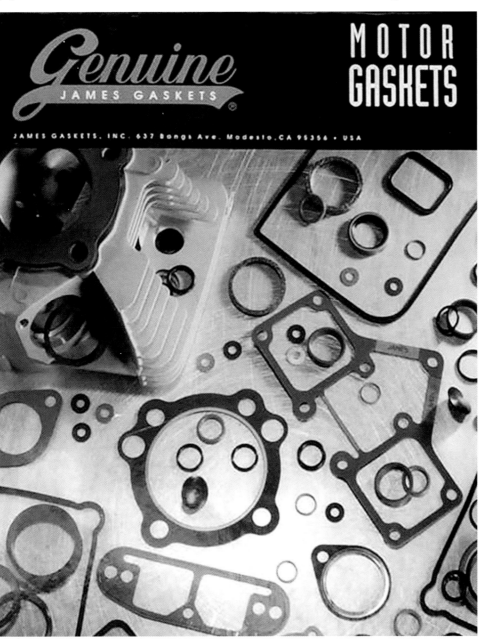

When dealing with gaskets, don't try to save a few bucks by using cheap products. If you go that route, I guarantee you will be sorry. There are several makers of quality gasket sets; Genuine James Gaskets is one brand that's given me good results.

only make it higher!

Second, to minimize the chance of the piston hitting the cylinder head by not permitting engine reach operating temperature before flogging it.

Kinetic-Karb Keihin CV recalibration kit
Cost: $38
Source: V-Twin Manufacturing
You will also need one 46, or possibly a 48, slow jet, because a slow jet does not come with this kit. I chose the Kinetic-Karb tuner's kit because it is very complete, works well, and is about half the cost of other kits. It's easy to install; just follow the instructions.

You will need to remove the stock slow jet and replace it with 46 slow jet. When you have the carburetor apart, you can gently radius the bottom edge of the front side (air cleaner side) of the piston. This will improve airflow under the CV piston. I showed you this trick in Chapter 4, Mixing Air and Fuel (in More CV Tips section).

Important tips: When you disassemble the CV piston, be very careful not to damage the rubber diaphragm that goes on the top of the CV piston.

The hole in the CV piston that you should drill (enlarge) is the aft—or inboard—hole, not the center hole into which the needle jet fits.

When drilling the plug to gain access to the idle mixture screw, drill slowly and stop as soon as you're through the plug. If you run the drill in too far, you will damage the face of the adjusting screw. The instructions say to start with the idle mixture screw out three turns. Be sure to adjust the idle mixture jet correctly after the motor is up to operating temperature. If it runs best with three turns or more, your slow-speed jet may be too small.

High-flow chrome teardrop air cleaner kit
Cost: $61
Source: V-Twin Manufacturing
This unit is basically the same as the S&S air cleaner except it doesn't have the S&S logo. I chose this air cleaner because it looks nice, is priced reasonably (about half the cost of the S&S unit), and it's a proven performer.

I recently had to install two air cleaners on two different Twin Cams on the same day. One TC-88 owner went with the S&S teardrop air cleaner kit, while the other owner went with the V-Twin brand clone teardrop air cleaner kit.

I hate to say this, but I have to call it the way I see it. The fit and finish of the V-Twin backing plate was noticeable nicer than the S&S brand. After installing both, I found the V-Twin mounting hardware to be more versatile and easier to install.

The Screamin' Eagle plain oval "ham-can" cleaner with

The V-Twin Manufacturing chrome breather pipe adds a nice touch over the top of the stock CV carburetor.

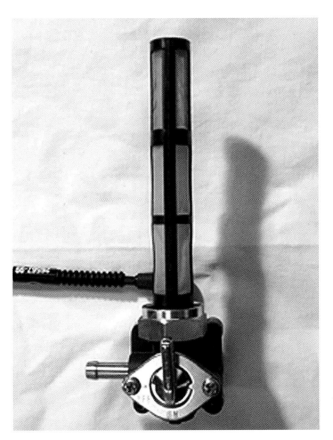

If you have one of these stock OEM vacuum-operated fuel pet-cocks, you should replace it, even on a stock bike.

its K&N style air filter is a slightly better-performing filter than the S&S teardrop style unit. I went with the teardrop unit because it's chrome and, to me, it looks better than the Screamin' Eagle unit. Run whichever one you want.

K&N high-flow air filter element
Cost: $39
Source: V-Twin Manufacturing
The K&N style air filters are high-flowing top performers, and they can last a lifetime if taken care of properly. Yes, they are expensive, but they're worth every penny.

For the stock Keihin carburetor, when using either the V-Twin or S&S brand of air cleaner, you will need to use the filter element made for the S&S Super B air cleaner. The S&S Super E and G air cleaners use a taller filter that will not fit.

Even though K&N says its B filter will fit the S&S Super B air cleaner, the filter is often too tall and will not fit under the cover properly unless you take a razor knife and trim one side of it down. If you try to install it without trimming it, you will crush the filter element. I have seen quite a few of these expensive filters crushed and damaged because the installer didn't take a few minutes to trim it to fit.

V-Twin Manufacturing chrome breather kit
Cost: $38
Source: V-Twin Manufacturing
The V-Twin Manufacturing breather kit is very complete, easy to install, and the chrome breather tube adds

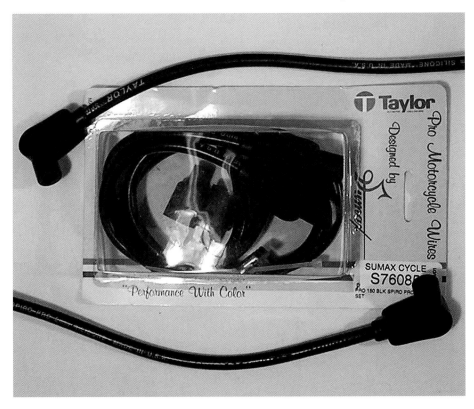

I highly recommend running spiral-core wire on all motors not equipped with points or magnetos. These wires are made by Taylor and are my wires of choice. Taylor's new Thunder Volt 50 wires at 10.4 millimeters are impressive and effective.

119

Autolite's fine-wire platinum spark plugs are true, no-hype, performance spark plugs. Consider this: If any of those fancy gizmo-type spark plugs really made a big difference in performance, wouldn't high-performance engine builders install them as on their motors?

a nice touch to the black plastic carb top cover.

V-Twin Manufacturing chrome gas petcock
Cost: $15
Source: V-Twin Manufacturing
If you haven't already replaced the stock vacuum-operated gas petcock, do so now. The vacuum operation makes it useless for performance work.

The V-Twin petcock is chrome and flows more than enough fuel to satisfy your motor's requirements. The stock vacuum-operated petcock can malfunction and shut you down. Also, think about this: It turns the fuel on when it is under vacuum. When you crank open your carb, your vacuum pressure drops, and if it drops below the gas petcock's required pressure, it could turn your fuel off when you're accelerating. You won't go very fast without gas!

Screamin' Eagle 1200-cc performance ignition module
Cost: $115
Source: H-D
I am going with the Screamin' Eagle module because it's plug-and-play. There's nothing for you to adjust or worry about, and it works well. There are bunches of modules to chose from, but just make sure the one you choose is designed to work with an 883 conversion.

We must change the module because the 883-cc timing curve is all wrong for the larger 1200-cc motor, and your modified motor will be operating with a higher corrected compression ratio than a stock 1200-cc Sportster. The higher corrected compression ratio can make better use of the slower advance curve of the 1200-cc performance module.

The Screamin' Eagle performance module (H-D part # 32633-96) uses the "Q" advance curve and works very well with this setup. It has a rev limiter set at 6,800 rpm. Check with your local Harley mechanic to see if it will work on your year's model. If not, find a Screamin' Eagle

1200-cc performance module that will work on your bike, preferably with the "Q" advance curve. You can install a module with a rev limiter that goes higher than 6,000 rpm, but this motor's stock heads will start to run out of airflow at approximately 5,500 rpm. Even so, my motor recipe will still produce good horsepower numbers even past 6,000 rpm.

This modified 1200-cc motor will perform poorly if you try to run the stock 883-cc ignition module and may even damage it.

Blue Streak 40,000-volt ignition coil
Cost: $46
Source: V-Twin Manufacturing
I went with this coil because it's rated at 40,000-plus volts, it's reliable, it's the same size and shape as the stock coil, and it is reasonably priced.

The Blue Streak coil is blue. I don't care for a blue coil, so I clean the coil, put a light coat of wrought iron black spray paint on it, and then it looks like a stock black coil. Be sure to mask off all connectors if you decide to paint yours.

One set of Taylor Spiro-Pro spark plug wires
Cost: $20
Source: V-Twin Manufacturing
I went with the Taylor Spiro-Pro wires because they have very low resistance and their performance potential is considerable compared to stock carbon-core wires. They work well, are priced right, and they even come in different colors to match your paint scheme, if you're so moved.

One set of Autolite MP4146
Platinum fine-wire center electrode spark plugs
Cost: $10 (set)
Source: V-Twin Manufacturing
I went with the Autolite Platinum fine-wire plugs because

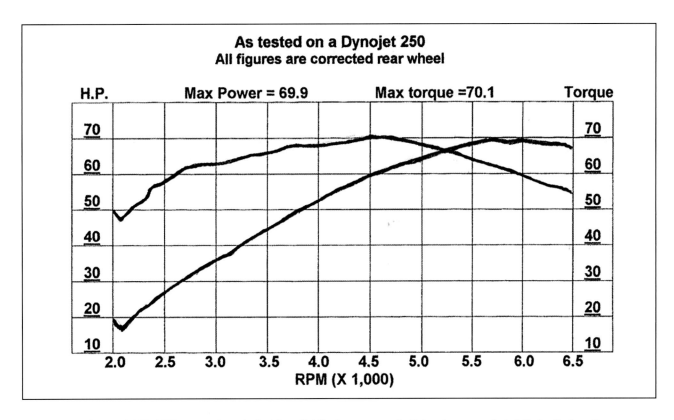

Actual dyno printout of 883-1200 conversion—look at how flat the torque curve is. Below is uncorrected air/fuel ratio from the same run.

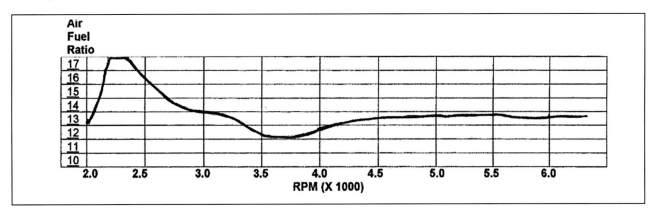

they are real-world (no gimmick) high-performance spark plugs and are priced lower than most gimmick spark plugs.

The folk at Zipper's Performance in Elkridge, Maryland, told me that they highly recommend the use of Autolite Platinum plugs for performance applications and even run them in their drag bikes. I also highly recommend using these plugs.

As this modified motor will have a high corrected compression ratio, I recommend that you set the plug gaps at a loose 0.035 inch and never more than 0.038 inch.

Two things interfere with a spark plug's ability to successfully fire:

1. When you compress hydrocarbons, they create a dielectric (insulating on non-conducting) field, and the higher the cylinder's compression, the stronger this field will be, making it harder for spark plugs to fire.

2. The faster you spin the motor, the less time the coil has to build up a sufficient magnetic field to produce a strong spark.

These interferences are the reasons why you should always use a high-output performance coil. Modified motors will often run higher corrected compression ratios and operate at higher rpm. Because of this, I strongly recommend you set the plug gaps on all Evo Sportsters, Big Twins, and Twin Cam motors at a loose 0.035 inch.

The large stock gap of 0.038 to 0.042 inch is mainly used to satisfy pollution requirements, not performance requirements. Always remember to use a small amount of high-heat, anti-seize compound on the spark plug thread. If you've ever stripped out a set of spark plug threads on a head, you already know how important this is.

Indexing the spark plugs to the cylinders is always a good idea, and it may yield some extra power. Magazines often tell their readers how to do this as a secret to hidden power.

The truth is that sometimes you may gain a little and sometimes not, but the important thing is to try. By indexing your plugs, you will at least be maintaining consistent plug positioning.

I always index spark plugs to the cylinders. What you want is the open end of the spark gap to be facing the incoming air/fuel mixture and the center of your combustion chamber. To do this, the ground leg of the plug should be on the bottom, with the open part of the gap facing up toward the top of the cylinder head and the intake valve.

To index spark plugs, use indexing washers. I find the store-bought ones unacceptably thick and a waste of money, so I make my own thin ones from brass or copper shim stock. When installing spark plugs, I always use a torque wrench set at 18 lb-ft, or 215 lb-in, for aluminum heads and 20 lb-ft, or 240 lb-in, for iron heads.

THAT'S EVERYTHING YOU NEED FOR THE 883 CONVERSION

All of these parts have been chosen because they are quality parts and are reasonably priced. Each part has been chosen to work with, and complement, the creation of a total engine package.

I did not include an exhaust system with this package. If you have already changed your exhaust system (hopefully not with drag pipes), you're ahead of the game.

If you still have the stock system, just fix and use them since they're already paid for. Just do the stock muffler baffle removal trick that we already discussed in Chapter 8, Do It Yourself at Home Head Fix.

If you have the stock crossover pipe, it is fine as is. Unless you just can't stand it, leave it be. The modified stock system won't do much for the low end, but it will do fine where this motor is the strongest, from 3,000 to 5,500 rpm.

We have also fixed the stock carburetor and that's all this motor needs. A larger carb will not help this motor much and may cause it to perform even worse. The stock carb flows plenty of air to satisfy its requirements until 5,500 rpm, at which the stock heads start running out of airflow. The modified stock carb will allow the motor to turn to 6,000-plus rpm, and there's little reason in pushing this combination any further than that. You have to be honest with yourself here!

These motors will definitely respond to the do-it-yourself at home head fix we discussed earlier. The stock heads are very flow limited, so spend the time to help this motor breath a little better. This motor will work alright with the stock unmodified heads; it just won't be as much fun.

Because of the reverse-dome pistons, you cannot install 1200-cc heads at a later date (unless you switch to Wiseco flat-top pistons), because the combustion chamber volume will be too big, and you will not have an adequate corrected compression ratio for high-performance work.

You also don't want to run a combustion chamber much larger than the stock 883's 51-cc chamber with the -11.2-cc reverse dome pistons.

CAM CONSIDERATIONS

I did not recommend a cam change with this recipe because the stock Sportster cam—with 223 degrees of intake duration (intake closes at 41 ABDC) and a 0.458-inch lift—is a decent cam and produces good low-to-midrange torque. The whole idea of this was a low-buck, only-what-you-need deal.

But if you really must spend the money on a cam set, the Andrews N8 cam with 256 degrees of intake duration (intake closes at 44 ABDC) and 0.490-inch lift should work well with this combination. You will only lose a little low-end torque with this cam, because the N8 only holds the intake open for 3 degrees more than the stock cam.

You will still have a good corrected compression ratio with the N8, and it should be good for about 5 more horsepower, but it will show up at the top end. The N8 cam may help your heads continue to make power up to the 6,000-plus-rpm range.

DYNO POWER RESULTS

So if you followed the step-by-step instructions of my 883-to-1204-cc recipe and used the stock cam, what kind of power results should you get? That's a good question. Here's what my wife got when I applied my recipe on her 883 Sportster motor.

This Sportster started out with around 42 horsepower and liked to backfire through the carb until it got good and hot. It had a hard time getting out of its own way and was, for me, a boring beast to ride. So with only about 500 miles on the clock, it went under the knife. The operation was a success; it's alive!

Here's a look at the un-tuned fuel curve. Now that we know about proper air/fuel ratios and carburetor tuning, we can see where a little more power could be extracted by flattening out the fuel curve so it stays at about 13:1 for the full run.

As I predicted, the motor started to run out of air around 5,500 rpm, but I was pleasantly surprised to see that at 6,400 rpm, the horsepower was still hanging in there at just under 70. Remember, this motor is still running stock cams and wearing stock 883 heads with their small valves. The do-it-yourself head fix we discussed is

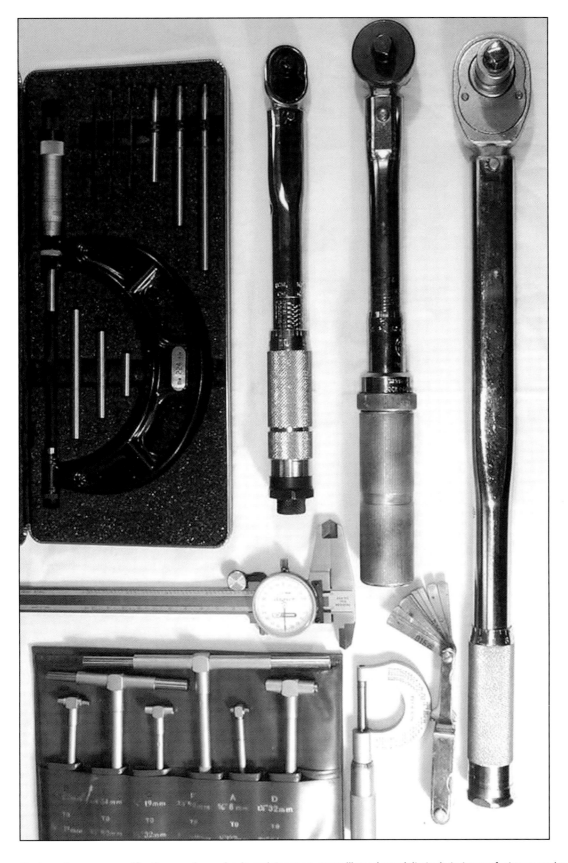

To do performance modifications, and even basic maintenance, you will need specialty tools to torque fasteners and measure parts. As with most things, quality tools are expensive, and cheap tools are often just that—cheap.

paying this bike back with usable power.

The thing that makes this bike a blast to ride is that flat torque band. Look at it: From about 2,500 to 6,000 rpm, this motor is pumping out over 60 lb-ft of torque and peaking with 70 lb-ft at 4,500 rpm. This motor combination is as loyal as a pet rock; no matter what speed you're at or what gear you're in, you just twist the throttle and go. Yah, well, power's nice, but what about gas mileage? How does 55 miles to the gallon sound? Last time I measured it, that's just what it got.

This was a reasonably priced do-it-yourself project; the parts were around $1,000. Remember in Chapter 4 in the Air/Fuel Ratio Meters section, we saw that this carburetor was not in optimum tune at the time this run was conducted? With a properly tuned carburetor, a tuned performance exhaust system, the Andrew's N8 cam, and a 0.030" head gasket, 80 lb-ft of torque and horsepower are a possibility.

The 883 Sportster has a smaller transmission belt drive sprocket than the 1200 Sportster. This smaller sprocket will allow you accelerate even faster. I recommend that if acceleration is important to you, don't change it for the larger 1200-cc sprocket. If reducing rpm at highway speeds is more important, do the sprocket change.

SPORTSTER COMPRESSION RATIOS
Here are some relevant compression numbers for my 883-to-1204-cc conversion.

Stock advertised mechanical compression ratio is 9:1.

The actual mechanical compression ratio of the stock Sportster, with the stock 0.050-inch head gasket is 8.8:1, and the more important corrected compression ratio is only 8.1:1.

It's easy to see how installing a performance cam, with its later intake valve closing event, in a stock compression 883 would be a big mistake, but people do this everyday. By doing so, you could end up with a corrected compression ratio as low as 7.5:1. Will a corrected compression ratio of 7.5:1 produce a desirable torque band? No! That's why knowledge and proper planning are so essential.

- My 883-to-1204-cc with stock cam and 0.040inch head gasket: mechanical compression ratio of 9.7:1 and corrected compression ratio of 8.9:1

- My 883-to-1204-cc with stock cam and 0.030-inch head gasket: mechanical compression ratio of 9.9:1 and corrected compression ratio of 9.1:1 (which is pushing the limit)

- My 883-to-1204-cc with N8 cam and 0.040-inch head gasket: mechanical compression ratio of 9.7:1 and corrected compression ratio of 8.75:1

- My 883-to-1204-cc with N8 cam and 0.030-inch

head gasket: mechanical compression ratio of 9.9:1 and corrected compression ratio of 8.95:1 (this one might be fun)

The 1204 cc with stock cam and 0.040-inch head gasket will be doing some serious squeezing. Cranking compression with stock 51-cc heads will be in the 185-psi range, plus/minus 10 psi depending on your head castings.

These motors should be run on high-test gasoline when available. The wife runs 90-octane gas (the highest we have up here in Alaska) in hers, and it runs fine with no signs of detonation.

We have increased the motor's displacement by 321 cc and raised the compression ratio on this motor.

Because of this, your stock starter will have to work harder to turn this motor over. You will hear the starter protesting about the increased workload, but it will still start the bike. The only time I have seen the stock starter fail to start these modified motors is when the battery's charge is low or the battery is shot. Switching to the new-style sealed batteries with this setup will make a big difference.

THINGS TO CHECK ON ALL MOTORS
There are four long studs in the engine case that hold the cylinders and heads to the bottom end. After removing the heads and cylinders, use a pair of pliers and exert a small amount of pressure to each stud. If you find a stud that turns freely, unscrew it, clean all oil from both threaded surfaces, and reinstall it with 271 red Loctite. Don't over-torque it. Just tighten it down until it's good and snug in the engine case.

The latest trend is to remove the used studs and replace them with new ones. I'm not sure what genius started this, but just about every magazine has picked up on it and has been preaching it as gospel. Although changing out the studs is not a bad idea, I have never had a problem with the stock studs on an 883 conversion motors, and neither should you as long as you do what I've just suggested.

If you do decide to change them, at least spend a few extra bucks and install heavy-duty studs. Then you'll be able to sleep at night.

GASKETS: TO GLUE OR NOT TO GLUE?
Most gaskets are designed to be installed as is, or dry. Most gaskets are also designed to absorb and swell-up with oil to aid them in sealing, but this doesn't always work.

Petroleum-based oils often build up a layer of junk on the gasket that will help them seal. On the other hand, synthetic oils do such a good job of penetrating and lubricating, they can, and do, wick through some gaskets.

Personally, I can't stand an oil leak anywhere on a Harley. So even though you're not supposed to, I always install things like a rocker box, primary chain case, and cam cover gaskets with a small amount of silicone sealant. The choice is yours. All I can say is that my gaskets usually don't leak. When you disassemble the parts, the silicone just rubs off.

SEALING HEAD GASKETS

As cylinders and heads expand and contract under heating and cooling, their shape can distort, making it difficult for head gaskets to seal. As head gaskets that seep oil are depressing, is there anything you can use to help prevent this? Yes!

One product that I routinely use on copper and aluminum head gaskets is available at your local National Automotive Parts Association (NAPA) automotive store. Called Perfect Seal JV66B sealing compound, this NAPA-brand product is designed to seal metal gaskets and, with a light coating applied, will help prevent head gasket oil leaks. It almost looks like thick oil. This tip is very important for early motors running copper head gaskets.

LOCTITE—THE BINDING BLOOD

Having watched parts and pieces fall off of Harleys for the last 30 years, I always use a thread glue. I use 242 blue (medium-strength) Loctite on just about every nut or bolt I install, that is, except for the ones requiring 271 red (high-strength) Loctite. The medium-strength blue 242 Loctite does double duty. Not only will it prevent fasteners from coming loose, but it also works like an anti-seize compound and will prevent fasteners from galling (fusing themselves together). Loctite and other similar products can be found in most automotive stores.

LOCTITE TIPS

Make sure you clean all the oil and old Loctite off of both surfaces before re-applying the Loctite. Whenever possible, use a tap or die to clean the threads. Removing the old Loctite is vital to get a proper torque value when tightening the fastener. Never let Loctite come in contact with plastic products, as it can destroy some types.

To remove a stubborn fastener that has had 271 red applied to it, try applying some heat. There is also a green Loctite, which is the only one of the three that has penetrating qualities.

TORQUE WRENCHES—A MUST

If you're going to perform service or performance work on your motorcycle, you must have a torque wrench. Always check your service manual for the proper torque values for all fasteners on your motorcycle, and always use an accurate torque wrench when tightening fasteners. Failure to do this could result in damaged parts or personal injury! For best all-around results when performing engine modifications, I recommend having three sizes of torque wrenches: 1/4, 3/8, and 1/2 inch.

Other important tools for taking measurements during performance work include feeler gauges, dial caliper, micrometers (inside and outside), and dial indicators.

Remember, a mechanic often is only as good as the tools and/or specialty equipment that he uses. So don't skimp, get quality tools! Performance modifications require more than just a pipe wrench, a hammer, and a roll of duct tape.

In addition to normal tools, many specialty tools are required for performance modification work. Before purchasing a specialty tool, always weigh the cost of the tool against the cost of having someone with the specialty tool perform the work for you. If you are only going to use the tool once, is it worth purchasing? I'll cover specialty tools in Chapter 12.

For example, instead of purchasing all of the specialty tools required to press the cams in and out of a Twin Cam's support plate, it may be more cost effective to take your cam support plate to someone who already has the proper tools.

CHAPTER 10 **TWIN CAM MOTOR RECIPE**

MY PERSONAL PERSPECTIVE
ON THE NEW TWIN CAM MOTORS

That I took the time to sit down and prepare the information you have before you demonstrates that I have a strong interest in performance V-twins. Thirty some years ago, when I had just turned 16, I purchased my first V-twin Harley, a modified magneto-equipped XLCH Sportster. I immediately got hooked on the Sportster's power.

The first thing I learned was that smoking Big Twins was so easy, it wasn't even any fun . . . that's a lie. It's always fun to smoke Big Twins!

At the time, the XLCH seemed to dominate most things on the street with two or four wheels; that is until the Japanese fours, like the 903 Kawasaki showed up. What can I say? It was fun while it lasted, and at least I still had the Big Twins to beat up on.

Even though the Sportster was no longer king of the hill, I still remain loyal to it. I have thoroughly enjoyed every Sportster I have owned, from my magneto XLCHs to my XR1000 and now my Evo Sportsters. To this day we still have more Sportsters than Big Twins in the garage.

The reason I have remained loyal to the Sportster is simple: power and weight. Today's rules are just as true as they were back then. If you perform the same modifications to a Sportster as you do to a Big Twin, the lighter Sportster will always be quicker. Since winning is always nice, I decided to stick with my Sportsters until something better from Harley comes along.

Over the years, I have spent a lot of time with Big Twins (Panheads, Shovelheads, and Evos) because there were a lot of them around for me to work on, modify, and ride.

But being a young perfectionist, I just couldn't get into them. Every time I worked on one or rode one, I kept comparing it to the Sportsters and analyzing its weak spots. For me the list was long: weak cases; poor valve-train geometry; ticking lifters; weak crank pins; no rigidity between the engine and transmission; oil-leaking cylinders; breathers oozing oil all over the right side of

This is what can happen if you ask me to fix a brand-new Twin Cam with zero miles on the clock. You can forget your warranty! Shortly after this picture was taken, the cams, lifters, motor sprocket, clutch pack, and ignition system were also removed from the motor. Other than the clutch pack, minus the clutch spring, everything else will be replaced with the performance goodies of my choice.

Except for the S&S air cleaner and the Rinehart pipes, this bike deliberately looks stock. What you can't see is over $4,000 worth of Branch, S&S, Andrews, JIMS, and Screamin' Eagle parts hiding inside. Just goes to show that you can't judge a motor by its covers.

the motor; a poor lubrication system; and on and on. (Actually, the Evo Big Twin motor isn't really as bad as I make it sound.)

Of course, the aftermarket has fixes for most of the stock motor's shortcomings, starting off with a new set of engine cases and flywheels, but why should you have to do that?

FAST FORWARD TO 1999

Harley introduced the new Twin Cam motor in 1999. I was skeptical at first, so I studied this new powerplant, and the more I saw, the more I liked it. Finally, a Big Twin I could live with. I couldn't wait to get my hands on one, so I ordered a new 2000 Dyna Low Rider to serve as my project bike.

I told myself I wasn't selling out, because Dynas are just big Sportsters for us senior citizen types. Delivery of the new bike came in January, and I trucked it 130 miles home. (Remember, I live in Alaska.) Once in the garage, I inserted the key and hit the starter button. The bike fired up, I let it idle for 30 seconds and turned it off. I looked at the wife and

said, "Cool, so that's what a new Twin Cam sounds like. I can't wait to fix it."

Thirty seconds of idling and zero miles. That's how long the bike lasted as stock. As there's not much riding going on in Alaska in January, I had time to play. By the same time the next day, the only thing left of the Twin Cam's motor was the short block with two connecting rods sticking out of it. Gee, I wonder if I voided my warranty?

Removed were a few stock parts like the cylinders, pistons, heads, pushrods, lifters, cams, carburetor, air cleaner, fuel pet-cock, ignition module and coil, motor sprocket, primary chain, and the clutch pack.

Other than the clutch pack, minus the clutch spring and the primary chain, everything else was replaced with performance goodies of my choice. To this day, I'm still impressed with what you can do to this new powerplant.

Anyway, my point is that the Twin Cam engine is a giant leap forward for the Motor Company, so much so that I had to go out and buy more HDI stock. If you're interested in Big Twin performance, you can really build reliable power with this motor.

Straight from the Motor Factory, this motor—with minor changes, i.e., free-flowing exhaust and air cleaner, recalibration jet kit in the carb—is a really good powerplant. Personally, I think the only mistake the Motor Company made was not allowing enough material in the cylinders or opening up the cases enough so it could run a 4-inch bore. A 4-inch bore, 4-inch stroke Harley would have been an instant marketing success! There's just something about a 4x4, 100-inch Harley that sounds so right. I can see it now: "Be the first kid on the block to own a 4x4 Harley to match your 4x4 Harley-Ford pickup truck." The folk in marketing and advertising should be kicking themselves in the butt for missing this. It would have only required a very small change in the design to make a 100-inch Harley a reality.

Of course, if you want a 100-inch Twin Cam, the aftermarket is ready for you. But because the designers missed this, it's rather expensive to do because you have to split the cases and have the cases bored. If you really want a big Twin Cam, S&S has a 124-incher all ready to go.

MOTOR RECIPE:
LOW-TECH, BARE-BONES TWIN CAM 88 FIX

With all that said, let's take a look at the Twin Cam. If you have read any of the V-twin-oriented magazines, you know all about the few bugs Harley had to work out of the new motors during the first year: lame cast cam-drive sprocket and weak rear cam bearing, Softail oil tanks draining into the engine cases, and B motor transmissions that didn't like to shift. To Harley's credit, these bugs were few and it found them quickly and engineered most of them out.

From a performance standpoint, I think that the Twin Cam A motor is an excellent building block to produce a truly high-performance street motor that can safely rev to 7,000 rpm. This is to due to its almost bulletproof lower end and its increased deck height and longer rods.

The B motor, on the other hand, is also suitable for performance work, but in a different way. When modifying the B motor, you should be looking at a big-torque motor that gets all its work done by 6,000 rpm, because the B motors have the crankshaft counterbalance weight system.

While the A motor is safe to 7,000 rpm or more, the B should be held to a 6,000-rpm limit if you want all of your parts and pieces to stay where they belong. Also remember that, for either engine, if you go with the Screamin' Eagle cast pistons, always keep your rpm at or below 6,200. If you need to go over 6,200 rpm, you'll need forged pistons.

Harley did an excellent job of keeping this new motor a secret. When Harley revealed it in 1999, it totally blindsided the aftermarket performance parts makers. But not wanting to be caught sitting on its duff, the aftermarket rolled up its sleeves and jumped into the Twin Cam with both feet. For the past seven years, the aftermarket has been unleashing a staggering amount of go-fast goodies for this new motor, with

more new stuff coming out everyday. By the time the aftermarket is done, you will be able to make your wildest Twin Cam dreams come true.

Unlike the low-buck 883 Sportster fix, the Twin Cam is not so cut and dried, because there are so many ways to go with it. The easiest thing to do is decide what you ultimately want it to do and then just do it. But due to the costs, not everyone can afford this option. Depending on what you want, you could be looking at a $4,000-plus investment in just parts alone; this is close to the cost of a new stock motor. If your budget is unlimited, it would be easier to just change motors and drop in something like the S&S 124-incher.

So what we'll do in this chapter is to try to get the most power for the least amount of money. A good thing about the Twin Cam is you can keep adding onto it in stages as your budget allows. Because of this, I will address modification using the "modifying it in stages" concept.

LET'S SEE WHAT WE HAVE
TO WORK WITH—THE GOOD AND THE BAD

Good: When compared with the Evo, the Twin Cam lower end is extremely tough and should be able to handle twice the stock motor's power without a problem. It's also designed to easily grow a few more inches. More inches are always good, so we will be doing that. Because its lower end is so strong, most power modifications will be limited to top-end parts. This makes the Twin Cam a better performance platform to work from than, say, an Evo with its weaker lower end.

Bad: As we have already covered, all stock Harley heads are flow restricted to increase flow velocity in the low to midrange, which creates that famous Harley torque band. Plus, it helps keep the pollution police happy.

But with the Twin Cam, small ports and valves have been taken to new extremes. Let's look at the numbers: As measured by Branch Flowmetrics, a stock 80-inch Evo head flows 127 cfm on the intake side, and the stock Twin Cam head flows approximately 118 cfm at 12 inches. What this amounts to is the 88-inch Twin Cam motor is 10 percent bigger than the 80-inch Evo, but the Twin Cam's heads flow 7.6 percent less air than the smaller 80-inch Evo's heads. If we convert this to the industry standard of 10 inches, the Twin Cam heads flow only 98.3 cfm at 10 inches on Branch's flow bench.

As a rule, Branch's one-of-a-kind flow bench always gives lower figures compared to, say, the popular SuperFlow flow benches.

So, the stock 80-inch Evo heads flow 127 cfm and our soon-to-be 95-inch Twin Cam with stock heads will only flow 118 cfm. Obviously, when running the stock heads, we have a clear case of an elephant trying to breath through a mouse's nose. Therefore, after we make the motor bigger, everything we do must address the issue of getting air and fuel into the cylinders and getting the exhaust gasses out. To make any real power with the 95-

inch Twin Cam motor, sooner or later the heads will have to be professionally ported or replaced with aftermarket performance heads.

When Branch Flowmetrics was done with my heads, they were flowing 159 cfm at 12 inches at 0.600-inch lift on the intake side. That's a large move up from the stock 118 cfm.

Let's say that budget constraints dictate modifying this motor in stages. Each stage must then be a building block for the next stage. You can jump through as many stages as your budget will allow at a time. We will be looking at the most cost-efficient (read "cheap") route to go. No bored-out cylinders, no adjustable ignitions to play with, no fancy and expensive exhaust systems, etc.

Again, I will list suggested retail prices (from 2001, when I wrote the book) from Harley-Davidson or from V-Twin Manufacturing so you have an idea of the cost. To keep cost down we will be shooting for a top rpm of only 6,200. If you ultimately want to spin your motor faster than my 6,200-rpm limit, you will need forged pistons, not the cast Screamin' Eagle pistons.

When we enlarge the motor, we will also be tightening up the squish band. We will use the 0.040-inch head gasket again to ensure a margin of safety. As stated before, I personally like and use 0.030-inch or less, but when set that tight, I have to let the bike warm up before riding, and I always keep the rpm down until the motor is up to normal operating temperature.

Remember that if you opt for the tighter squish band, your corrected compression will go up. Always recalculate it to see if it's still in the safe range.

Let's get to work!

STAGE I

Stage I will be the usual: replace or fix the air cleaner; install recalibration kit or re-jet carburetor; fix the stock mufflers; and replace the stock plug wires and spark plugs. To ensure a hot spark, gap the plugs at 0.035 inch; indexing them to the cylinder heads can't hurt. We will also lose the stock vacuum-operated fuel petcock.

PARTS LIST

- Kinetic-Karb Keihin CV carburetor recalibration kit
  Cost: $38
  Source: V-Twin Manufacturing

- One 46 and 48 slow speed jet
  Cost: $2
  Source: Harley-Davidson or V-Twin Manufacturing

- V-Twin high-flow teardrop chrome air cleaner kit
  Cost: $61
  Source: V-Twin Manufacturing

- K&N high-flow air filter (for S&S B) element
  Cost: $39
  Source: V-Twin Manufacturing

- Chrome breather kit
  Cost: $38
  Source: V-Twin Manufacturing

- Chrome gas petcock
  Cost: $15
  Source: V-Twin Manufacturing

Tip: If you're planning on major modifications down the line, go with a high-flow fuel valve now.

- **Spark plug wires:** Taylor, Spiro-Pro
  Cost: $20
  Source: V-Twin Manufacturing

- **Spark plugs:** Autolite MP4146 platinum
  Cost: $10 (set)
  Source: V-Twin Manufacturing

- **Optional:** Change the motor sprocket from the stock a 25- to a 24-tooth sprocket. You can't go wrong with this change if you want better acceleration.
  Cost: $100
  Source: Harley-Davidson or V-Twin Manufacturing

Stage I will get you going. It will correct the EPA-mandated restrictive equipment and fix the carburetion jetting problem. Your stock bike will be much happier this way. As long as you have the carburetor off, you should remove the intake manifold and work it over with 60- to 80-grit sanding paddle wheels connected to a drill. You're not going for a mirror finish here. Just smooth out the lumps, bumps, and casting flaws.

If you want better acceleration, the sprocket change does help and it doesn't affect your speedo's calibration. The 1-tooth-lower sprocket change works well on both heavy and light bikes. The sprocket change will drop the Dyna from a 3.15:1 to a 3.28:1 ratio. If you go this route, reread the sections in Chapter 5 containing Jerry Branch's comments on the stock overgearing problem and my instructions on modifying your primary chain adjuster to work with the smaller motor sprocket.

If you can't find a Twin Cam breather kit, or if you already have a kit for an Evo lying around, or if you just enjoy hard work, you can use a kit designed for an Evo.

The main difference with the Twin Cam is it uses a smaller 3/8-inch breather bolt, while the Evo B-T uses a 1/2-inch bolt. Before the Twin Cam kits were available, I turned down 1/2-inch stainless-steel bolts on a lathe and bored and threaded them. It's very labor intensive and is not for the average Joe.

The breather pipe fits under the gas tank. On some

If you can find a safe place to mount one, an inline gas filter is always a good insurance policy to protect your carburetor.

Twin Cams it fits well and on others it's too tall. If it's too tall, I usually cut the breather pipe just above the banjo fitting on one side.

Then I drill out the banjo fitting with a 5/16-inch drill bit and solder it back together. When done correctly, the chrome is not marked and you can't tell it was ever shortened.

The cheap (I mean reasonably priced) V-Twin Manufacturing chrome gas petcock will flow enough fuel for most applications, but if you plan to go whole-hog down the line, buy an expensive (Pingel, Accel, etc.) high-flow fuel valve and install it now.

STAGE II

In stage II, we will enlarge the motor to 95 inches and tighten up the squish band.

Tightening up the squish band will improve turbulence, power, and gas mileage, and will also increase the compression ratio.

The true stock TC-88 compression with the carburetor cam and sock head gasket: The mechanical compression is 8.8:1 and the corrected compression ratio is only 8.1:1.

On our modified 95-inch motor, our compression with the 0.040-inch head gaskets: The mechanical compression ratio will be raised to 9.5:1 and corrected compression ratio with the stock cam will be raised to 8.8:1. At 8.8:1 corrected, we are starting to do some serious air/fuel squeezing that will make more power.

To reduce the possibilities of detonation and to ensure good spark in our higher compression environment, we will change to a performance ignition module with a slower advance curve. We'll also install a high-voltage coil.

PARTS LIST

- **Screamin' Eagle big-bore kit with flat-top cast pistons**
  Cost: $420
  Source: Harley-Davidson or V-Twin Manufacturing.
  The Screamin' Eagle big-bore kit comes with everything you need including gaskets. The only downside to its cast piston is its limited to a maximum of 6,200 rpm.

- **0.040-inch head gasket**
  Cost: $30
  Source: V-Twin Manufacturing
  The head gasket that comes with the kit is 0.055 inch, which is too thick to develop a good squish band. So toss it your spear parts pile, we'll use a different gasket at a thinner 0.040 inch. I like the EST head gaskets made by Cometic Gasket.

- **Screamin' Eagle 6,200-rpm performance ignition kit**
  Cost: $200
  Source: Harley-Davidson
  It comes with the 6,200-rpm performance ignition module and a high output coil. I went with the Screamin' Eagle ignition kit because it's plug and play and it works. With the Screamin' Eagle ignitions, there's nothing for you to mess with or to worry about. Note: There are many good adjustable ignition modules on the market. If you feel comfortable with their small added complexities, you can substitute at will. The truly reliable way to find the correct curve to use is by spending money on dyno testing.

The "do it yourself at home head fix" from Chapter 8 should also be done here. At 95 inches, anything you can do to help this motor breathe is extremely important. Also remember, you do not use the O-rings on the top cylinder dowels with the 95-inch cylinders.

STAGE III

Time for a mild cam! When we change the cam, we will also install adjustable pushrods. We will need the adjustable pushrods anyway, when we upgrade the heads. So this will save us from having to remove the gas tank, rocker boxes, and rocker arms again when we do.

The reason we'll change the pushrods has to do with clearance problems we may encounter later on. Depending on the modifications we make, the stock pushrods might end up being too long, and could damage the motor. Also, the stock pushrods are fixed in length so we can't adjust them. Properly adjusted pushrods are very important when tuning to maximize power output.

To make any real power, all these stock ignition components will need to be replaced with either aftermarket performance parts or Harley Screamin' Eagle components.

First, remove the pushrod retainer clips, cut the pushrods in half with a set of bolt cutters, and remove them in two pieces. If you don't have bolt cutters, you can rent a set for a few bucks from a tool rental place.

The instructions that come with most aftermarket cam kits tell you to adjust the pushrods by lengthening them until they can no longer spin freely, then further lengthening the pushrods by three full turns of the adjusting nut, then tightening the lock nut against the adjusting nut. In most applications this will work okay.

But, from a performance standpoint, is there a better way? I think so. That's why I do it a different way, ensuring I get all I can from the new cam I just bought and installed.

Here's how I adjust hydraulic lifters (it takes time to do it this way, but it's worth it):

First disconnect the battery.

Then make sure the pushrod you're adjusting is on the low side of the cam lobe. You can do this simply by looking at the pushrod as you slowly rotate the motor. You will see the pushrod rise up, lifting the valve, then you'll see it come back down. When the pushrod stops moving down, you are on the low side of the cam.

Now we will collapse the lifters by manually bleeding them down. Loosen the two jam nuts and lengthen the pushrod until you can no longer turn it with your fingers. Take a 5 minute break and wait for the lifter to bleed down. Now check the pushrod. You should be able to turn it again with your fingers. Extend the length of the pushrod by one turn of the adjusting nut. Take another 5 minute break. Repeat as necessary.

Only lengthen the pushrod by one turn at a time, or you

Cometic's new EST head gaskets are a three-piece metal affair, with two rivets holding the gaskets together. I have had good luck with these gaskets and recommend them for stock or high-output motors. To install them on heads that have been milled, you may need to cut the rivets off before you install them. They fit fine as is on stock unmilled heads.

could bend and/or otherwise damage parts. Eventually, you will come back after one of your five-minute breaks and find you can no longer turn the pushrod. When that happens, the pushrod has been bled down and the lifter spring has collapsed. Now we start shortening the pushrod by turning the adjusting nut one sixth of a turn at a time until we can once again turn the pushrod with our fingers.

Stop here because this is your baseline to correctly adjust the pushrod.

Now decrease the pushrod length from this point by one full turn of the adjuster nut, hold the top adjusting nut and

tighten the bottom lock nut.

Before you move on to the next pushrod, rotate the motor again watching the adjusted pushrod lift and lower the valve. When it's back on the low side of the cam, check it again. If it's correctly adjusted, you should still be able to rotate the pushrod. If you can't, you have to start all over again;, if you can, you're done.

Now for the bad news: you still have 3 more pushrods to adjust. This process can take two hours or more to complete, but from a performance standpoint it's time well spent. If you want to ensure you're getting the most from your new cams,

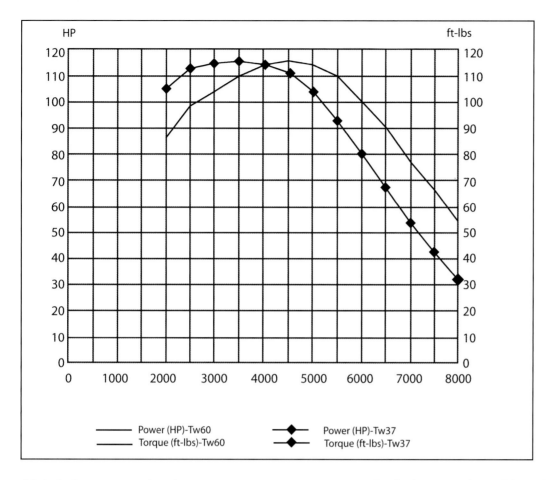

Power (HP)-Tw60
Torque (ft-lbs)-Tw60
Power (HP)-Tw37
Torque (ft-lbs)-Tw37

this is the best way to make it happen.

At this stage, the only thing really holding us back is airflow. Earlier, I stated that no cam change would increase the cfm flow rate of your heads. This is a fact. But, what we can do is open the intake valve a little earlier and close it a little later. This keeps the valves open longer, and the longer they're held open, the more air can flow through the port and into the cylinder.

Remember, there is a point of vanishing returns where this stops working for you and starts working against you.

While we can increase the overlap to take advantage of scavenging, we can also lift the valve higher for more flow. However, as you will see from Branch's head flow data, airflow stops increasing at a lift of only 0.400 inch. Lifting the valve much higher than the stock 0.473 inch is not going to help you gain much of anything. The maximum height you can safely lift the stock valves on a stock Twin Cam head is 0.510 inch.

When it comes to cams, mild is always better than wild with our flow-restricted heads. Plus, we are trying to make a motor with lots of torque in the low and midranges. A wild top-end-only cam will not accomplish this, and can make your motor less street-worthy.

As stated earlier, the aftermarket geared up big time to make Twin Cam parts. At the time of this writing, there were over 50 cam grinds available for Twin Cams, with more coming out every day. But no matter what brand you choose,

avoid radical cams, as they will be useless at this stage. Since it is impractical to cover every cam that would work, I will pick two candidates from the Andrews cam line. The two we will be looking at are the TW-26A and the TW-37B cams.

CAM TIP TIME

I touched upon computer-based engine building software. Whenever someone asks me about a cam recommendation, I head for my laptop computer. Although these programs don't deal in absolute numbers as far as torque and horsepower are concerned, they do work well for matching cams and compression ratios, and for comparing torque bands and peak torque locations.

The torque band and the location of peak torque will only be relative to the cam you are comparing it to! In other words, the relative shapes and locations of torque and horsepower will be useful, but the numbers themselves will not be correct. For cam and compression match-ups, I like to use Accelerator Pro III software.

For modeling and comparing torque bands for cams, I like to use Desktop Dyno 2000. Since it is an auto-based program, some fudge factor is involved in using it for V-twin motorcycles. Once you get around the fudge factors, it works very well for comparing power bands. Update: A new version of Desktop Dyno 2000 has been released—Desktop Dyno 2003.

If you're new to using one of these programs, take the time to understand how they work and what they are telling you

While you have the cam case opened up, it would be an ideal time to replace the two inside cam bearings.

before you spend money on parts! Approximate costs: Desktop Dyno 2000, $50; Accelerator Pro III, $150. Note: Accelerator Pro III is a disk operating system (DOS) based program, but you can run it with Windows.

To give you an idea of what Desktop Dyno 2000 looks like, I have modeled torque bands for a modified 95-inch Twin Cam motor using the Andrews TW-37B and TW-60A cams. The numbers are not that important; it's the shape of the torque bands, and how they compare with each other.

In this motor combination, we can see that the TW-37B should produce a nice, broad torque band.

The TW-60A is geared more for top-end horsepower. Its peak torque and power will happen higher in the rpm range.

In this motor combination, the TW-60A will make more horsepower, but the average rider will probably enjoy the torque band of the TW-37B a lot more.

PARTS LIST
- **Andrews cam kit**
  Cost: $262
  Source: V-Twin Manufacturing

- **Genuine James cam gasket kit**
  Cost: $40
  Source: V-Twin Manufacturing

- **Andrews 7/16-inch adjustable aluminum pushrod set**
  Cost: $139
  Source: V-Twin Manufacturing
  For street use, I like the large-diameter lightweight aluminum pushrods, because they have adequate rigidity for all but maximum-effort motors and help minimize valvetrain noise. If you plan eventually to build a maximum-effort engine, you would be better served with the heavier rigid moly steel pushrods.

CAM BEARING TIP
While you have the cam case opened up, it would be an ideal time to replace the two inside cam bearings. The stock bearings are INA brand and have a reputation for failing under hard performance use. If this happens, we're talking really big money to repair the damage caused by a $10 part. Replacing the stock bearings with the reliable Torrington brand bearings will correct this. The bearings you need are two Torrington B-148 bearings. Buy these from a motorcycle aftermarket shop, and they could cost you as much as $15 a pop. I went to a bearing supplier and purchased both bearings for $6. That's more money this book just saved you.

STOCK CAM REFERENCE INFO
The stock INA bearing is on the left, the Torrington bearing right. The stock bearing uses a cage to separate the needle rollers

If you can't find someone who will lend you the tools, you'll need to take your bike to a shop that has them and pay to have the bearings replaced. These particular tools are from JIMS.

inside of the bearing. The superior Torrington bearing does not utilize the cage setup and it has almost twice as many needle bearings and bearing surface than the stock cam bearings.

Now for the bad news, it only takes a few minutes to replace the bearings but you need specialty tools to replace them. These tools cost about $200, here's a look at the tools

I use, they're from Jim's USA.

It's important to remember when working with bearings, like oil seals, many are directional, that is they a designed to only be installed and work only one-way. Always check and note the positioning of the bearing or seal before you remove it. Always reinstall the bearing or

137

Here, the stock INA inner cam bearing is being removed using the JIMS tool.

seal in the same orientation as the one you removed. Of course this relies on the fact that the original one was installed correctly. In the case of the Twin-Cam's inner cam support bearings they are directional, when correctly installed the name and number of the bearing faces out so you can read them after they are installed.

TWO TWIN CAM CAMS ANALYZED

Stock cam reference information: Stock Twin Cam with carburetor (A) cam: mechanical compression is 8.8:1;

corrected compression is only 8.1:1; intake valve closes at 38 degrees; intake duration is 216 degrees; and overlap is only 2 degrees.

The Andrews TW-26A: This cam is geared for low-to-midrange torque. It closes the intake 1 degree sooner than the stock cam for a tad more compression. At 226 degrees of intake duration, it will keep the valve open 10 degrees longer than the stock cam for a little more flow volume.

Given its 16 degrees of overlap, it has 14 more degrees of overlap than the stock cam, so it can take better advantage of

A different tool is then used to install the new Torrington B-148 inner cam bearings. The bearing swap, as far as the cost of bearings goes, is an inexpensive upgrade that I highly recommend you perform whenever the cam chest is opened up.

scavenging. The TW-26A, with the big-bore flat-top piston kit and a 0.040-inch head gasket, will give us a mechanical compression ratio of a 9.5:1 and a corrected compression ratio of 8.85:1.

The TW-26A would work fine for both a heavy touring bike and a light sportbike. Personally, I'd recommend this cam for the heavy touring bike, because it will produce a strong low-range torque band, although it will run out of air at higher rpm.

The Andrews TW-37B: I like this cam because it's a good compromise. Using the stock heads, this cam will work well on the lighter Dynas and Softails. With performance heads

and carb, it will work well on a heavyweight dresser.

The TW-37B cam closes the intake valve 4 degrees later than the stock cam, so we will lose some corrected compression. Its 236 degrees of intake duration keeps the intake valve open for 22 more degrees than the stock cam for greater cylinder refill. Given its 26 degrees of overlap, it has 24 more degrees than the stock cam and will make good use of scavenging, but this will happen in the middle of the rpm band and not at the bottom.

The TW-37B, with the big-bore kit and 0.040-inch head gasket, will give us a mechanical compression ratio of 9.5:1 and a corrected compression ratio of 8.65:1.

Although this is a little short of our target 8.8:1 corrected compression, it's still better than the stock 8.1:1 ratio. Using a thinner 0.030-inch head gasket will help get back some of the compression. The nice thing about the TW-37B is that it has a broad torque band that does not fall off as quickly as the torque band on the TW-26A cam. That means you can keep making power further up the rpm band.

Another thing I like about this cam is that it works well when you upgrade your heads and carburetor. This cam, with the stock heads, will cause a heavy bike to lose some low-end grunt, but when you upgrade to performance heads, this cam will produce more than enough torque to power a heavy touring bike. I have run this cam with the 95-inch big-bore kit, 0.040-inch head gasket, performance heads, and S&S E carb. It produced a very strong, broad torque band (from 2,500 to 5,000 rpm) and peaked out with over 95 lb-ft of torque. That's more than enough torque to get even a loaded-down bagger moving. This cam also provides a nice smooth idle.

STAGE III CONCLUSION

Everything depends on the parts you choose to assemble and how fast you want to go. Done correctly, you could end up with about 16 percent more horsepower and about 20 percent more torque. Although this does not sound like much, a 20 percent increase in torque will make a big difference the next time you twist the throttle to pass that big rig. Our modified motor will have a much stronger and broader torque band than the stock motor, and torque is what it's all about.

The problem with the stock motor's torque band is that it comes on strong down low and then disappears just as fast.

STAGE IV: THE FINAL FRONTIER
Cost: $750 to $1,500.
Stage IV is where we fix the number one thing that has been holding this motor back from the start: the heads. In this stage we will remove the mouse's nose and install the correct size trunk on our elephant.

We have kept the re-jetted small stock carburetor up to this point. I would have suggested replacing it sooner, but with the low flow rate of the stock heads, the cost to install it may not have been worth the little performance improvement we would have gained. At this stage we must install a larger carburetor so we can take advantage of our high-flow heads. Depending on what kind of a torque band you want, a cam change may also be called for in order to utilize your new head's flow capabilities fully.

TWIN CAM HEAD CONSIDERATIONS

As we covered before, you have two options: send your heads out to a professional head porter to be modified, or buy a set of aftermarket performance heads. So what's best?

Well, the truly professional head porter has the advantage of custom modifying your heads to match your engine's size and your intended performance goals. He can also match flow rates and combustion chamber volumes.

In the past I have always gone this route. Is it cost effective? Maybe not. Today, there are a number of excellent, off-the-shelf, aftermarket high-performances heads to choose from, especially those manufactured by Edelbrock, STD, S&S, and others. Even Harley has its own Screamin' Eagle brand heads, which are priced reasonably and work well, but don't flow quite as well as most of the other aftermarket heads.

For the Twin Cam motors, the Screamin' Eagle line has the high-torque combustion chamber (HTCC) cylinder heads and pistons. These heads utilize the effective angled dome-piston squish bands. Although I haven't seen any flow data on these new heads yet, they rate investigating.

Remember, once the stock heads are modified, there's no way to turn them back into stock heads. For the same money, you can buy a set of complete, ready-to-run aftermarket performance heads, and you'll still have your stock heads. Then, you could sell the stock heads and recoup some of the money you invested in the aftermarket heads.

REQUIRED AIRFLOW

To achieve 100 percent volumetric efficiency in our 95-inch motor, at 6,200 rpm we must be able to flow 155 cfm at 10 inches of H_2O on the intake side through the heads and intake system, and 7,000 rpm requires 175 cfm at 10 inches of H_2O.

Even if the intake tract can flow the required amount of air, the cam you run will always control the amount of volumetric efficiency and the range where your engine will achieve it. Without a power adder (turbo or blower) it is almost impossible for a street bike to realize 100 percent VE—especially at lower rpm.

CARBURETORS
Cost: $300 to $500 plus.
Carburetor airflow requirements are the same as those for the heads. When I say carburetor, I mean the entire intake tract system including the intake manifold and air cleaner assembly.

As stated before, it's always a good idea to choose a carburetor (total intake system) that will flow only about 10 percent more than the required flow rate. If you go much over that, it will cause low-speed tuning problems and poor low-speed drivability. At this stage, many carburetors will suit our requirements, but I'm only going to mention a few. If we stay with the mild cams and limit rpm to 6,200, carbs like the S&S Super E, the Mikuni HRS 42, or the Keihin CV 44-millimeter will work fine. If you want to run a more radical top-end cam or plan to spin your motor over 6,200 rpm regularly, larger carbs like the S&S Super G or Mikuni HRS 45 may be better suited for your needs.

CARBURETOR RULES

A carburetor that is too big will not perform well at low speeds, where you spend most of your time. I know I have mentioned "low-speed tuning problems and poor low-speed drivability" time and time again in this book, but it's a reality.

A smaller carburetor will give you good performance and will respond faster to the demand changes of normal every-

140

day riding, but the smaller carb may run out of air at the very top end. Worrying too much about the last part of that statement is often what causes people to get carburetors that are too big for their motors.

So unless you plan to spend most of your time on the dyno or the drag strip, you may want to lean toward a smaller carb for the best all-around street performance.

For example, in the course of my research for this book, I decided to deliberately screw up a perfectly good combination. My plan involved removing the smaller S&S Super E and replacing it with the larger S&S Super G carb on the Twin Cam project bike; the objective was to see what would happen. Going into this test, I knew two things that made me want to try it:

1. Even though this motor combination was happy and performed well with the smaller E carb, I knew that the larger G carb would produce higher top-end numbers on the dyno. So for a maximum-effort 95-inch motor, the larger S&S Super G would be a logical choice.

2. If the larger G carb could be easily tuned to work on the Twin Cam project bike, I—with my bag of S&S carburetor tuning tricks and modifications—should be able to do it.

Before starting the test, the S&S Super G carb had all the tuning modifications we discussed earlier, except for the addition of a ThunderJet. Once installed and tuned, the carb idled fine, and the motor accelerated well and felt strong holding a fairly steady air/fuel ratio of about 13:1. On maximum acceleration above 5,000 rpm, the mixture started to lean out a little bit, but that could be easily fixed with a T-Jet. That's where the goodness stopped, because no matter what I tried, I could not dial in a proper fuel curve for this motor when operated in a steady state.

Remember, the project bike had an air/fuel ratio meter installed on it, so I could see exactly what the air/fuel ratio was doing every second the motor was running. No matter what I tried, the air/fuel ratio would wander all over the place when the motor was in steady-state operation, like riding through town doing 25–30 miles per hour in third gear or a steady 50 miles per hour in fifth gear. In other words, it would do this when I was looking at an rpm of around 2,200 rpm. By ear, I could hear that the motor was laboring and not running well. Looking at the air/fuel ratio meter told me why. At low-load, low-rpm, steady-state operation, the fuel mixture was fluctuating all over the place and was often in the dangerously lean area of 15 to16:1. Sometimes all the lights would go off, indicating the mixture was going leaner than 17:1. The carburetor was starving the motor of fuel.

Operating an engine with an air/fuel mixture that lean produces very high temperatures and leads to catastrophic engine damage. When I twisted the throttle open a little

and asked the motor to accelerate, the air/fuel ratio instantly settled back to a normal and safe 13:1. I tried different intermediate jets and different air bleed combinations with no luck. I even tried the Sifton Bombsight booster that worked so well on the E carb, still with no luck.

Was there something wrong with that particular S&S Super G carburetor? No, I would say not. My guess is the problem was the size of the carburetor in relationship to the motor combination itself. The culprit that caused this problem was probably intake tract reversion. When that particular motor, with that particular large carburetor, was asked to operate in a steady state, it created intake reversion that negatively affected the jetting circuits. In other words, the carb was getting mixed signals, so it didn't know what to do. When I asked the motor to do something other than operate at a steady state, like accelerate, the point of reversion changed and the carb operated normally. Of course, a motor is required to operate at a steady state quite often. So, I found that running that particular large carburetor with that motor combination was both dangerous and unacceptable.

The only possible cure might have been experimenting with the plenum area of the G carburetor by adding spacers between the carb body and the intake manifold. Of course that would have caused the carburetor to stick farther out from the gas tank; not an option I wanted to pursue.

I reinstalled the smaller S&S Super E and everything went back to normal. The air/fuel ratio stayed within a half point of 13:1 from idle to redline, under load and during steady-state operation, like fuel injection. It's a wonderful thing to watch and ride.

TWIN-CAM CAMS COMPARED

The reason why I can't throw power figures around at this stage is because of the wide variety of cams out there now. With the flow-restricted stock heads, only mild cams would have provided satisfactory results. Now that we are running free-flowing performance heads, the field's wide open. At this stage the more radical top-end cams can be used. Even though we can run these more aggressive grinds, the rules of cam usage have not changed.

The low-to-midrange torque cams will still do all of their business in the same power band, but their torque figures should be even better.

Top-end high-horsepower cams will still be doing all of their business in the upper rpm range with the sacrifice of low-end torque.

When running an aggressive cam, you will need to increase your compression ratio.

By running the proper corrected compression ratio, you may be able to gain back some of the lost low-end power, but you will never be able to reproduce the strong low-range torque that milder cams will provide. Reversion also tends to raise its ugly head with aggressive cams, further complicating low rpm tuning. And as we just discussed, reversion can be problematic.

When we compare the TW-26A and TW-37B Andrews cams with the TW-60A, at a glance we can see that the TW-60A is aimed at making power in the upper end of the power band by its timing and its lift of 0.560 inch. A 0.560-inch lift is on the conservative side when comparing it with today's trend of lifting valves ever higher.

The duration on the TW-60A is 260 degrees (stock is only 216), it has an overlap of 46 degrees (stock is only 2), and it doesn't close the intake valve until 56 degrees ABDC (stock is 38). An intake valve-closing event at 56 degrees ABDC will cause intake tract reversion. This reversion will interfere with low-speed tuning, so this cam won't hit its sweet spot until 4,000 rpm. We'll need to run a mechanical compression of about 10.5:1 or higher with this cam to get our desired corrected compression ratio of 8.8:1 or better.

So what can we expect from these three cams—the TW-26A, TW-37B, and the TW-60A—if we set our corrected compression ratio to a safe 8.8:1?

The TW-26A will produce the best low-to-midrange torque band. Its peak torque will happen around 3,500 rpm, and then it will quickly diminish due to lack of cylinder refill (VE) at higher rpm. This cam should produce a peak torque in the range of 95 lb-ft and close to 80 horsepower at the rear wheel. Horsepower will peak at about 5,000 then drop off. Low-speed idle and tuning will be good. It would be a good candidate for the heavy touring bike.

With our high-flowing heads, the TW-37B will also provide a strong broad torque band, although it will be a little softer between 2,000 and 2,500 rpm than the TW-26A. Its peak torque will happen around 4,000 rpm, but unlike the TW-26A, it will stick with us further up the rpm band because its VE will not fall off as fast. This cam should also produce peak torque in the range of 95 lb-ft and about 85 horsepower at the rear wheel. Horsepower will peak at about 5,300 to 5,400, and then remain fairly steady to redline at 6,200 rpm, because torque should be falling off at about the same rate as the rpm will be increasing. Low-speed idle and tuning will be good. It would be a decent candidate for both the light bike and heavy touring bike.

The light bike will accelerate hard in the low to midrange with this cam. This cam will provide an excellent power band over a wide rpm range. This is a good, mellow street cam grind, not a drag racing or dyno queen cam.

This cam has also worked well for me on heavy touring bikes. It provides the heavy bike with a more performance-oriented power band. It should produce the same amount of torque as the TW-26A, but you will need to turn the motor 500 rpm more to get to it. Once there, though, the TW-37B cam will provide a much wider torque band, and will also allow the heavy bike to reach a higher road speed than the TW-26A will.

The TW-60A is a top-end oriented horsepower cam. It is designed to make its power in the upper rpm ranges. Because of its late intake-valve closing event (56 degrees ABDC), intake tract reversion will interfere with its ability to perform very well below 3,000 rpm. Reversion will not disappear until around 4,000 rpm. Because of this, the idle will be rough and may not be possible below 1,200 rpm. Low-speed carburetor tuning may be difficult and low-speed power will be down. Increasing the compression will help recover some of the lost power, but doing so will only make the low-speed reversion problem worse.

This cam should produce a peak torque in the range of 95-plus lb-ft and 95 to 100 horsepower at the rear wheel. Maximum torque with this cam will happen at about 4,700 rpm. Horsepower will continue to build all the way up to, and even beyond, our rev limiter's setting of 6,200 rpm. This cam would work best on a lighter bike with 10.5:1 mechanical compression or better. It is ideal for the biker who loves to go really fast, turn good numbers on the dyno, and collect lots of speeding tickets.

COMBUSTION CHAMBER VOLUMES

With our stock heads we were stuck with the stock 83-cc combustion chamber. The only way we could increase compression was by running a thinner head gasket or using dome pistons. When it comes to piston shapes, when used in conjunction with a compact, efficient combustion chamber with a properly set-up squish band, the flat-top piston will always be the most economical type to use. Why?

Let's take yet another quick look at squish bands, cylinder heads, and pistons. There are basically two types of squish band designs. The simpler of the two is the flat-top piston and the flat-base cylinder head. The stock Twin Cam cylinder head comes with a flat bottom. If we use a flat-top piston to match the flat bottom of the cylinder head, setting up the desired squish band is as simple as choosing the head gasket with the right thickness.

Here are a few things that the flat-top piston setup has going for it. The flat-top piston doesn't interfere with the progression of the flame front, which a dome piston can do. The flat-top piston also has less surface area, which means it will absorb less heat. The less heat we waste heating the top of the piston, the more heat we have for making power.

The other type of squish band involves machining the inside of the cylinder head at an angle (usually 30 degrees) and running a piston that is designed with an identical angle to match the cylinder head. The piston is often only angled on the sides to create the squish band and is flat on the top. Properly set up, this type of squish band can outperform flat squish bands. Harley's new Screamin' Eagle HTCC heads use this arrangement.

How does it work? A flat squish band creates mixture turbulence, when the mixture reaches TDC, by forcing the mixture from the flat area under the cylinder head to the center of the piston and into the combustion chamber. Angled squish bands often utilize the flat ledge and add another squish area between the cylinder head and the angled sides of the piston, thus creating a secondary squish band. It can generate more mixture turbulence by forcing the mixture directly into the combustion chamber, unlike the flat squish band that just forces the mix-

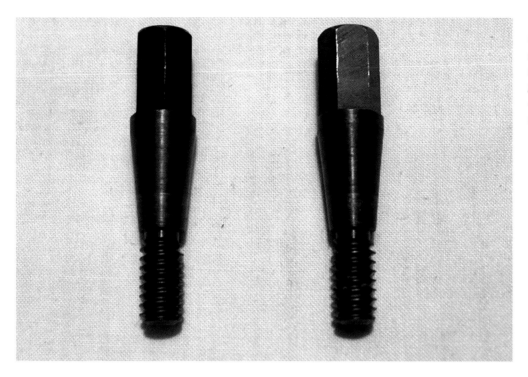

Using these Evo tappet base alignment tools (H-D #33443) to align the oil pump on the Twin Cam motors may prevent premature oil pump failures.

ture toward the combustion chamber at right angles. This can yield a more efficient burn, which equals more power. The only downside to the angled squish bands is that they can cost more to create than the flat squish band.

When we move into the realm of performance cylinder heads, we also have the option of modifying the shape or volume of our combustion chamber. On a stock head we could mill off some of its deck surface to get the desired combustion chamber size or, as Branch does, we can weld up the chamber and reshape it with our desired volume. Aftermarket heads are available with different combustion chamber sizes, so it is often easy to choose the head according to our desired corrected compression ratio.

The camshaft is often referred to as the personality of your motor. This is a very true statement. The cam you decide to run will control how your bike performs and how, and where, it will make power.

PROPER MOTOR DESIGN STEPS

1. Decide on the motor's displacement.

2. Calculate the amount of intake airflow needed to satisfy requirements for your targeted maximum rpm, and be sure to include the entire intake system: heads, intake manifold, carburetor, and air cleaner.

3. Decide on the type of power (torque) band you want the motor to create.

4. Select a cam that will create your desired power band, thus satisfying your displacement's intake and exhaust airflow requirements.

5. Match your chosen cam to the correctly sized combustion chamber volume to achieve the proper corrected compression ratio.

Now that you have chosen your displacement and your cam, your next job will be to calculate the total combustion chamber volume required to achieve your desired corrected compression ratio. As stated, I like to run 8.8:1 to 9.0:1 maximum. This should work for you, too, especially if you live in a place like Alaska, where 90-octane is called high-test gasoline . . . if you can find it.

You will find that utilizing one of the computer-based simulator programs will make this job a piece of cake.

Here's an example. We have decided that on our Twin Cam we will use the Screamin' Eagle big-bore kit with flat-top pistons. We have also decided that we only want to build a mild street performance bike and that the TW-37B cam will meet our torque band needs. The TW-37B closes the intake valves at 42 degrees ABDC. We don't want this motor to be prone to detonation, so we will shoot for an 8.8:1 corrected compression ratio. With the pistons and cylinders installed on our motor, we will lightly tighten the cylinders down.

We will need four spacers to do this. They can be as simple as pieces of 1/2-inch copper pipe that are long enough to reach from the top of the cylinder to the threaded part of the studs. We will then rotate each piston to TDC and measure the piston-to-cylinder deck height.

To keep things simple, let's say the pistons are flush with the tops of the cylinders. Our deck height would be zero.

We have decided to run the safer 0.040-inch head gaskets because we don't want to wait around for five to ten

You can see the above bolts being used to center a Twin Cam oil pump.

minutes for our motor to warm up before we can ride. To figure out our required combustion chamber size quickly, we will use the compression tool in the Accelerator Pro III software. Entering the correct bore, stroke, cam timing, and deck height information into the advanced compression ratio tool, we find that we will need a combustion chamber with a volume of 81 cc to get our desired corrected compression ratio of 8.8:1.

If you were sending your heads out to a professional head porter, the porter could machine your heads to achieve your required combustion chamber volume. Remember, when milling heads, always check your valve-to-piston clearances!

Another choice would be to find a set of aftermarket heads that already have your required combustion chamber volume.

As a rule, Twin Cam aftermarket heads run between 88 to 72 cc. Edelbrock offers a version of its Performer RPM series heads with only 72 cc of combustion chamber volume, one of the smallest available.

If we used these 72-cc heads on our example motor, with the TW-37B cam and 0.040-inch head gasket, this head would yield a 10.7:1 mechanical compression ratio and a 9.74:1 corrected compression ratio. If you ran a tighter squish band and used the 0.030-inch head gasket, your corrected compression would be 9.92:1!

If you attempted to run either one of these corrected compression ratios on pump gas, it would cause enough detonation to end your motor's life in very short order. This is why it is so important to plan every detail of your motor before you assemble it. The penalty for not doing this will be either disappointing performance results or a motor that spills its guts all over the ground!

TWIN CAM OIL PUMP FAILURES

There have been a number of reports of premature oil pump failures on the new Twin Cam motors. The Twin Cam uses a gerotor oil pump that is mounted inside of the cam case and located behind the cam support plate. This is the same oil pump that has been used successfully on Sportsters for years, and is far superior to the early stock, externally mounted Big Twin oil pumps.

Personally, I believe the problem with the oil pump is not a design problem, but an alignment problem. The early factory shop manual describes a rather dubious method for aligning the oil pump. You first install the four oil pump bolts and snug them down. You then loosen the bolts, rotate the motor a few times, hoping the oil pump will magically align itself, and follow the recommended sequence to torque the oil pump bolts. The problem is, if the pump is not properly aligned when it's torqued, the result will be oil pump damage. This may be the cause of the reported premature oil pump failures.

A more reliable method to align the Twin Cam oil pump is to use the same tool that is used to align the Evo tappet bases, the H-D tool 33443 (Evo tappet base alignment tool). Simply insert the two tools in two of the bolt holes on opposite sides of the oil pump, and then snug them down. Now insert and torque two of the oil pump bolts. Remove the two alignment tools, and torque the last two bolts. This may keep the oil pump straight and happy for many years of use.

TWIN CAM IGNITION MODULES

The rev limiter on stock Twin Cam ignition is set at 5,700 rpm. This limit is okay, because the small ports and valves in the stock heads on an 88-inch motor will run out of air flow at approximately 5,400 rpm, and even sooner on a 95-inch motor. When you can no longer supply the maximum required airflow volume, torque starts to fall.

The stock Twin Cam heads will not flow enough air to satisfy the airflow requirements to reach the stock rev limiter's setting of 5,700 rpm. Once you have exceeded your motor's peak required airflow location, your motor's volumetric efficiency will drop off substantially. You can spin your motor beyond this point, but due to a poor cylinder refill percentage, it will not be producing much torque, and when your torque starts to fall off faster than your rpm are increasing, horsepower also starts to decrease.

Harley sells several different ignition modules in its Screamin' Eagle line, which include usage recommendations. The two modules I'll address here are listed as the performance and the race ignition modules for Twin Cam 88.

The Screamin' Eagle performance ignition has the rev limiter set at 6,200 rpm, and it's listed for use with stock compression ratios only. It is to be used on the stock 88-inch displacement or with the big-bore kit with flat-top pistons and a 9.3:1 mechanical compression ratio.

There're two main differences between the stock and performance ignition module: The rev limit is set 500 rpm higher and it has 5 degrees less advance at full advance.

Screamin' Eagle race ignition has the rev limiter set at 7,000 rpm, and it's listed for use with the big-bore kit with high compression ratios and other performance enhancements. The race ignition module rev limit is set 1,000 rpm higher than stock and has 5 degrees less advance at full advance than the performance module, or 10 degrees less than stock.

Other than the different rev limit settings, the only real difference is that the race module has a slower (by 5 degrees) advance curve than the performance module, to reduce possible detonation. If you believe everything you read, a performance street bike with cams, carb, high compression, and added displacement would require the race module.

Branch Flowmetrics says, "Not so!" The folks at Branch told me that after dyno testing with Branch heads, they have found that the performance module, with its faster advance curve, works better on hot street motors than the race module.

Therefore, the performance street module is recommended over the race module. Note that Branch heads would equal any correctly designed cylinder heads that have large, generous squish bands.

I fully agree, and I utilize the performance module on my highly modified 95-inch Twin Cam, which has 10:1 mechanical compression and an 8.8:1 corrected compression with a tightly set-up squish band. And it runs fine, even on 87-octane pump swill.

Why? When set up properly, the large squish bands on Branch modified heads, and similar performance heads, will create excellent combustion chamber turbulence. Because of this, they can make good use of the 6,200 rpm performance module's faster advance curve. The performance module has the ability to make more power than the slower advance curve of the 7,000-rpm race module.

Remember that good chamber turbulence is one way to control detonation when running high compression and/or faster advance curves. It can also increase power and gas mileage.

We have already discussed that we can increase power by reducing parasitic loss. S&S discovered that when a Twin Cam is run at high rpm for extended periods, it suffers excessive oil buildup around the flywheel in the crankcase. So S&S has come up with a simple breather device that corrects this problem. Its breather consists of four reed valves that fit over the crankshaft in the cam case. When the pistons move down the cylinders, pressure is created in the crankcase. When this happens, the reed valves open, allowing the oil in the crank to flow into the cam chest. When pistons move back up the cylinder, the reed valves close, trapping the oil in the cam chest where it is removed and sent to the oil tank.

Here you can see the breather installed. This is a very easy installation and, just like with the inner cam bearings, you should do it when you're doing a cam change.

TWIN CAM DYNO TEST INFORMATION

This information is from Branch Flowmetrics. An 88-inch Branch test mule motor dyno results (before and after).

This stock Twin Cam 88 A test motor's power numbers are very good for being stock. The Branch modified motor is 88 inches, has a 10.5:1 compression, and has Branch heads and a Branch T-55 cam, Mikuni HSR45 carb, White Bros. E pipes, and Screamin' Eagle 6,200-rpm module. Note: This Branch combination is a top-end horsepower setup. (Peak horsepower and torque numbers in bold.)

TWIN CAM HEAD FLOW INFORMATION

Mph	Rpm	HP Stock	HP Branch	Torque stock	Torque Branch
47	2,000	28.2		74.1	
59	2,500	36.7	31.2	77.0	59.7
71	3,000	44.4	46.5	**77.8**	81.4
82	3,500	51.8	56.5	77.7	84.7
94	4,000	58.1	69.8	76.4	91.7
106	4,500	61.5	80.2	71.8	**93.6**
118	5,000	**63.6**	86.1	66.8	90.4
130	5,500	62.1	92.1	59.3	87.9
141	6,000	rev limit	96.0	rev limit	84.8
147	6,200	rev limit	**97.7**	rev limit	82.1

Combustion chamber stock = 82 to 85 cc, depending on the source
Branch says stock chamber = 83 cc
Branch bathtub chamber = 82 cc
Stock valves: intake 1.840 inches, area = 2.658 inches; exhaust 1.570 inches, area = 1.935 inches
Branch valves: intake 1.930 inches, area = 2.924 inches; exhaust 1.632inches, area = 2.091 inches
Cfm flow rates: Stock compared to Branch heads
Percent = Percentage of exhaust to intake ratio (**Note:** An 80 percent ratio is considered ideal!)

TWIN CAM HEAD FLOW INFORMATION
This information is from Branch Flowmetrics.

Lift in inches	Evo intake	Stock TC intake	BranchTC intake	Evo exhaust	StockTC exhaust	BranchTC exhaust
0.050		20.4	23.3		20.5	21.8 = 93%
0.100	36	44.2	46.5	30	37.3 = 76%	39.2 = 84%
0.150		67.5	69.2		57.7	58.5 = 84%
0.200	76	86.8	89.7	61	72.5 = 69%	76.1 = 85%
0.250		101.0	104.4		79.7	82.9 = 79%
0.300	108	110.6	116.3	77	86.1 = 73%	90.2 = 77%
0.350		116.6	128.3		94.3	98.2 = 76%
0.400	122	118.6	137.3	89	98.1 = 73%	103.3 = 75%
0.450		118.6	145.9		101.9	110.7 = 76 %
0.500	126	118.6	151.0	95	109.7 = 75%	119.2 = 79%
0.550		118.6	153.2		111.3	125.4 = 83%
0.600	127	118.6	158.9	99	111.3 = 75%	132.8 = 83%
No valve		118.6				

The stock Twin-Cam cams have a lift of 0.473 inch for both valves.
The Branch T-5 cams have a lift of 0.560 inch for both valves.

CHAPTER 11 MAGNETOS: MAGIC OR MADNESS, IGNITION SYSTEMS AND A BUNCH OF OTHER STUFF

INTRODUCTION

I originally composed this magneto chapter back in the early 1990s. I have updated it and made changes to the original for inclusion in this book. In addition to the secrets of magnetos, this chapter also touches on electricity, performance information on ignitions systems in general, and information useful for older V-twins. This information may be useful for the rider who holds steadfast to the adage of "See no Evo, hear no Evo, ride no Evo." Of course I was one of these people, too. Then Harley came out with the new Twin Cam, and what more can I say?—other than I sold out to the dark side for a shot at 100 lb-ft of torque and 100 horsepower.

My magneto madness started when I wanted to replace the old condenser in my 1959 Harley XLCH hot rod. I always knew the condenser in my magneto was larger than the stock condenser, but up until that time, I never gave much thought as to why this larger condenser was in there or what kind of magic was going on inside that magneto in general.

So I decided to replace the condenser. Not because it was bad, but because I just thought that, after many years of use, it was about due.

Thus began my quest to find out why this larger-than-stock condenser was in there. This magneto was originally set up for me years ago by a professional motorcycle drag racer—the 1969 National Drag Racing Champion Guy Leaming, to be exact. Guy won the national championship on a magneto-powered Sportster. So I figured Guy must know something about those magnetos that I didn't know, and I wasn't going to give up until I discovered what it was.

What did I discover? Unlike today, magnetos were once a common ignition system. You could find them on airplanes, automobiles, motorcycles, outboards, snowmobiles, and even your lawn mower. Today, ignition systems using capacitor-discharge electronic sensors, and computerized ignition modules are commonplace. The use of magnetos, in this ever-complicated world of ours, is slowly fading away. Sadly, the information I was looking for was also fading away! Luckily, I was able to record some before it was completely lost.

My goal here is not to make you an expert on how or why the magneto works—although you may become one—but to cure what I call magneto illiteracy. Having dealt with magnetos for about 30 years now, I consider the operating principles of the magneto to be simple, so I decided to put this information into print.

The first thing I realized was that explaining the operation of the magneto in a way that could be easily understood was not going to be as easy as I initially thought.

ELECTRICITY

Much of the information in this chapter will deal with electricity and ignition systems. To better understand this information, it will be useful for you to have a basic understanding of electricity and some of the most commonly used electrical terms. I will once again use the KISS rule to explain the basic electrical terms you will need to know.

Most people have a better understanding of the dynamics of water than electricity. After all, you can see water, but you can't see electrons flowing through a conductor. After giving it some thought, I have decided to use water as an analogy to help explain the basic principles of electricity.

Of course, water and electricity are not the same things, and the two should never be mixed.

Consequently, by presenting electricity this way, I need to take some liberties. In other words, I will keep my explanations simple and present them in a way that will make them easier to comprehend. Someone with a degree in electrical engineering may find my explanations simplistic and possibly not 100 percent technically accurate. But if you can grasp the subject as I have presented it, you will be able to understand the basic concepts and principals of electricity without wasting time obtaining a degree.

CURRENT

Current is a generic term for the flow of electricity. Electricity involves the flow of negatively charged electrons, usually through a conductor. Electricity has voltage (pressure), amperage (volume), and flow direction characteristics (either in the form of alternating current, or AC, or direct current, or DC). To help explain electricity, we will substitute the image of water for the flow of electrons that make up the current.

VOLTAGE

An easy way to think of voltage is to visualize it as water pressure, or the amount of pressure water is under as it flows through a pipe. The more pressure (or voltage) you apply to the water in the pipe, the more water you could flow through the pipe, and the faster you could perform the work of filling up a bucket.

In other words, increasing the pressure (voltage) would increase the amount of work we can get from our pipe. The more pressure you apply, the more water you would get through the pipe. If you reduced the water pressure, it would take longer to get the same amount of work out of your pipe, thus it would take longer to fill your bucket.

AMPERAGE

Look at amperage as water volume, or the amount of water flowing through our pipe. Let's say you were to pump water through a pipe at 10 psi (voltage), so in one minute you would have 1 gallon of water in your bucket. If you were to flow water at the same 10 psi through a pipe that was twice as big, your bucket would fill much quicker because you would have increased the water's volume (or its amperage).

ELECTRICAL WORKLOAD
The required amount of voltage and amperage are proportional to your workload, or the amount of work you need to perform.

In our case, that would be the amount of water we would want to flow through our pipe. If you increase the water pressure (voltage), you could use a smaller pipe with less volume (amperage) to fill your bucket at the same rate. If you were to decrease the water pressure (voltage), you would have to use a pipe with more volume (amperage) to fill your bucket at the same given rate.

In other words, to maintain a given workload, if you increase the voltage, it will reduce the amount of amperage required to maintain the same workload. Conversely, if you decrease the voltage, you will have to increase the amperage to maintain the same workload. Ignition coils use very high voltage to fire the spark plugs. Because the output voltage of the coils is very high, they require very little amperage to operate and are often only operating in the milliamp (1000th of an amp) range.

WORKLOAD EXAMPLE
This is an example of how workload, voltage, and amperage relate to each other. These figures are only approximations; I'm going to use them because it will be easier for you to understand the proportional values of voltage and amperage.

We have an electric motor that requires 10 amps of power at 110 volts to perform a given workload. If we wanted to run it on 220 volts, it would now require only 5 amps of power at 220 volts.

If we wanted to run the motor with only 55 volts, it would now require 20 amps of power to run and perform the same workload.

DIRECT CURRENT (DC)
Direct current, or DC, is like the water flowing through your home. The water comes from a source (the city or a well) and it flows from this source to, and out of, your faucet. The water, like DC current, always flows in the same direction. With DC current, you have one pole that is always positive and one pole that is always negative.

DC TRIVIA
Most people assume, draw, and describe voltage as flowing from the positive terminal to the negative terminal, with voltage flowing to ground, and everyone knows that your ground leg is the negative terminal. But in reality, the opposite is true. It is the flow of negatively charged electrons that actually make up the current, flowing in reverse. Remember, this is only trivia. Unless you're planning to be a contestant on the Who Wants to Be a Millionaire, don't dwell on it!

We know now that a lot of this misnomer stuff goes on. When we want to describe power, we quote horsepower numbers, instead of torque bands. If someone asks you what your compression ratio is, you state your mechanical value instead of your corrected compression ratio. We sometimes describe torque in ft-lb, when it's actually lb-ft, and we call the CV carburetor a constant-velocity carb, when it's correctly a constant-vacuum carb. But in spite of all this, life still goes on.

ALTERNATING CURRENT (AC)
Alternating current, or AC, does what its name describes. With alternating current, the flow of electricity—or in our example, the flow of water through our pipe—would be constantly changing direction between flowing to your faucet and flowing away from your faucet.

With AC current, the polarity of the two poles constantly switches back and forth between positive and negative. The rate at which the poles change is usually measured in the amount of times it changes directions in one second. These are called cycles.

As an example, normal U.S. house current changes its flow direction 60 times every second, so it's rated at 60 cycles.

DIODE
A diode is a one-way electrical valve, and it does the same thing a check valve does in a water pipe.

The check valve will only allow the water to flow one way through the pipe. If you turn the check valve (or diode) around, the water (or electricity) will only be able to flow in the opposite direction. Diodes will only allow direct current (DC) to flow through them in one direction. One of the most common uses of a diode is to change AC current to DC current.

Here's an example. Your bike operates on DC electric current, but your bike has an alternator which, as its name implies, produces alternating current.

A diode is used to force this AC current to flow in only one direction. By doing this, the current coming from the alternator is now converted to direct current, or DC.

Depending on your motor's rpm, the voltage in your alternator is constantly fluctuating up or down. In addition to the diode, a voltage regulator is also used to control the output voltage of the alternator. Without it, batteries would cook and light bulbs would pop.

CONDUCTOR AND CONDUCTANCE
A conductor is something electricity flows through. In our water example, it would be the pipe.

Conductance usually refers to how well electricity can flow through a conductor. The amount of resistance to the flow of current through a conductor represents the conductance of a material.

An unobstructed water pipe would be a good conductor and have good conductance because there is nothing

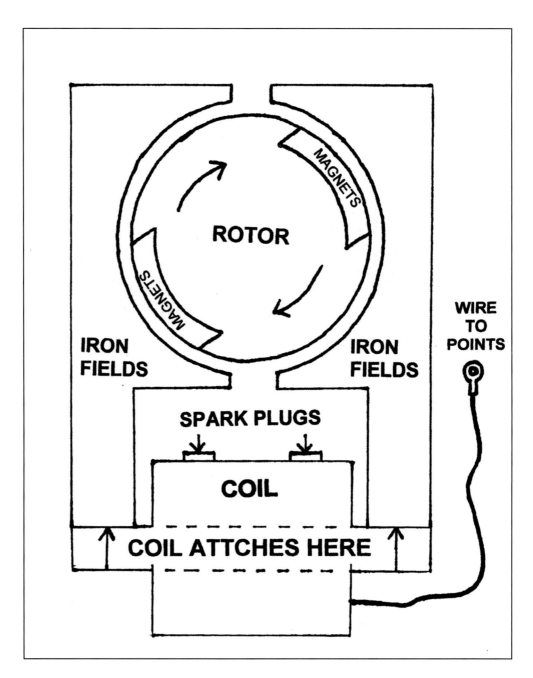

to resist the flow of water through it.

The same water pipe filled with stones has the potential to be a good conductor, but because the stones are resisting the flow of water through the pipe, it will have poor conductance. The best conductor would be one with the least amount of resistance to the flow of current. This conductor would have excellent conductance properties.

CAPACITANCE, CAPACITORS, AND CONDENSERS

Capacitance is the ability to store electrical energy. Capacitors and condensers are basically the same things. They are devices we can store electrical energy in.

We can think of a capacitor as our bucket. If we hold the bucket with the open end up, we could fill it up with water and store water in it. The size of the bucket, or the capacitor, regulates how much water or electrical energy we could store in it.

If we ground the capacitor, it will unload its stored energy. This would be the same thing as turning the bucket upside down and dumping the water out.

Capacitors are used in ignition systems to reduce point arcing. This, in turn, reduces the burning of contact point surfaces and extends the lifespan of the points. On a normal battery/coil-type ignition system, the size, or capacitance, of the capacitor needs to be large enough to prevent, or at least reduce, the point arcing.

On a magneto, the capacitor provides an added bene-

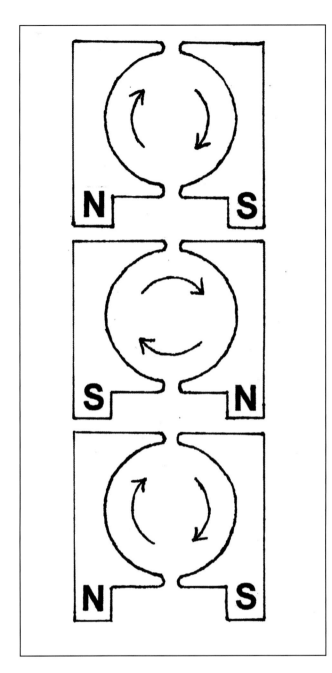

Likewise, the more resistance a conductor has, the harder it will be to flow electrical energy through the conductor. One common byproduct of resistance is heat.

INDUCTANCE

Inductance involves producing, or changing the properties of, current by using a magnetic field or an electromagnetic force. Inductance does not use direct physical contact; it relies on the force of magnetism to interact with the object it's trying to influence. This magnetic force can come from a permanent magnet (like the rotor in our magneto) or from an electromagnetic source.

An ignition coil uses the principle of inductance to fire the spark plugs by transferring an electromagnetic field from the primary windings to the secondary windings. This, in turn, fires the spark plugs.

A transformer utilizes inductance to change the properties of AC into DC.

Using water to explain inductance is difficult, because water has physical properties and inductance uses magnetic properties, so a little creativity is in order: A baseboard heat register in your home has hot water flowing through the pipe. The heat energy of the hot water radiates out of the pipe and warms you. You are being warmed up, or induced, by the heat energy from the water in the pipe, even though you are not physically touching the water. We could also say that the inductance of the hot water's energy has changed the properties of the air around us, by changing it from cold to warm air.

MAGNETOS: THEORY OF OPERATION

The Fairbanks Morse, Morris Magneto, and Joe Hunt magnetos are called spinning magnet magnetos, which are often referred to as German Bosch magnetos. As the name implies, spinning magnet magnetos operate with a magnet spinning inside the magneto.

To help us understand this magneto, I'll divide it into its two main parts.

1. The spinning magnet part of the magneto—this part consists of a spinning rotor, its magnets, and the two soft iron fields that surround the rotor.

2. The coil—the magneto coil consists of three main parts: an iron bar that runs through the center of the coil; the primary windings (low voltage); and the secondary windings (high voltage) that fire the spark plugs.

All three of these items are combined into one unit that we call the coil. For illustrative purposes I will later divide the coil into two parts: the primary and secondary sides.

When you look inside a magneto, you see a rotor with magnets on it. This rotor is spinning around inside two iron fields.

fit. When the magneto's points close, energy is stored in the condenser; when the points open, this energy unloads to the coil. This helps to build up a stronger magnetic field in the primary winding side of the magneto's ignition coil. So, a large condenser would be beneficial on a magneto. (More on this later in the chapter.)

RESISTANCE

Resistance impedes the flow of electrical energy through a conductor and reduces its conductance. If we were to take a pipe and fill it with stones, it would impede, or restrict, our ability to flow water through the pipe. This will cause our pipe to have less water conductance. The more stones we put in the pipe, the harder it will be to flow water through the pipe.

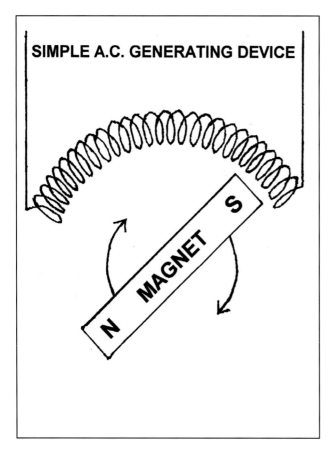

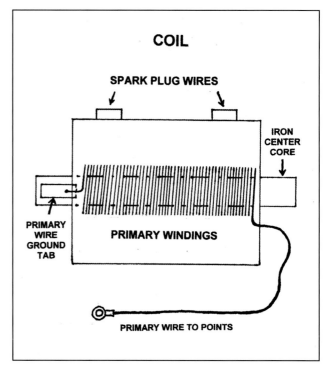

A common mistake is to think that the spinning rotor is generating electricity.

Electricity is being produced as a byproduct of the spinning rotor, but it is not being produced at the rotor. The generation of electricity, for our purposes, is happening inside our coil. It is being produced by the primary windings that are wrapped around the iron core located in the center of our coil.

Let's start at the beginning. As the rotor and its magnets revolve inside the two iron fields, they are inducing, or transferring, magnetism (hence the name "magneto") to the two iron fields. One side of the rotor's magnet has a north pole and the other side of the rotor has a south pole. As the rotor revolves around inside of the fields, it is constantly alternating (as in alternating current) the presentation of the magnetic poles to the two fields.

This causes the induced magnetic poles on the iron fields to be constantly alternating back and forth between north and south. (See illustration.)

Above, I have illustrated a simple electric generating device. In this example, we are spinning a bar magnet through a wire coil or field. When the north pole slices through the coil, the current will flow in one direction; when the south pole slices through the field, the current will flow in the opposite direction. This is an example of an alternating current (AC) generating device.

This concept is very important for you to understand, because the way the magneto operates and the way we will manipulate the magneto in the future revolve around this simple principle and the fact that we are dealing with AC current.

If we were to connect a diode to either side of this field, the current would only be able to flow in one direction. This device would then produce direct current, or DC. The direction of the current flow would depend on which way we positioned the diode.

THE MAGNETO'S MAGIC

Our magneto operates differently than the simple electric generating device in the last illustration, because our magneto does not utilize a physically spinning magnet slicing through a field to produce current. Review the rotor and iron field illustration. On the magneto, the spinning magnets only transfer, or induce, magnetism to the two iron fields surrounding the rotor.

Now review the coil illustration. The iron bar in the center of our coil connects directly to the two iron fields. As the rotor rotates, the alternating magnetic field is induced, or transferred, first to the two fields and then to the iron core in the center of our coil.

As the rotor rotates, it causes the poles on our coil's iron bar to switch back and forth between north and south. Although the bar inside the coil is not physically moving, it is producing the same results as the illustrated spinning bar magnet. Induction from the fluctuating magnetism of the iron bar causes the primary winding to produce a current each time the bar is magnetized by the spinning rotor.

Again, the poles on the bar are constantly switching

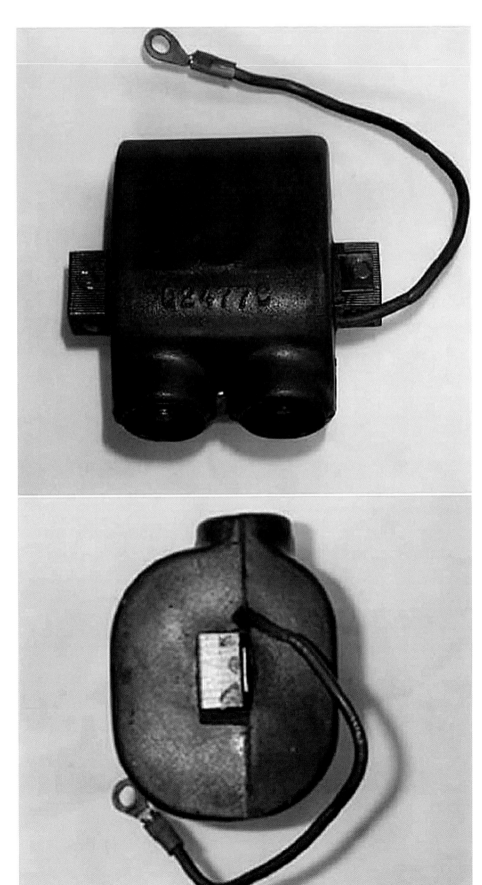

You can spot a real Fairbanks Morse magneto coil because it will have the part number Q2477C molded into its housing.

back and forth between north and south. Each time the poles of the bar switch, the direction of the current flow in the primary windings changes. As the flow direction of the current is constantly changing, the magneto's coil is producing AC current.

If we spin the magneto at 1,500 rpm, the current would change direction 1,500 times per minute, or 25 times per second. So at 1,500 rpm, the magneto would be operating at 25 cycles. At 3,000 rpm, it would be operating at 50 cycles.

In addition to the cycles changing, the voltage also varies with rpm. The faster you spin the magneto, the more voltage it puts out. This makes the magneto very attractive for high-performance use.

Unlike the DC operation of a standard ignition system, the fact that the magneto operates with AC will become very important when we move on to more advanced magneto functions.

COILS ILLUSTRATED

The coil in a magneto works like most coils, by using the principle of induction, and it functions as a transformer by transforming low-voltage current into high-voltage current.

The coil transforms the magnetic energy from the iron core, with its magnetic poles switching back and forth, to AC electrical energy. This happens because the wires of the primary windings slice through the magnetic field created by the bar at the core of the coil. This magnetic field is induced into the primary windings and produces current.

When the power to the primary windings is shut off suddenly by the points opening, the electromagnetic field it was producing collapses.

The principle of induction transfers this magnetic energy from the primary windings to the secondary windings. The secondary windings have many more turns than the primary windings, inducing high voltage for the spark plugs. Review the coil illustration.

If you look closely, you can see both ends of the primary windings. The wire to the points is one end, and the flat tab on the center bar is the other. In the top picture, the grounding tab is on the right side of the core bar. In the lower picture, it is still on the right side of the core bar, and you can see how the secondary windings surround the primary windings.

The illustration on page 157 depicts the simple wiring diagram that makes up the magneto. The only thing missing is the rotor and the two surrounding iron fields that connect to the coil's center core.

PEAK MAGNETIC FLUX

Most coils rely on dwell time, or the time the points are closed, to build up a strong magnetic field for maximum coil performance.

Magnetos, on the other hand, use what is referred to as

COIL

SPARK PLUG WIRES

IRON
CENTER
CORE

PRIMARY
WIRE
GROUND
TAB

SECONDARY WINDINGS

PRIMARY WIRE TO POINTS

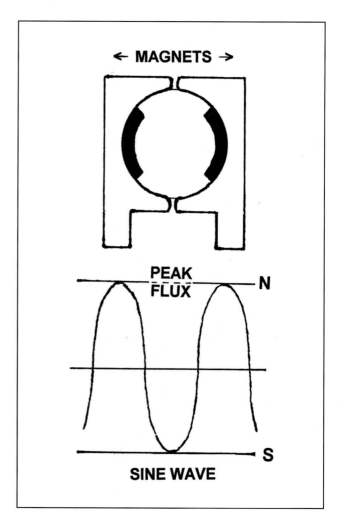

← MAGNETS →

PEAK
FLUX — N

SINE WAVE

S

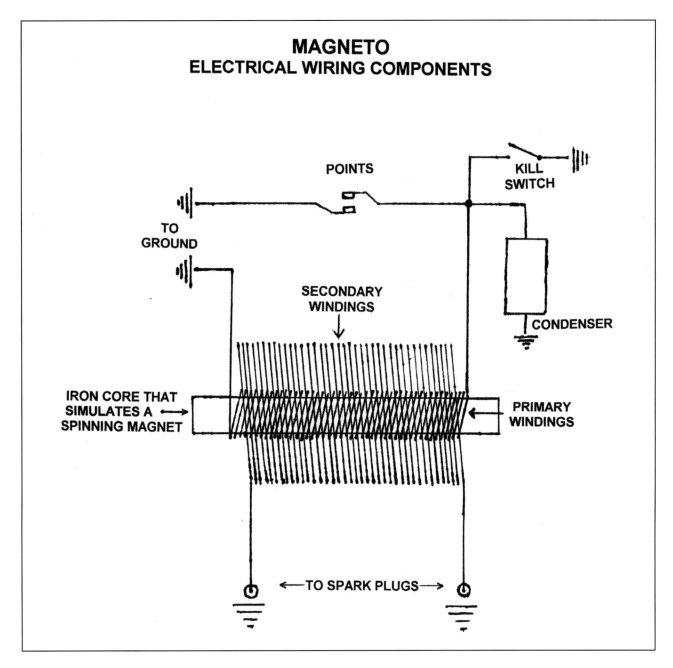

MAGNETO
ELECTRICAL WIRING COMPONENTS

POINTS

KILL SWITCH

TO GROUND

SECONDARY WINDINGS

CONDENSER

IRON CORE THAT SIMULATES A → SPINNING MAGNET

PRIMARY WINDINGS

←—TO SPARK PLUGS—→

peak magnetic flux. You want the points to open when the magneto reaches its point of peak flux. In theory, peak flux is reached when the rotor magnets are directly centered between the two soft iron fields. At that time, you will be producing the maximum magnetic field and power to the primary coil windings.

Ideally, you want the points to open when the primary coil is producing its strongest magnetic field. Then, when this magnetic field collapses, it transfers that energy via induction to the secondary windings and then to the spark plugs. See magneto wiring illustration.

IMPORTANT NOTE ON MAGNETO COILS
The secondary windings on the magneto coils are open-ended (that is, they're not grounded). See secondary windings illustration. This is common with most Harley wasted-spark coils. Because of this, both spark plug wires must go to a common ground or to themselves to complete the circuit.

Normally the motor itself acts as the ground between the two spark plug wires that complete the circuit. If either one of the wires is not grounded to the other by some means, neither spark plug will fire! This has tripped up many amateur troubleshooters.

POINTS
The cam that opens and closes the points is fixed to the rotor. There's no adjustment there.

157

Setting the gap distance of your points now becomes very important toward ensuring the points will open at the location of maximum peak flux. If you have access to a tester that measures the high voltage to the spark plugs, you could experiment with different ignition point gaps to find the one where your magneto works best. If you don't (like me), try to keep the points gapped as close as possible to the recommended 0.015 inch.

I've looked at several aftermarket point sets, and I recommend that you stick with real magneto point sets from manufacturers like Fairbanks Morse and Morris Magneto. The Morris Magneto P-5 points seem to be of the same quality as the stock Fairbanks Morse points. Harley-Davidson points are made by Fairbanks Morse, and the part numbers are Fairbanks Morse B2437A, or H-D 29533-55A.

Real magneto points are not the same as regular ignition points. The difference is that real magneto points are designed to be more durable and should have platinum-plated contacts. Regular 12-volt ignition system points usually don't.

Let's look at the difference. On standard ignition system, a battery powers the coil's primary windings. The voltage is held at a regulated 12 volts (actually 13.6 volts). On the magneto, the voltage is not regulated; the speed of the turning rotor regulates the voltage in the primary windings of the coil. This fluctuating high and low voltage requires a more durable point contact surface.

Another problem to consider is that we may be running an extra-large condenser, which also adds stress to our points.

To acquire a sufficiently durable surface, the points should be platinum plated. This is similar to the reason why some valve stems are often chrome plated—to make them more durable in the valve guides.

Of course, this makes real magneto points more expensive than standard points. Through my aftermarket dealership, I can purchase aftermarket magneto points for about $2.50 per set. I highly recommend that you do not use these El Cheapo aftermarket points in your magneto.

I only run, and recommend that you run, real Fairbanks Morse points, part number F-M B2437A. These points hold up very well and can last for years if not abused. If you can't obtain the Fairbanks Morse points, Morris Magneto P-5 points are of the same quality. Actually, the last time I saw a set of Morris P-5 points, they appeared to be made by Fairbanks Morse and were possibly repackaged by Morris.

The Morris points may cost you more money than a set from Fairbanks Morse. Today, I'd expect to pay over $20 for a set of real Fairbanks Morse points. Ten years ago, I saw a set of Morris P-5 points at an H-D shop in Alaska with a $30 price tag on them. Needless to say, I passed!

Rule of thumb: cheap points are trouble. If the points are cheap, chances are their quality is, too. You get what you pay for.

CONDENSERS

One of the main jobs of a condenser in a standard ignition system is to soak up and store electrical energy.

This, in turn, helps prevent the points from arcing and burning when the points open. It all adds up to longer point life and more precise timing.

On a magneto, the condenser provides another benefit. When the points are open on a magneto, energy is stored in the condenser. When the points close, this energy is unloaded and helps to build up the electromagnetic field in the coil's primary windings. The amount of power a condenser can store and discharge (when the points open and close) can definitely influence how fast the primary windings of a coil can re-establish its magnetic field. Reasonably, the bottom line is that the more the capacitance, or storage capacity, a magneto's condenser has, the better.

A large capacity magneto condenser should cause

- A faster rise time of the magnetic field in the primary windings side of the coil due to its increased storage capacity

- Easier starting due to its larger capacity to store and discharge electricity to the primary windings of the coil

TESTING CONDENSERS

I perform two tests on condensers.

1. Condenser capacity test: This test tells you how much energy (in microfarads) the condenser can hold. You then compare your test reading to the manufacturer's listed capacity. If it's not within its specified range, the condenser needs to be replaced. I have included for you a Fairbanks Morse condenser specification chart in this book.

2. Condenser leakage test: This test loads the condenser and checks for leaks or shorts.

If your condenser passes these tests it's okay, right? Not necessarily.

The problem is that you're testing a cold condenser. When the engine gets hot, so does the condenser. A hot condenser may give you different readings than a cold condenser.

So if you really want to be sure, you could always perform the hot-condenser torture test. Connect the condenser to the ignition analyzer, use a hair dryer to heat the condenser, and retest it. Remember, you just want to heat the condenser, not melt it.

Condenser failure is often easy to see on a magneto if you run a clear magneto cap. If you notice lots of sparks coming from your points, your condenser is history.

When you replace your condenser, don't forget to change your points, because when that condenser went south, it more than likely took your points with it. Luckily, condensers are rather simple devices, and failures are rare.

Although running a larger-than-stock condenser can produce a little more noticeable arcing at the points than a normal size condenser, using large condensers has never caused me significant extra point wear.

MAGNETO MAGNETS
Another thing that can cause a magneto to perform poorly is a weak rotor magnet.

As a magneto gets older, the magnets on the rotor can, and will, lose some of their magnetism. Weak magnets will, in turn, cause a weak magnetic field to be produced in the primary windings of the coil, and a weak magnetic field will produce less spark plug voltage. If the magnetic field becomes too weak, your spark plugs will not fire at all and will cause you much embarrassment, not to mention a sore leg, when you try to start your bike. Luckily, magneto magnets can be re-magnetized.

Morris Magnetos performs this service, and Joe Hunt probably does, too. Auto electrical shops that have been in business for a long time may also provide this service, because they may still have the specific equipment needed for servicing magneto magnets. And if you're really lucky, they may even have someone who knows how to use that equipment. You could also check with your local certified airplane mechanic, because older airplanes ran magnetos, and an airplane is no place for magneto problems. But then again, neither is your Harley-Davidson!

Harley-Davidson had a high-performance rotor for its XLR and KR racing bike magnetos, whose part number is H-D 29536-56R. More than likely, the main difference in this rotor may be that it features a shorter driveshaft, so it can be mounted up front, where the generator is normally mounted. The stock rotor is H-D 29623-55A.

FAIRBANKS MORSE PARTS AND SERVICING
The last place I purchased a large-capacity RX-2433 Fairbanks Morse condenser was at Blanchard Auto Electric, 640 South Spokane Street, Seattle, WA 98134, (206) 682-2981.

This condenser wasn't cheap, but at least I found one. While I was at it, I also grabbed a few sets of Fairbanks Morse points. Blanchard said it had, or could get, most parts for Fairbanks Morse magnetos. At the time, this shop also serviced them, including re-magnetizing the rotor magnets. This was a few years back and sometimes things change, so you'll have to check it out for yourself.

The last time I was in Seattle, I was informed that Ballard Electrical—at 930 NW 49th Street, Seattle, WA 98107, (206) 789-4050—also stocks, or can order, parts for Fairbanks Morse magnetos. This shop may also perform some magneto servicing.

Another source for parts is American Electric Ignition; 1-800-654-3932 extension 2.

Or, you could try contacting Fairbanks Morse directly at Fairbanks Morse Engine, 701 White Avenue, Beloit, WI 53511, (800) 356-6955.]

OTHER CONTACTS FOR PARTS
Morris Magnetos, 103 Washington Street, Morristown, NJ 07960, (973) 540-9171

Joe Hunt Magnetos, 11333 Sunco Drive, Suite 100, Rancho Cordova, CA 95742, (916) 635-5387

V-Twin Manufacturing, Tedd Cycle Inc., P.O. Box 473, Vails Gate, NY 12584 Ph. (845) 565-2806

Nostalgia Cycle, 15681 Commerce Lane, Huntington Beach, CA 92649, (714) 891-6263

There are still a lot of places that have the equipment and the knowledge to service magnetos. You'll just have to pick up the phone and start calling around.

Remember to look for the shops that have been around for a long time. Parts and servicing prices vary from shop to shop, so call around for the best deal.

Except for re-magnetizing rotor magnets, you can do most of the routine service that a magneto requires. One of the strongest selling points for using a magneto is its simplicity and reliability.

TESTING DOUBLE SECONDARY COILS
Testing a double secondary magneto coil is different than a standard automotive coil. I have diagramed the method in the accompanying illustration. You must perform two tests on the coil.

1. The continuity or low-power test: Your coil should start arcing before it reaches its operating amperage. The lower the amperage when it starts to fire, the better the coil.

2. The full-power test: Here you'll check your coil at full power and run your coil to full amperage (1.70 amps). Your spark should remain constant, without irregularity (missing). If it does miss, the coil is bad and needs to be replaced.

In addition to the above tests, performing a coil surface insulation test may be a good idea to check for leaks or cracks.

NOTES ON MAGNETO PARTS
Stock H-D magneto: The stock standard Harley-Davidson magneto was a Fairbanks Morse FMZ2-2C63A.

These are the real things. Fairbanks Morse points have FM molded into the black composite piece.

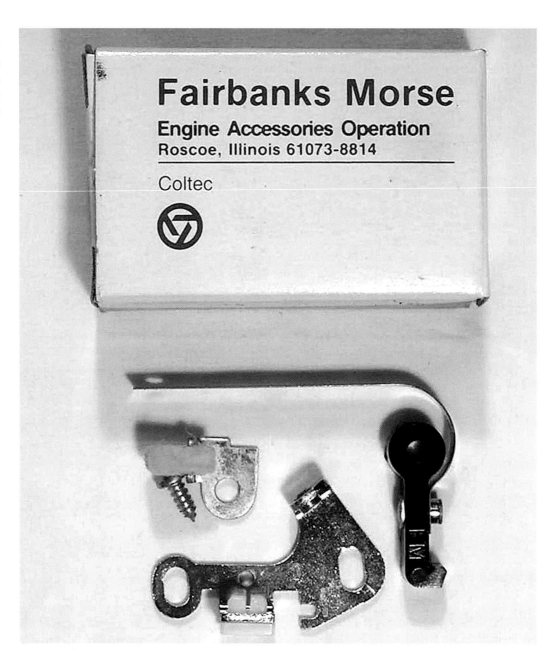

H-D racing magneto: The high-performance (racing) Harley-Davidson magneto was a Fairbanks Morse FMZ2-2B63B. This magneto used a different rotor and a larger condenser.

Stock H-D points: The stock points used by both magnetos were Harley-Davidson 29533-55A (Fairbanks Morse B2437A). You can save yourself some money by purchasing your points from a Fairbanks Morse dealer. Warning, these points are not cheap!

STOCK H-D COILS
The stock coil used by Fairbanks Morse Harley-Davidson magnetos is Fairbanks Morse Q2477C (Harley-Davidson 29524-55A). Old stock Harley-Davidson coils should have the Fairbanks Morse

Q2477C molded onto the side of the coil. This type of coil is known as a double secondary lead coil.

COIL SPECIFICATIONS
The operating specifications for the stock coil are as follows:

- Operating amperage: 1.70 amps

- Secondary winding continuity: 50 ohms minimum and 70 ohms maximum

STOCK H-D CONDENSER
The stock condenser used by Fairbanks Morse Harley-Davidson magnetos was the Fairbanks Morse AXMR2433 (Harley-Davidson 29534-55A).

Condensers are another component where size can matter. Left, the stock AXMR2433; center, the one I run, the RX243; right, Morris Magnetos P-6. See my capacity test results of these condensers.

An old stock H-D magneto condenser will be marked Fairbanks Morse 2433 MR (AX), signifying that it is the AXMR2433 condenser.

MORRIS CONDENSER
The new Morris Magneto (high-voltage) condenser is Morris P-6; this condenser is marked AXMR2433. Due to the number, the Morris P-6 condenser appears to be the stock low-capacity Fairbanks Morse AXMR2433 condenser.

FACTORY RACING CONDENSER
The racing condenser used by the model FMZ2-2B63B magneto was a Fairbanks Morse SXY-2433 (Harley-Davidson 29534-55R).

Remember, Harley-Davidson no longer sells parts for its Fairbanks Morse magnetos.

I have a Fairbanks Morse magneto on my little hot rod that was set up for me by professional drag racer Guy Leaming in 1976. All of the parts in this magneto appear to be stock, except for the condenser. Guy took advantage of the benefits of running a large-capacity condenser by using the much larger Fairbanks Morse RX2433 condenser.

This condenser is almost twice the physical size of the stock Harley or Morris P-6 condenser, and it holds over

Above: The large capacity Fairbanks Morse RX2433 condenser.

Below: It's a tight fit, but the large RX2433 will fit under the magneto cover.

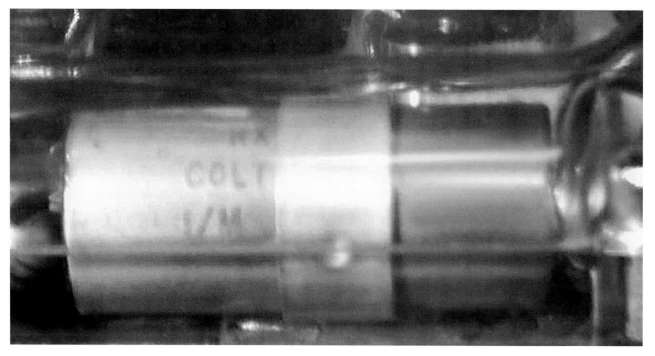

twice the amount of electricity.

I have tested five different magneto condensers on my Merc-O-Tronic Model 73 ignition analyzer. If they're still in business, you can contact them at Merc-O-Tronic Instruments Corp., 215 Branch Street, Almont, MI 48003.

Different batches of condensers may read slightly differently. After reviewing the test numbers, you will see that the RX2433 condenser easily wins the capacity test.

	Microfarads
The stock H-D 29534-55A or F-M AXMR2433	0.22
Accel's high performance	0.26
V-twin's stock replacement	0.25
Morris Magnetos P-6	0.20
Guy Leaming's F-M RX2433	0.48

The Fairbanks Morse condenser RX2433 holds over twice the energy as Morris P-6 condenser or the stock H-D condenser. I got 20 years of use out of the same RX2433 condenser before I changed it.

One good thing about condensers is they can last a long time, although I wouldn't recommend going for 20 years before you change yours. In an older H-D publication, I found a listing for a high-performance magneto condenser, H-D 32722-64R (Fairbanks Morse SXY2433). The 64R stands for a 1964 racing part. This part was probably for the XLR, one of Harley's racing bikes at the time.

FAIRBANKS MORSE CONDENSER CHART
The following is an old list of all Fairbanks Morse condensers, along with their minimum and maximum capacity specifications in microfarads. Note: The stock condenser is AXMR2433, and the factory racing condenser is SYX2433. Guy's large-capacity magneto condenser is RX2433.

TROUBLESHOOTING TIPS
If your magneto stops making juice for no apparent reason, here are two things to check:

1. Check for chafed wires, both inside the magneto and also on the kill switch and kill wire.

2. Check the grounding lug for a short or a worn-out insulator.

The grounding lug is located on the inboard side of your magneto, by the coil. This lug is insulated from the magneto body by running through a fiber grommet (washer) and is connected to the points on the inside and to the kill button on the outside. When you push in the kill switch, it grounds your points, your magneto stops producing spark, and your motor stops. As the washer gets old (yours may be over 40 years old already) it can chafe through and short out. This won't hurt the magneto, but it will stop you cold.

What to do? Remove your magneto cap. Disconnect, at the points, the wire running from the lug to the points. Connect one end of an ohmmeter (or continuity tester) to the lug and the other end to a ground on your bike. If you get a complete circuit (a short), disconnect the wire to the kill switch and test again. If you no longer have a short, your kill switch, or the wiring to it, is shorted out. If you still have a short, your insulator block (washer) on your lug is worn out and needs replacing.

I have seen this happen a few times and, if it only happens on an intermediate basis, it could drive you nuts trying to figure out what's going on.

Remember, magnetos are very reliable. Often when one stops, the problem can be traced to something that is as simple as a chafed or loose wire, a shorted kill switch, or a worn-out insulator on the grounding lug.

IGNITION SYSTEMS AND RADIO FREQUENCY ENERGY
Your basic ignition system consists of the follow items:

- A power source (commonly a DC battery)

- A triggering device (mechanical or electronic)

- A condenser to store and absorb electricity

- A coil to amplify the low-source voltage to high spark plug voltage

- Transmission lines (spark plug wires) to carry the voltage from the coil to the spark plugs

- A spark gap device (spark plugs) used to produce and control the length of the spark

The standard old ignition systems used a DC battery for source voltage; a set of mechanical points to control when the spark would accrue; a condenser to stop the points from arcing and burning up; and a grounded coil to amplify the low DC source voltage into high spark plug voltage.

The coil was technically grounded because it was connected to both sides of the battery. Multistrand solid-core spark plug wires carried the high voltage to the spark plugs, and solid-core spark plugs produced and regulated the spark.

This system worked very well for what it was designed

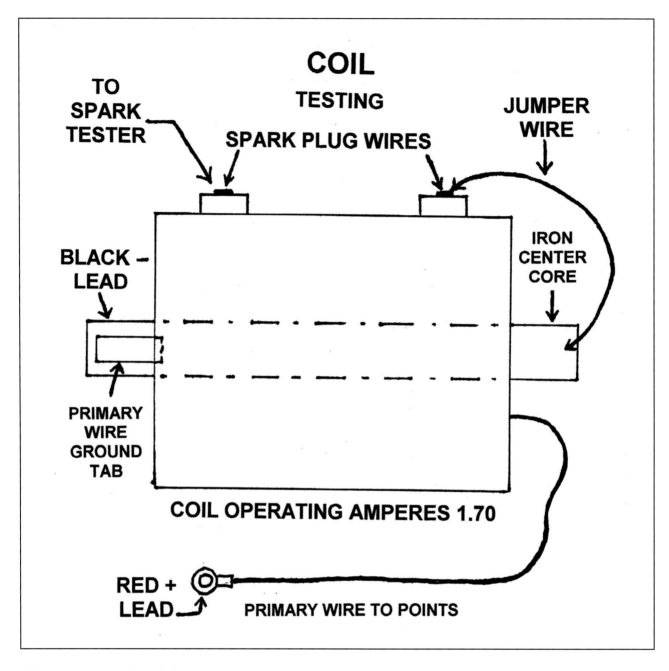

COIL TESTING

TO SPARK TESTER

SPARK PLUG WIRES

JUMPER WIRE

IRON CENTER CORE

BLACK – LEAD

PRIMARY WIRE GROUND TAB

COIL OPERATING AMPERES 1.70

RED + LEAD

PRIMARY WIRE TO POINTS

This is how you connect your tester.

to do: successfully provide an ignition spark to the cylinder at the proper time. Due to its inherent design flaws, it had one nasty byproduct, and that was that it radiated radio frequency (RF) energy.

This basic type of ignition system closely resembled one of the earliest types of radio transmitters called a spark gap transmitter.

The spark gap transmitter contained all of the same elements as our ignition system. The main difference between the two was where we connected the spark plug wire to our spark plugs. With the spark gap transmitter, they were connected to an antenna.

On the old-style ignition system, we used multistrand solid-core wires to carry the voltage to the spark plugs. Not only did the solid-core wire efficiently carry the voltage, it also radiated RF energy just as the antenna did on the spark gap transmitter. Simply put, this type of ignition system was both an ignition system and a radio transmitter.

In days of old, the RF energy emanating from engine ignition systems was not a big deal, but as we started to rely more and more on sensitive electronic devices, the RF energy transmitted from these ignition systems started to become a problem, so the radio waves had to be

The Merc-O-Tronic 73 ignition analyzer I use for testing magneto parts.

neutralized. The two most common ways to limit stray RF energy waves are by resistance and by inductance.

SPARK PLUG WIRES

Resistance is the most common type of noise (RF) suppression used in spark plug wires and ignition systems today.

This system uses resistance built into both the spark plugs and spark plug wires, which are made with carbon- or graphite-impregnated resistive cores. The inherent design of these wires not only resists the flow of electricity, it also suppresses the wire's ability to radiate radio waves.

As we discussed earlier, resistance impedes, or inter-feres, with the flow of electricity. This level of resistance is fine for a stock engine, but for performance work, we want the maximum amount of energy to reach our spark plugs. Anything that interferes with getting the maximum flow of electricity through the wires and to the plug's spark gap is a bad thing.

There are many carbon-core resister wires that are sold as high-performance wires. This has always been a misnomer to me. How can you say that you have truly high-performance wires if they are designed to resist the flow of electricity?

There is a more electrically friendly way to suppress RF energy, which is through inductance, not resistance.

165

Inductance-type spark plug wires do not directly suppress radio waves by resisting the flow of electricity; they instead suppress the radio waves by physically changing the properties of the electricity itself. These inductance-type wires are often referred to as spiral-wound, or spiral-core, wires.

They utilize a spiral-wound wire (like a spring) in their core to reduce the RF energy. These wires do have some resistance, but it's only about one-tenth of the resistance of carbon-core wires. Taylor's excellent 8-millimeter Spiro-Pro wires are an example of this type of spark plug wire.

LEAKAGE AND SPIRAL-CORE WIRES

Another major problem with spark plug wires is leakage and crossfire. Professional auto racing engine builders have known how bad this is for performance and have gone to great lengths to stop it.

A motor is a motor, be it in a car or bike, so we must also be concerned about this problem.

Sadly, I can't remember anyone voicing much concern on this subject with regard to performance V-twin engines. So, I will.

When it comes to getting voltage from the coil to the spark plugs, nothing outperforms solid-core wires, but they have two drawbacks. One is the transmission of RF energy, which we have covered. The other is voltage leakage.

People may think that new spark plug wires are constructed in some high-tech way, so leakage is a thing of the past. I wish that were true. I will admit that the newer wires are getting better. That's why the dielectric covering of the spark plug wires keeps getting fatter.

When high-voltage electrical energy passes through solid-core wires, it causes electromagnetic radiation (the source of RF) to flow in all directions around the wire, creating a phenomenon called secondary induction. You may want to review my section on inductance near the beginning of this chapter.

This secondary induction is desperately looking for ground, and it's not very interested in waiting around until it gets to your spark plugs. This is why it is extremely important to always separate the wires from each other, or any other source of ground, by a minimum of 1/2-inch.

If we were to construct the conductive core of the spark plug wire by tightly winding a fine wire around a medium that forms a foundation at its center, we would have a spiral-core plug wire.

This spiral core physically looks like a tightly wound spring. The inner foundation of the core is not part of the conductor and is usually constructed out of a material that adds strength to the wire. When we flow voltage through this type of wire, radiation is suppressed by the inductance properties created by the spiral core, and this greatly reduces the leakage problem caused from radiation and secondary induction. The electrical energy now flows along the spiral core, instead of radiating outward from the core.

F-M number	Microfarads	
Condenser No.	Minimum	Maximum
AX2433	0.17	0.23
AXMR2433	0.18	0.23
BX2433	0.16	0.19
CX2433	0.28	0.36
DX2433	0.28	0.36
EX2433	0.17	0.23
FX2433	0.28	0.36
GX2433	0.16	0.19
HX2433	0.37	0.43
JX2433	0.17	0.23
K2433	0.16	0.24
KX2433	0.28	0.35
LV2433	0.38	0.43
M2433	0.17	0.23
MX2433	0.28	0.35
PX2433	0.28	0.35
QX2433	0.28	0.35
R2433	0.17	0.23
RX2433	0.37	0.42
S2433	0.28	0.32
SXY2433	0.28	0.33
SYX2433X	0.28	0.36
TX2433	0.28	0.35
WX2433	0.28	0.35
X2433	0.28	0.36
Y2433	0.28	0.36

Note: The HX2433 condenser is a feed-through type.

SPIRAL-CORE WIRE REVIEW

1. They have one-tenth of the resistance of standard carbon-core suppression wires.

2. They suppress RF without sacrificing much electrical energy.

3. They come close to totally preventing wire leakage. (**Note:** No matter what type of wire is used, you should always try to separate spark plug wires from each other, or any source of ground, by 1/2-inch.)

All three combined mean one thing: more power to your spark plug!

I highly recommend you run these spiral-core wires for performance work on all motors that require resistor wires.

I like these wires so much, I run them on everything, except magnetos. These wires will also work well on older battery point-type ignition systems, where radio wave suppression is important.

For performance work, I would prefer the use of solid-core wires on all motors with points. Even though spiral-core wires do have low resistance and resist leakage, I recommend that you never run these wires on a kick-start-only bike that has a magneto.

The use of any type of resistor spark plug wires or resistor spark plugs can make a magneto-equipped kick-start-only bike very difficult, or near impossible, to start.

The popularity of using inductance-type spark plug wires for performance work is growing. I predict that soon—just like with synthetic motor oils—many after-market performance spark plug wire manufacturers will offer their own versions of spiral-core inductance-style suppression spark plug wires.

TROUBLESHOOTING PLUG WIRES

As discussed previously, you should use only solid-core wires on a Harley-Davidson with a magneto.

If the ignition system has points in it, you are better off using solid-core wires. Do not use suppression-type spark plug wires with a magneto. If you do, your motor may not start, due to the magneto's low voltage at cranking speeds.

Experience has taught me that carbon-core wires, magnetos, and Harley-Davidsons add up to trouble. On numerous occasions, I have come across motorcycles that have broken up or lost a cylinder for no apparent reason. I tested the carbon-core wires with an ohmmeter and they appeared to be fine, but the problems were still there. I replaced the wires with solid-core wires and then the bike ran fine. Old Harley motors are known to shake around a bit; this vibration is not good for carbon-core resistance wires.

To save yourself some grief, if it's a Harley and it has points, use solid-core wires whenever possible! Leave the carbon-core wires to the electronic ignitions where they're needed.

The old solid-core Packard 440 wires were standard on magnetos for years. Any of today's modern solid-core performance wires will work fine on the magneto. Always be sure to check your wires to ensure they are in good shape.

Because the magneto operates at very high voltage, a small crack in the outer insulating shield could cause voltage to escape the wire (leakage) and short out to ground before finding its way to your plugs.

It is common to have spark plug wire leakage and not lose a cylinder. If this happens, the leakage will be bleeding off a percentage of your spark plug's voltage, causing a reduction of power output from the affected cylinder.

Remember, electricity is lazy, and it will always take the path of least resistance to get to a ground.

SPARK PLUGS

H-D magneto coils, like other older Harley coils, use an open-ended double secondary lead coil that generates the wasted spark ignition system, so both plugs fire at the same time.

Because the plugs fire at the same time, try to keep both plug gaps as close as possible to each other. The spark plug gaps on the magneto need to be small and should be set at 0.018 to 0.020 inch maximum.

It's important to understand why you need such a small spark plug gap with the magneto. It all has to do with starting the bike.

A magneto has no constant external power source, as it relies on the speed of the spinning rotor to produce its electrical power. As its speed increases or decreases, a big change in the magnetic field occurs in the coil's iron core. This fluctuating magnetic field causes an even greater change in the voltage going to the spark plugs from the secondary windings. Voltage to the spark plugs can vary greatly depending on the velocity of the magneto armature and the type of coil used.

At slow rotating speeds, like when you're trying to start your engine, the magneto may not be able to overcome a large spark plug gap, due to its low voltage output.

Spark plugs also have to overcome the increased dielectric field (an insulating field) caused by the compression of hydrocarbon gasses between the spark plug electrodes on the compression stroke of an engine.

Sadly, this small spark plug gap is another one of the many compromises that we live with. As we have already discussed, the main reason for the short gap distance is to aid in starting.

When the magneto is turning at very slow speeds, it's struggling to produce enough voltage to fire both plugs. The faster you spin the magneto, the more voltage it will produce. When operating at high rpm, the magneto can put out twice the voltage of a stock ignition coil.

With this high voltage output, the spark plugs could, and will, produce more power from the cylinder by running a wider gap of say 0.040 inch. I have witnessed magneto sparks jumping distances as long as 1 inch. Unfortunately, if you run a plug gap of much over 0.020 inch on your magneto, you'll never get your beast started.

Here's something else that most people forget about. With the individual spark plug gap set at 0.020 inch, the total distance the spark has to jump is 0.040 inch. Let's take a closer look.

The magneto coil, like some other Harley coils, is open-ended—that is, it has no ground.

Because of this, both terminals on the coil have to ground back to themselves to complete the circuit and fire the spark plugs. If you set the individual spark plug gaps at 0.020 inch, to fire both of the spark plugs, the voltage must jump a total distance of 0.040 inch.

Depending on the location of the magnets on the rotor, one side of the coil will be positive and one side will be negative. The voltage will flow from one side of the coil, through a plug wire, to one of the spark plugs. The volt-

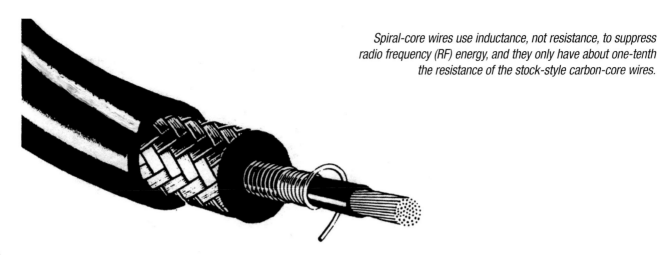

Spiral-core wires use inductance, not resistance, to suppress radio frequency (RF) energy, and they only have about one-tenth the resistance of the stock-style carbon-core wires.

age will then jump the spark plug's gap. The voltage will continue to flow through the motor until it reaches the other spark plug. The voltage will now have to jump the gap on this spark plug, too. After it has jumped the gap of this second spark plug, it will flow though the spark plug wire back to the coil completing the circuit.

When the magneto's rotor magnets turn 180 degrees, the polarity of the coil will be opposite, the voltage will then make the same trip, but in the reverse direction.

So if the voltage has to jump two gaps of 0.020 inch, it would be the same distance as running one spark plug with a 0.040-inch gap.

Since the time I purchased that first Sportster until the time the Motor Company stopped making them, I always ran straight Harley-Davidson number 4 spark plugs. They worked well over the years and I was satisfied with their reliable performance. But the straight number 4 plugs have not been available from H-D for many years, and Harley has replaced them with the 4R plugs. These plugs have the same heat range, but they are resistor plugs. Do not use the 4R plug or any other resistor-type spark plugs with a magneto.

As stated earlier, one of the few drawbacks of using a magneto is the fact that at low speeds (like when trying to kick-start your bike), the voltage output is low. The same thing that causes resistor plugs to be resistor plugs will impede the flow of this already low voltage to your spark plug electrodes. The end result may be a motor that will not start easily, or may not start at all.

The Champion H8 and H8C (the C stands for copper) plugs are the equivalent to the old H-D number 4 plugs and they will work about the same. If you want to run an even better plug than the old stock ones, try Autolite's fine-wire platinum spark plugs.

For the Ironhead Sportsters, I now use the Autolite AP4316. They are real, no gimmick, performance plugs that work very well. In fact, they're all I run today.

An Autolite side note: About nine years ago, I installed a new set of Autolite plugs in a Twin Cam. After the motor ran for about 10 minutes, the engine started breaking up and running very roughly. I pulled the plugs, and found that the porcelain insulator inside of one of the spark plugs had broken off and fallen down over the electrode.

I was bored, so instead of tossing the plug in the trash, I sent it back to Autolite with a letter explaining what had happened. Finally, after waiting for months, I received a nice letter from Autolite. In a longwinded way, it said it could find nothing wrong with the spark plug (other than it was broken!), and that I must not know how to install spark plugs properly. With that being said, Autolite said that it would still send me a new replacement plug.

It's been over nine years now, and I sure hope I get that replacement plug before I'm too old to ride. Maybe I should will it to my daughter, just to be safe.

If you own a bike with a magneto, or any bike for that matter, spend a few dollars and buy yourself a small spark plug cleaner. It will pay for itself 10 times over.

Some so-called experts have put in print that you should never use a spark plug cleaner. I guess that means I've been doing something wrong for the last 30 years! All I can say is that these people obviously must have deeper pockets than I do, and they sure as hell don't ride a kick-start-only bike with a magneto!

Magnetos, because of their low cranking voltage, love clean spark plugs, and they will often refuse to start with dirty ones. Always be sure to remove all blasting material from the plugs after they have been cleaned. Hose them down with brake cleaner, and then blow them out with compressed air. Don't forget to apply a small amount of anti-seize compound to the threads. If you have ever had to repair a stripped out head, you'll know why!

Cold V-twin motors with magnetos are somewhat sensitive to dirty spark plugs, or at least, all of mine have been.

If you jump up and down on your bike a dozen or more times and it won't start, try a clean set of plugs. I've done this for years and it does help. If nothing else, it gives this old man a chance to rest. Remember, spark plug cleaners should only be used to clean plugs that are in very good condition. A spark plug cleaner will not fix a worn-out plug.

TIMING

Motors, like people, are not all the same. Each motor has its own personality dependant on cam timing, compression, and combustion chamber shape.

Some XLCH Sportsters run well with 45-plus degrees of advance, while others may prefer less than 40 degrees to be happy.

The stock timing for the 900-cc Ironhead is 45 degrees advanced, meaning the piston is 11/16 inch before TDC when it fires. By today's standards, this is an awful lot of timing advance, but it is necessary due to the inefficient design of hemi-shaped combustion chambers.

I wish I had some magic timing number to could give you, but I don't. You'll only find out what's best by dyno tuning. At full advance, I run my 1959 CH at about 36 to 38 degrees of advance for normal use, but my motor is far from stock. It displaces 1,011 cc and has dual-plugged heads and on and on.

The timing for the stock 900 calls for 45 degrees advanced, and the 1,000, with its slightly larger bore, calls for 40 degrees. If you move your timing mark to the front of your timing window, it will retard your timing by 3 to 5 degrees. If you move the mark to the back of the timing window, it will advance your timing by 3 to 5 degrees. Only testing will tell you what will work best for your motor combination.

Back in days of old, we often adjusted the timing on magneto Sportsters using the timing-by-ear method. To do this, you would set the idle to a fast 1,200 to 1,300 rpm. You would then loosen up the two 1/4-inch magneto hold-down bolts and, with the motor operating at a fast idle, advance the magneto by rotating it counterclockwise. While listening to the sound of the motor, you would search for the location where the motor sounded the best and produced the highest rpm. Then you would shut the motor down and tighten down the two hold-down bolts. The magneto would now be timed for maximum power and ready to go.

Compared to more sophisticated timing methods, like using a timing light, this method sounds pretty crude. In reality, this method worked very well for making power and was, more often than not, the way the timing was set on many of these old motors.

Because the hemi-shaped combustion chamber is not as efficient as the new combustion chambers of Evos and Twin Cams, it takes longer for the flame to travel (the time it takes to burn all of the air/fuel mixture).

You do want to burn all the air/fuel mixture in your combustion chamber before you open your exhaust valve. Since the Ironheads use an awful lot of timing advance, though, the faster you spin your motor, the sooner your spark plugs will need to fire to burn all of the mixture. This is why the old Ironhead Sportsters require that excessive timing advance, and it's also the reason why you advance the timing as you increase the rpm of the motor—that is if you can. (More on that later.)

TEMPERATURE

Old V-twin motors seem to tolerate more advanced timing in cold weather than they do in warm weather. If you retard your timing too much, your motor will run too hot and you'll burn your exhaust valves and seats. Your exhaust pipes will also blue. The faster you want to spin your motor, the more timing advance will be required. The less timing advance you use, the easier your motor will start and the smoother it will idle.

ADJUSTABLE MAGNETO ADVANCE

The Fairbanks Morse magneto has no provision for an adjustable advance curve.

You physically set your timing, and once it's set, it stays at that setting from startup to redline. But all is not lost. You can do as I have done and convert your magneto to the manual advance used on the stock XLCHs from 1965 to 1969.

There are three main parts you'll need to accomplish this: the control arm H-D 29607-65, the upper adapter plate H-D 29600-65C, and the lower adapter plate H-D 29604-65A or 29603-67. The lower adapter plate is the part that bolts to the bottom of the magneto, and there are two different types. H-D 29604-65A was used on the 1965 and 1966 CHs and is identifiable by both the adjusting screw that sets the timing advance and the lack of a roll pin. H-D 29603-67 was used on the 1967 to 1969 CHs and had a roll pin to control the advance and retard timing. Replacement parts had both, so they could be used on all years. The same applies to the upper adapter plate that bolts to the cam case cover.

You'll also have to change your handlebars, because you'll need a way to control your spark advance. These parts used to be almost impossible to find, but today you are in luck! V-Twin Manufacturing now has reproductions of all of the stock parts needed for this conversion.

The more you retard your timing from 45 degrees, the easier it will be to start your motor because it reduces the possibility of kickback, and it will also idle easier.

When the timing is fully retarded (10–15 degrees BTDC), try not to rev your engine much above an idle. If you do, you won't be able to burn all the air/fuel mixture. If you run your timing too retarded at high rpm, two things will happen:

1. You'll lose lots of horsepower because you're not burning all of your fuel mixture.

2. When your exhaust valve opens on that unburned fuel mixture, a ball of fire will shoot through your exhaust valve, and this heat will, in time, destroy your exhaust valves and their seats.

When setting your timing advance, your goal is to find a happy medium. I would start at 45 degrees and work down a little.

If you want speeding tickets, then push it up to 45 or so. Remember: The more you advance your timing, the harder it is on your motor at low rpm. It will also be harder to start because your bike may protest by kicking back and trying to throw you over the handlebars. Have fun and be prepared for the unexpected!

DUAL-PLUG HEADS

We already discussed some of the drawbacks inherent with Harley's old fashioned hemi-style combustion chamber design; problems like an offset spark plug, poor flame front, poor mixture turbulence, too much heat-absorbing surface area, and combustion chamber shrouding caused by the dome piston all affect performance.

In my opinion, if you are running an old Knucklehead, Panhead, Shovelhead, or an Ironhead Sportster with a hemi-style head, the most important modification you can do to increase power and performance is to run dual-plug heads. This is an inexpensive option that will yield a significant power increase that you will really feel.

The dual plugs (one plug on each side of the cylinder head) will burn a larger percentage of the air/fuel mixture in your cylinders. Not only will this produce more power, but by burning a greater percentage of the mixture, you should also see an increase in gas mileage.

When I dual plugged my first set of Sportster heads, the first thing I noticed was the smell of the exhaust gasses—or should I say, the lack of smell. Before installing the dual plugs, if I had run this bike in my small shop with the garage door closed for more than a minute, it would have asphyxiated me! With the dual-plugged heads, it now takes a couple of minutes before I have to head for fresh air.

Here are several things you'll want to take into consideration when running dual-plugged heads:

- With spark plugs mounted on both sides of the cylinder head, the mixture will be ignited from two opposite locations at the same time.

- With two ignition points, the mixture will burn more thoroughly, produce more power, and you will have fewer unburned hydrocarbons coming out of your exhaust pipes.

- Burning a larger amount of the mixture in your cylinders can increase your gas mileage and power.

- With dual plugs, the mixture will require less time to burn fully, but in order to take full advantage of this potential power increase from the quicker burn rate, you must retard the spark advance by approximately 5 degrees.

- Failing to retard your spark advance with dual plug heads will negate any increased power potential.

- By retarding the spark advance, the mixture will be compressed and homogenized a bit more before the plugs fire, which can increase power while reducing detonation

- Running dual plugs will require the mounting and installation of an additional ignition coil and spark plug wires

INTAKE MANIFOLD LEAKS

When discussing things that can cause a Harley to run irregularly, the subject of manifold leaks should always be at the forefront. Harleys have always been susceptible to intake manifold leaks, and the older the Harley, the bigger the problem is.

Even the new sealing method used on the Evos and Twin Cams is still susceptible to intake manifold leaks. Believe me, I know this to be a fact! Whenever your motor starts running erratically, until you can rule it out, always suspect an intake manifold leak. This is especially true if the problem appears to be carburetor-related.

If your carburetor develops an unexplained or intermittent lean condition, suspect an intake seal problem.

If you add into the mix different size head gaskets, milled heads, or stroker plates, the sealing problem only gets worse. Be aware that there are intake manifold adapter rings available for running taller-than-stock cylinder heights.

I have been dealing with, and trying to prevent, intake manifold O-ring leaks on magneto Sportsters since day one. Sometimes I've met with success, and sometimes failure. One of the first tricks people try is the tape fix. This involves wrapping a heat resistant tape, like electrical tape, over the O-rings to prevent leaks. This works to some degree, but I don't recommend it. The main problem is that the tape gets heated, and the adhesive starts to ooze. Not only does this make a mess, it also makes the sealing surface very slippery.

If a separate and secure carburetor brace is not utilized, the carburetor will slip all over the place. Of course, when this happens, the tape gets chafed through.

Another trick is silicone sealant. Don't go there, it only makes a mess and you can't ensure a good seal.

So other than installing the seals just as they come out of the pack, is there anything you can try to cure the leak problem? My answer is yes . . . well, sort of.

First, always use new, good-quality O-rings or rubber

These are the original, and valuable, new old stock (NOS) parts required to convert the magneto to manually adjustable advance. V-Twin Manufacturing now sells reproductions of all these parts.

Unfortunately, many adjustable magnetos were converted to run the simpler fixed base plates, and the original adjustable parts were lost over time.

171

This is what the NOS magneto conversion parts look like when installed on the motor.

band seals. Never reuse old seals unless it's an emergency. Avoid using the stock intake clamps; they looked slick 40 years ago, but not today.

I prefer using bridge-type, 360 degree sealing, aircraft-style clamps. V-Twin Manufacturing (Tedd Cycle) and others sell this style of clamp. The ones I have been getting from V-Twin Manufacturing work well and are reasonably priced. As far as adding a foreign object, about the only thing I have found that sort of works is Teflon pipe tape. You will want to use tape that is wide enough to cover the entire sealing surface; 3/4-inch may be a good choice. You will want to put about five wraps snugly over the gap and install the aircraft-style clamps over it, while trying not to disturb the tape. The downside to this is that it requires three hands to do it, and you only have two, so you'll need help. Although I am not saying

this is the solution, I have never experienced an intake manifold leak when using this Teflon tape trick. The choice to try it is totally up to you.

I am including the Genuine James late model seal because it has an extra sealing lip that works quite well on stock applications. Unfortunately, if you have milled your heads or are using shorter-than-stock head gaskets to set up your squish band correctly, depending on your application, there my not be enough room for them to fit. Also, depending on how much your heads have been lowered, you may find that your intake manifold may be too wide to fit between your cylinder heads, and you may need to shorten your intake manifold. Example: Because of the milled heads and the thin head gasket I run on the Twin Cam project bike, I had to grind off about a 1/16 inch off of both sides of the stock S&S manifolds before

There's a spark plug on the wrong side of this cylinder head. Dual plugging works, and it's one of the modifications for which you do get your money's worth.

they would fit in-between the cylinders.

I'VE CHECKED EVERYTHING, BUT SOMETHING IS STILL NOT RIGHT

Onto the dreaded backfire-through-the-carburetor scenario: Why does it happen and how can you stop it?

You've checked everything. Your magneto's working fine and your timing and pushrods are adjusted right, so what gives? The answer is as simple as the fact that you're dealing with a 45-degree V-twin and it's running the wasted-spark ignition system.

As a rule, this back firing is most common at startup and at low rpm. At higher rpm, it goes away.

Backfiring through the carburetor is a sign of two other possible problems, so you'll need to rule them out first:

1. A leak at your intake manifold causing air/fuel mixture in one or both of your cylinders to be too lean

2. Improper settings on one or more of your carburetor jets, causing an air/fuel mixture that's too lean

So, you've ruled out the two most common causes and it's still backfiring. What now?

Remove your carburetor and intake manifold and look at the rear intake valve. See all that junk on it? That's the source of your problem, and it's caused by that good old wasted-spark ignition system I've been mentioning.

Here's what's happening. The wasted-spark system fires the spark plug twice (one for each revolution of the flywheel) for every complete cycle of your four-stroke engine.

173

Intake seals clockwise from top left: early-style O-ring seal; rubber-band-style seal; Genuine James Gaskets blue silicone late-style seal; and stock late-style seal.

The only problem is, you only need one spark on the compression stroke of each cylinder. So the other spark (the wasted one) must be happening on some other stroke.

When the back cylinder fires, the intake valve on the front cylinder is closed, so there's no problem there. When the front cylinder fires, though, the rear cylinder is on its intake stroke, which means your rear cylinder's intake valve is open. So, let's see: We have the carburetor, intake manifold, and head full of air and gasoline. The intake valve is open, the cylinder is starting to draw this air/fuel mixture in and the spark plug is firing, all at the same time. The end result is often a loud "ka-bang" followed by serious pain in your kneecap!

Now you know where the backfiring comes from, and it's also why all that junk is on your rear intake valve.

When the fuel is ignited in an unrestricted environment, it can't fully burn. That goop on your valve is the fuel's unburned byproduct.

SINGLE-FIRE MAGNETOS
If the wasted-spark ignition system is causing the problem, then we need to fix it. The only way we can is to stop that spark from happening in the first place. Here comes Morris Magneto to the rescue!

Yes, we're talking about single-fire ignition for the magneto. Some new stuff can make that old magneto even better. Morris Magneto's single-fire ignition module does work. The module is very easy to install and it requires no work be done to the magneto, as the module is mounted externally.

Now for the bad news. The module will set you back a little over $100, the last time I checked. I know, that's a few dollars, but it's worth it if you really want to stop that backfiring.

If you have never tried single-fire ignition, you should. I personally did not notice my motor starting easier (although it should have, because the spark now only has to jump half the distance), nor did I notice it making any more power.

But when it does start, you don't have to run your rpm up as high to keep it running while it warms up. You will also be able to idle your engine slower, without having it coughing and stalling. Most importantly, it helps to hold the backfiring at bay!

HOW RELIABLE IS THIS MODULE? HOW LONG WILL IT LAST?

The components that make up this module are very simple. Barring abuse, I can only speculate that they should be relatively durable. I have been running two of them for over five years, and so far no problems. You can purchase them from Morris Magnetos or from the aftermarket. For information on its single-fire module, contact Morris Magnetos at 103 Washington Street, Morristown, NJ 07960, (973) 540-9171.

IT SOUNDS LIKE MAGIC, SO HOW DOES IT WORK?

I'll show you how it works and even tell you how to make your own for a fraction of the cost.

Before we start, you may want review how the magneto produces current, and what a diode does, which I explained near the beginning of this chapter. The secret to the whole concept of how the single-fire module works is right there!

The secret is that the magneto operates on AC power. On the other hand, battery-coil systems all operate on DC power.

I warned you that the fact that the magneto utilizes AC power was important to remember. Because the magneto's coil is running on AC current, the polarity on the magneto's coil is constantly switching back and forth between positive and negative, whereas in the battery/coil system, the current always flows in the same direction.

When the points open for the front cylinder to fire, the current is flowing in one direction. When the points open the second time for the rear cylinder to fire, the current is flowing in the opposite direction. This situation is just begging for a couple of diodes!

Although the principle of how this module works is quite simple, explaining it may be a little harder, so please bear with me!

The magneto runs at half the engine speed, which means each time the motor makes two revolutions, the magneto's rotor only makes one revolution.

The rotor in the magneto has two poles, just like all magnets do: one side is north, and the other side is south. Remember that the magneto coil is open-ended and operates with the wasted-spark system, so no matter which cylinder is on the compression stroke, both spark plugs must fire to complete the coil's circuit.

For explanation's sake, let's say that when the front cylinder is on the compression stroke, the north pole magnet on the rotor is slicing the field.

When this happens, the current flowing through the wire to the spark plug on the front cylinder would be positive and the current flowing to the back cylinder (the wasted spark) would be negative.

Now the motor turns one revolution and the magneto turns one-half of a revolution. The back cylinder is now on the compression stroke, but this time the south pole is slicing the field. This would cause the current to flow in the opposite direction as it did the last time. So when the south pole slices the field, the current flowing to the back cylinder would be positive and the wasted spark going to the front cylinder would be negative.

This polarity reversal is consistent with each 180 degrees of rotation of the magneto rotor. Because the polarity reversal is consistent, we can easily exploit it to make our magneto a single-fire unit.

To do this we use two diodes mounted in opposite directions. Remember, the diode operates as a one-way DC electrical valve, so it will only let current flow in one direction. If you send current to it in the opposite direction, the diode will not let the current through.

If you try mounting one of these modules on a standard ignition system that is powered by a battery, only one cylinder will fire. In other words, it won't work!

MAKE YOUR OWN SINGLE-FIRE MODULE

You can make your own single-fire module for a fraction of the cost. Here's what you'll need:

- A couple of feet of solid copper-core spark plug wire

- Two metal spark plug connectors and two rubber boots

- Two coil end connectors and two rubber boots

- Two diodes rated for 75,000 volts and at least 250 milliamps

- A durable plastic tube about 4 inches long with an o.d. of about 1 inch

- One tube of silicone sealant

- Some heat-shrink tubing big enough to fit over the spark plug wire

- One crimp-on wire terminal with an eyehole that's big enough for a magneto cap hold-down screw to fit through

This sounds like a bunch of stuff, but it's all inexpensive. If you do much work on motorcycles, you may have most of these things lying around already, except for the diodes. I know I have enough to make several of these things.

Study the diagram on page 177. Start off by cutting three pieces of spark plug wire about 1 foot or so long. Two will go to the spark plugs and one will go to the coil.

Take one end of one diode and the opposite end of the other diode and solder them together. The diodes' polarities must be in opposite direction! Now, connect the joined diode ends to the coil wire, and solder each of the diodes' other ends to a spark plug wire.

Insert the wires into the plastic tube, and slide the tube over the two diodes. Make sure the diodes are separated from each other. Fill the tube with silicone sealant, and allow it time to dry.

Cut the spark plug wires to the appropriate lengths and install connectors and boots.

Next, you will need to make up a coil ground wire. This short spark plug wire will go from one side of the coil to one of the four magneto cap screws for a ground.

That's all there is to it. Connect the module to one side of the coil and to the spark plugs. Connect the short plug ground wire to the other side of the coil and to one of the magneto cap screws. This is needed because the coil is open-ended, so the other side of the coil that is not going to be used must be grounded to complete the coils circuit.

HERE'S HOW YOU CONNECT IT

Once connected, attempt to start your bike. If it starts, you have your polarity correct and you're good to go. See the diagram on page 178.

If it does not start, you may have the spark plug wires polarity reversed. If so, just reverse the connection of spark plug wires to the opposite spark plugs.

Now that you have verified that the wires are connected to the correct plugs, it would be a good idea to mark one of the spark plug wires for future reference.

If at some point you change the side of the coil you have your module plugged into, you will need to reverse the order of the spark plug wires to correct the polarity.

I've asked two friends in the electronics field to provide me with a source where you can obtain these diodes. Unfortunately, neither of these fellows is into bikes, so I'm still waiting for them to get back to me!

So far, the only information I have received back is that Motorola and Philips both manufacture the required diodes and they are carried under their OEM automotive ignition parts. You'll just have to go to an electrical parts suppler and explain what you're looking for and what you're going to do with them.

The 75,000-volt power rating is good and 250 milliamps should be adequate. But I will admit, not being an electrical engineer, I'm guessing the milliamp rating.

RUNNING DUAL MODULES

We have already discussed how beneficial dual plugs are on motors with hemi-shaped combustion chambers.

The only thing I can think of that might be better than single-fire from our old magneto is a magneto that will operate dual spark plugs in the single-fire-only mode. Can you do this? You bet!

All this involves is properly connecting two single-fire modules to your magneto. Although it's somewhat complicated to illustrate, installation and operation is really very simple.

HERE'S WHAT IT WILL LOOK LIKE

As shown in the diagram on page 179, the two modules feed through each other and complete the coil's circuit, so no additional ground is needed.

WELL, THAT'S IT.

Hopefully you are now magneto literate.

I would like to close by saying that ever since Harley-Davidson stuck a magneto on one of its engines, magnetos have been praised and pissed on by motorcyclists.

If the magneto is maintained properly and set up right, it will give you years—and I mean a lot of years—of reliable service. But no matter how good the magneto works, your engine will not perform acceptably unless everything else is right. Timing, carburetion, valve adjustments, spark plugs, compression, and even the wrong octane of gasoline will cause an engine to operate poorly. Too often, the magneto is falsely blamed for these tuning errors.

Over the years, I have seen a lot of bad press and heard a lot of bad words being passed around about magnetos. All I can say in response is, "Don't sell your magneto short!"

The magneto has been doing what it was designed to do for over 100 years now—and doing it very reliably, I might add.

Yes, there are drawbacks to the old Fairbanks Morse magnetos. The lack of a useable automatic advance curve is one, and low starting voltage is another. But on the plus side, the magneto is self-contained and requires no external electrical source to support it. If you fry your bike's electrical system, you'll still be able to ride it home and fix it. On the other hand, if it happens to the guy who put your magneto down, he'd have no choice but to spend some time standing on the side of the road trying to think of some way to get his electrically fried and deceased motorcycle home. Maybe some nice guy on a magneto-powered bike will give him a ride to a phone.

Some of this bad press has come from motorcycle racing tracks. The XR-750 racing bikes were using Fairbanks Morse magnetos. One person reported that some racers would bring a basket full of magnetos to the racetrack, because they knew the magnetos were going to break. Why were they breaking? The reason was simple.

Your Fairbanks Morse magnetos are nothing more than a

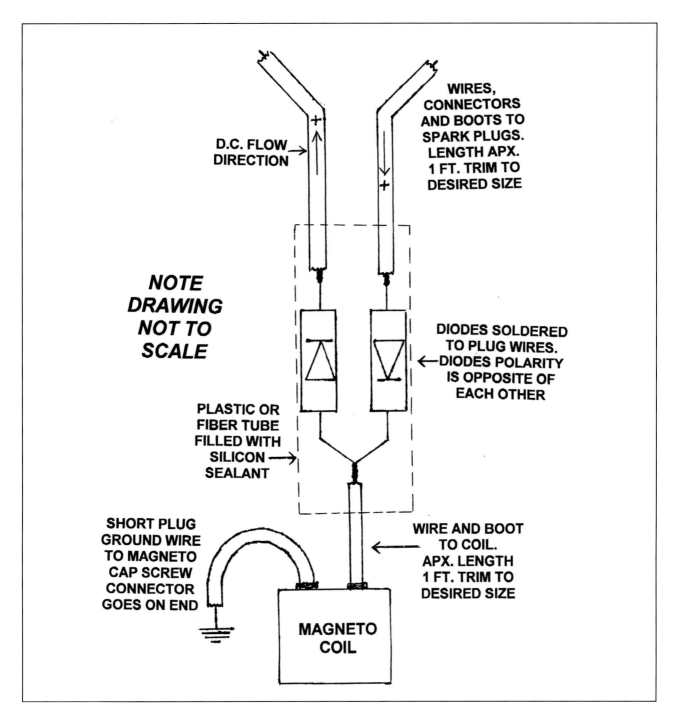

D.C. FLOW DIRECTION

WIRES, CONNECTORS AND BOOTS TO SPARK PLUGS. LENGTH APX. 1 FT. TRIM TO DESIRED SIZE

NOTE DRAWING NOT TO SCALE

DIODES SOLDERED TO PLUG WIRES. DIODES POLARITY IS OPPOSITE OF EACH OTHER

PLASTIC OR FIBER TUBE FILLED WITH SILICON SEALANT

SHORT PLUG GROUND WIRE TO MAGNETO CAP SCREW CONNECTOR GOES ON END

WIRE AND BOOT TO COIL. APX. LENGTH 1 FT. TRIM TO DESIRED SIZE

MAGNETO COIL

modified farm tractor magneto. How fast do you think farm tractor motors turn? The XR-750 racers, on the other hand, were turning their motors over 9,000 rpm! The magnetos were just not designed to spin that fast. At normal maximum rpm, let's say less than 7,000 engine rpm (which would be 3,500 magneto rpm) they should hold up fine. But who runs an old Ironhead at 7,000 rpm anyway? Not me. I like my old motor in one piece, thank you!

If you are lucky enough to own one of the old 1957–1969 Sportsters, please pamper it, as it's a non-replaceable piece of history!

Remember: The title for the bike goes with the left engine case, not the frame. If you break your cases and they can't be expensively fixed through welding and machining, you're out of business. The factory stopped making replacement cases in the 1970s, and there are no aftermarket replacements for these early engine cases. If you destroy your cases, you've also destroyed a piece of Harley history!

A FEW LAST WORDS ON MAGNETOS

The next time someone tries to put your magneto down, ask him, "What are the fastest—or should I say quick-

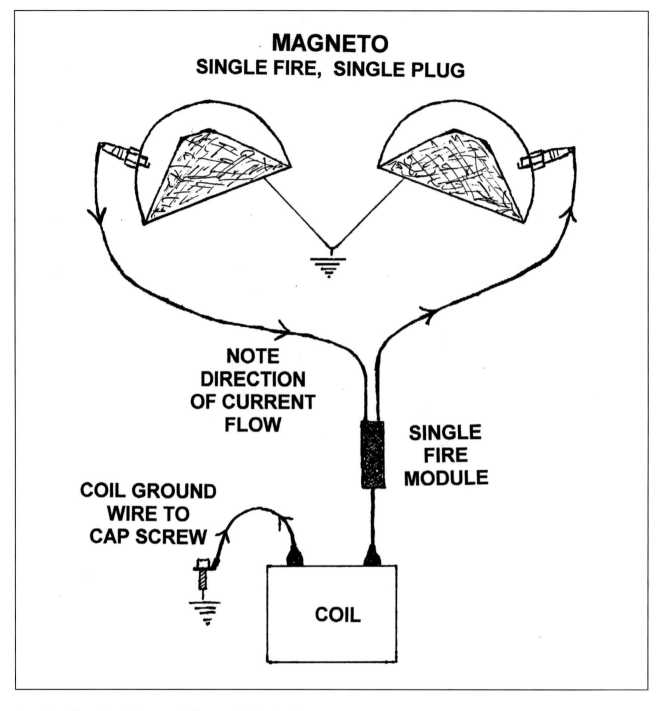

One side of the coil must be grounded to complete the circuit.

est—cars in world?" You know, the 5,000-plus horsepower top fuel dragsters and funny cars. (Go, John Force!)

Anyway, they're the ones that turn the quarter-mile in less than 5 seconds at over 300 miles per hour. Guess what kind of ignition system they use? You got it: Magnetos are the only things that will keep those monsters lit. Hell, the dragster guys like them so much that most of them run two magnetos on their engines. So, double your pleasure, double your fun.

One major advantage that magnetos have over standard battery/coil ignition systems is their extremely high output voltage. As you spin your V-twin motor faster, you should also be increasing the coil's output voltage to your spark plugs.

Magnetos do exactly that! Coil systems powered by batteries do the exact opposite. As their rpm increase, their output power decreases. The average output of a battery/coil ignition system is approximately 25,000

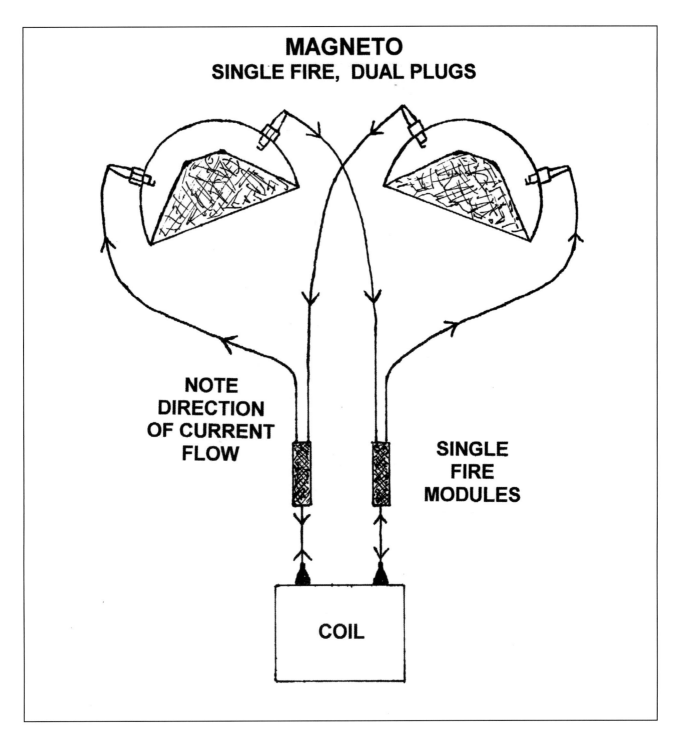

volts at 1,000 rpm. As rpm increases, the voltage to the spark plugs decreases, which is the exact opposite of what we want.

On the other hand, the magneto can pump out close to 50,000 volts at normal rpm. As you increase the rpm of the magneto, the output voltage to the spark plugs also increases to as high as 60,000 volts! On a high-compression, high-rpm motor, what do you want: the battery-and-coil's 25,000 volts or the magneto's 60,000 volts? Enough said. I rest my case!

MAGNETO PARTS

Parts for the Fairbanks Morse FMZ magnetos that were used on Harley-Davidson motorcycles are no longer available from the Motor Company. Morris Magnetos now produces the Fairbanks Morse FMZ magnetos, along with modified models of its own design. Morris Magnetos would be a good company to contact for stock Harley magneto parts. Joe Hunt Magnetos also sells the old type FMZ magnetos.

One reason I perform all my own work is to save

money. I don't mind spending money when I have to, I just don't like wasting it. One way I found to save money on magneto parts is to purchase them from automotive parts suppliers, instead of motorcycle magneto suppliers. It's been a few years since I purchased magneto parts this way, but the last time I did, I was able to find what I needed at reduced prices.

The main problem you have when doing this is you're working with Harley part numbers, and they mean nothing to the person at the auto parts store. But if you're armed with the Fairbanks Morse (Colt Industries) part numbers, it's a different story. To aid you in locating these parts and, hopefully, saving a few dollars in the process, I have included in the appendix a magneto parts breakdown and a table containing the hard-to-find (as I have never seen them in print anywhere) Fairbanks Morse part numbers you will need to locate parts.

These magnetos are similar to old farm tractor magnetos, so agricultural areas may be a promising place to locate parts. To increase your chances of finding what you're looking for, seek out businesses that have been established for a while. The last time I purchased magneto parts, I was in Seattle and found several places that either had the parts in stock or could order them for me. You shouldn't need to go to the ends of the earth to find parts. But time's running out, so good hunting!

In 1991, my research ship was deployed to Hawaii for seven months. I was able to dig through enough dumpsters there to assemble a perfectly serviceable, although somewhat ugly, 1965 XLCH Sportster, which I used to terrify myself and the tourists. The entire time I was stationed in Oahu, I never saw another old magneto-equipped Sportster on the road.

NOTES:

CHAPTER 12 **TOOLS**

 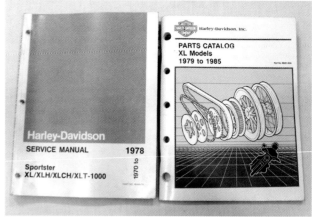

The service and parts manuals are the two most important tools you can own.

My main objectives when writing this book were to assist you in making the right choices, so your performance goals can become reality, and to help you save money in the process.

I stated early on that the two most important tools in your arsenal are the service manual (also referred to as the shop manual) and the parts book for your bike's year and model. Even if you're not a do-it-yourself type, you should still have these two publications. The service manual will let you know exactly what's involved in conducting the work you want preformed to your motorcycle.

Sadly, when you go to purchase your dream bike, you are often told that it will take months before the specific model and color you want will arrive. To add insult to injury, the dealership often requires you to put down a large chunk of change to get on its waiting list to get a new bike.

Luckily, the Motor Company has been increasing production every year, so the waiting period is not as bad as it used to be. Unfortunately for us consumers, some shops have used this supply and demand problem as a tool to extort money from their customers, and many shops will mark the bikes up from hundreds to thousands of dollars over Harley's suggested retail price.

Here's another trick they use. They tack on a couple of thousand to the manufacturer's suggested retail price (MSRP), and when you take delivery of the bike, they give you a voucher for $500 to $1,000 worth of free merchandise from their shop. If you already paid for it, it's not free! Or when an ordered bike comes in and the person who ordered it can no longer purchase it, the dealership quickly bolts on two or three thousands of dollars worth of accessories and pushes the bike out on the display floor. If you want the bike, you also have to buy all the expensive junk they bolted onto it. What can I say . . .

I highly recommend that when you make the financial commitment to buy a new bike, you also purchase the two most important tools you will need to work on it, the service manual and parts manual for your intended dream machine. Instead of just staring at the calendar while you're waiting for your bike to arrive, you can be doing your homework by studying the books.

A wealth of information can be obtained from the parts book, because it will show you every part used on your bike.

The parts book is very helpful when putting things back together, as it also shows the order of assembly.

The main reason the parts book exists is to provide you with the part numbers for every part on your bike. If you have the correct part number, it will increase your chance of getting the right part from the parts department. People who run parts counters love people who come in with part numbers! I've often wondered about this. After all, their job description is to relieve you of your money by providing you the correct parts, is it not? My guess is that having to deal with customer after customer saying "I need the thing-a-ma-bob that goes on that what-do-you-call-it" could get old.

The service manual is an even better tool! It will tell you how your bike works and lists the steps needed to conduct the required scheduled maintenance. It will also explain in detail how to disassemble, troubleshoot, repair, and reassemble the various components that make up your motorcycle.

After reading through the service manual, you will realize that most of this stuff is not rocket science. If you're mechanically inclined, and have the desire and the correct tools, you can perform most of the required work on your bike, and you can do almost everything I have covered in this performance book yourself!

By doing so, you will not only save money, but you will have the satisfaction of knowing that the work was done correctly and you did it yourself. Saving money and doing the work yourself is what this book is all about.

I am totally baffled when people drop over $18,000 on a new bike and don't even blink an eye when they hand over the money. Shortly after buying the bike they rush back to the dealership and pile on a couple of grand's worth of chrome doodads or whatevers, but they absolutely refuse to purchase a service manual and parts manual! Yes, Harley thinks a lot about these books, and you'll find out just how much when you go to buy them.

All too often, people come to me with a simple problem, and after checking out their bike, I'll say something like "it's

Face it, you're going to need more than a hammer, duct tape, and baling wire to work on your Harley.

just a leaking gasket, and the service manual will tell you how to change it," or "it's just out of adjustment, and the service manual will tell you how to correctly adjust it." What's their response? "I don't have a service manual. I never bought one." Well, the dealerships do buy service manuals and they actually read them, so they'll be more than happy to help the fellow out, at a cost of say 75 or 100 bucks an hour. This is your money, and you can do a lot of the work yourself. You may even find out you enjoy doing it. It's not work; it's a hobby!

Here's the bottom line: If you do your own work and it saves you only one or two billable hours of labor at the dealership, you have just paid for the books. It's your call, and it's also your money!

SPECIALTY TOOLS

A specialty tool is a tool that has been specifically designed to do a particular job that no other tool will do or that is designed to do the same job another tool could do, but will make the job easier, safer, or more reliable to perform.

As you read through the service manual you will notice that in order to work on Harleys, some specialty tools are needed. Actually, a lot of specialty tools are needed! Many of them are expensive, and sometimes it's not cost effective to purchase them if you're only going to use them once.

In addition, other equipment is required to work on bikes that most people don't have access to, such as an arbor press, a hydraulic press, a lathe, a drill press, a milling machine, a boring bar, an oxyacetylene torch, a welding machine, and on and on. Don't let this discourage you, there's still plenty of work you can do without all the fancy tools.

Earlier when I discussed changing cams, I explained that the tools required to press the old cams out and the new cams in are rather expensive. I mentioned that it would be more cost effective to take your cam-support plate to someone who has the specialty tools and have them do the work

for you. I still stand by that. So let's take a look at what's required to do that job.

I like to take my time when I work. A rushed job often results in a bad job.

For a cam change on a Twin Cam, I'd budget six hours, more if the heads were coming off. Most of this time will be spent dealing with things that have nothing to do with the cams, like removing and installing exhaust systems, carburetors, gas tanks, foot pegs, cleaning parts, etc.

Here's a gas tank tip: Removing the gas tank, gauges, and other parts can get quite involved and take a lot of time. You can save yourself a considerable amount of time by not removing the tank at all. If you remove the rear bolt and loosen the front bolt, you can lift the back end of the gas tank up and slide a piece of wood between the tank and the frame. This should provide you with enough access to work on the motor without totally removing the gas tank.

Once you get into the cam case, to remove the cam-support plate you only need a sprocket-locking tool and a way to hold the spring-loaded shoes open.

Several simple items can be used to open up the shoes and, as far as the shoe-locking pins go, a clean finishing nail will work just fine.

In place of the sprocket-locking tool, you could place the handle of a small screwdriver between the sprocket and chain. All it takes is a little imagination and ingenuity. Now that the cam-support plate is off, you can take it to someone who has the specialty tools to press the old cams out and the new ones in.

How long does it take me to change the cams on the press with the specialty tool? If I work slowly, it takes me about 5 minutes. My point here is, if you do the work yourself, except for the pressing of the cams, you save a bundle. How to do this job is covered step by step in the service manual.

Here's a horror story: Recently, I was talking to one of my acquaintances, who is a factory-trained and certified Harley

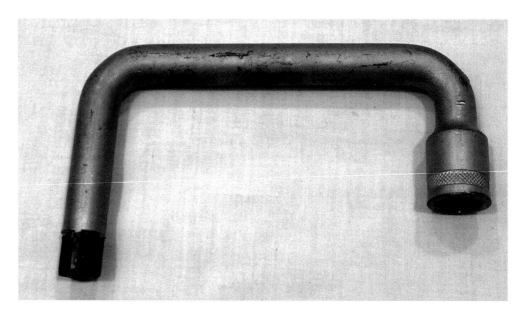

This simple device, when attached to a right-handed torque wrench, will reverse its direction. In my case, it turned my right-hand-only torque wrench upside down, so it now works in reverse and has become a left-handed torque wrench, as well.

mechanic. He told me how people were changing the cams on their Twin Cams by using blocks of wood, a hammer, and a couple of sockets. I place a limit on ingenuity, so I'm not going to tell you how they did it. Like I said, it's a horror story! He said it obviously works, because they're out riding. The question is, for how long?

Imagination and ingenuity are the keys to success. Here's another simple example. Many years ago, my research ship was working in Hawaii, and I needed to disassemble a set of Sportster shocks.

There's a specialty tool for compressing the shock springs so they can be disassembled, and I didn't have one. No problem, I simply put the shock in an upright position on our large drill press and had someone hold the shock while I pulled down on the drill press lever. When the weight was off the keepers, I pulled them out and eased off on the drill press lever. One disassembled shock. They went back together just as easily. You'll never know what you can do until you try.

Looking around my small shop, I see several specialty tools hanging on the walls. Some of the tools are store-bought items, but many are homemade. Tools are wonderful things, so I'll spend the next few pages explaining how to make some specialty tools (inexpensively) and other useful things that will make working on your Harley a little easier.

TORQUE WRENCH DIRECTION REVERSER

As stated earlier, if you plan to do a lot of work on your bike, you will need both a 3/8- and 1/2-inch torque wrench. Note: The 1/2-inch torque wrench needs to be able to torque up to 150 lb-ft.

A 1/4-inch torque wrench, although not mandatory, is very handy for getting into those tight places, so I recommend you get one. I usually always buy quality tools, but I did get a nice little 1/4-inch torque wrench from JC Whitney on the cheap.

Every fastener on your bike has a torque value, and most of them are listed in your service manual. Some fasteners have not only a torque value, but also a proper torque sequence that you must follow exactly as indicated or the part might not work properly or, worse, might be damaged.

Some torque wrenches will torque in both directions and work with both right- and left-hand-threaded fasteners. But some wrenches, like my 1/2-inch Proto torque wrench, will only torque right-handed fasteners.

One day I was in the process of installing the entire clutch assembly on an early Sportster, and when it came time to torque the mainshaft nut (which is left-hand threaded) to 150 lb-ft, I reached for my new fancy Proto torque wrench. I set the wrench to 150 lb-ft and started to tighten the nut, but something wasn't right. This is when I learned that my new expen-

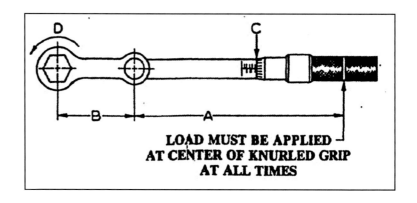

LOAD MUST BE APPLIED AT CENTER OF KNURLED GRIP AT ALL TIMES

sive torque wrench only torques right-hand-threaded fasteners. My first thought was, why did I sell my old torque wrench in the garage sale? It worked both ways. Then I remembered it was to help pay for my fancy new Proto wrench.

Oh well. It's time for a little Yankee ingenuity. Let's see, what could I do?

I reached in the toolbox and grabbed an old 1/2-inch drive extension and fired up my oxyacetylene torch. A bend here, a bend there, and a new homemade specialty tool was born. I then proceeded to torque the left-handed mainshaft nut using my new tool with my right-handed-only torque wrench without any problems.

USING EXTENSIONS ON TORQUE WRENCHES

I now had a new tool to reverse the way my torque wrench worked, but with the extension connected, when I set the wrench to 150 lb-ft, it would torque the nut too tightly. So I needed a formula to figure out where to set the wrench to get the desired 150 lb-ft at the end of the extension.

Here's the formula to figure it out(refer to the diagram on page 186):

$$[A \div (A + B)] \times D = C$$

A = the distance from the socket end center to the center of the torque wrench's handle

B = the distance from center to center of the extension

C = our new torque wrench setting

D = our desired torque value.

Here's an example: We want to torque a mainshaft nut to 150 lb-ft using an extension on our torque wrench.

Our torque wrench measures 18 inches from the center of the socket shaft to the center of the torque wrench's handle. Our extension is 6 inches long from center to center.

18 inches + 6 inches = 24 inches
18 inches ÷ 24 inches = 0.75 inch
0.75inches x 150 lb-ft = 112.5 lb-ft

With the 6-inch extension on our 18-inch torque wrench, we would set the torque wrench to 112.5 lb-ft, and it will torque our mainshaft nut to 150 lb-ft. It's hard to get this wrong, because the new torque value will always be less than the desired value. If it's more, you screwed up the math.

You may want to flag this area of the notebook and/or write this formula down and stash it in your toolbox. I often use extensions on my torque wrenches, so this is one formula I use frequently in my shop.

TORQUE WRENCH EXTENSIONS

Welding a custom-bent, open-end, or box wrench to an old socket will allow you to get into those hard-to-reach places to torque fasteners. I made the tool on the right[Designer: Make sure the photo he's talking about is placed on the right of this paragraph.] just to torque cylinder base bolts.

The first two tools are pretty simple, but they get the job done. That's all that matters.

A few homemade torque wrench adapters.

Here's the torque wrench extension in action while connected to a 3/8-inch torque wrench.

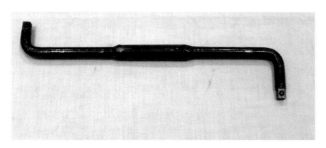

This tool will allow you to remove and install cylinder heads on older motors while the motor is still in the frame.

CYLINDER HEAD WRENCH

This is a copy of a Harley specialty tool that I believe dates back to the 1930s. It's used to remove and install cylinder heads in older V-twins, when the motors are still in the frame.

I made it by cutting the female ends off of two old 3/8-inch drive extensions. A piece of pipe connects the two pieces and is welded in place. You will need to heat the extensions up with a torch until they turn red before bending them. Note that the lengths of the extension, under the bend, are different. To connect it to your torque wrench, you simply put a 7/16-inch 12-point socket on the torque wrench end and plug the tool into the 12-point socket. As the ends on this tool face in different directions, it will not reverse the direction of the torque wrench. Use the formula to set your desired torque value.

There's a little story about this particular tool. Originally, I acquired a store-bought version of this tool, and the first time I used it, it bent up like a pretzel. Well, that ticked me off, so I made my own. This tool has been used and abused for years, and it's still in one piece. This just goes to show you that sometimes you can make better stuff than you can buy.

HOMEMADE LEAKDOWN TESTER

Now let's look at a more upscale homemade tool, a leakdown tester. I discussed leakdown testers in Chapter 7, Compression 101. Leakdown testers are used to monitor how well your motor is sealing, and can also troubleshoot problems if your rings, valves, or both are not sealing properly.

I've seen leakdown testers that sell in the $150 range. I made the one in the photo about 10 years ago for less than $30. I had some pipe fittings and an old valve lying around, so all I needed were two 100-psi gauges from the plumbing store, a spark plug hose from the auto parts store, and some ingenuity.

Although it looks fancy, the leakdown tester is fairly easy to make. You'll need the following:

1 male air hose chuck
1 small metering value (the one I used was an old hydraulic oil metering valve)
2 pipe Ts

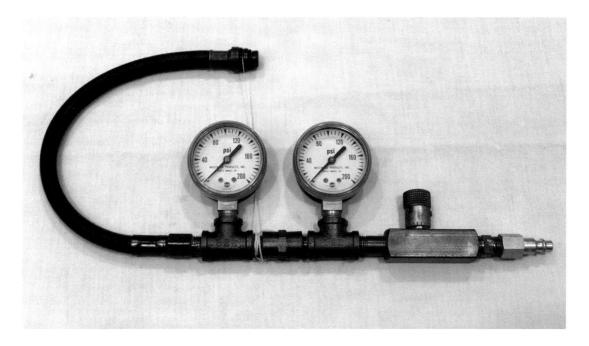

This is my homemade leakdown tester. When I made it, my out-of-pocket expense was less than $30. It may not be as pretty as a store-bought one, but it works just as well.

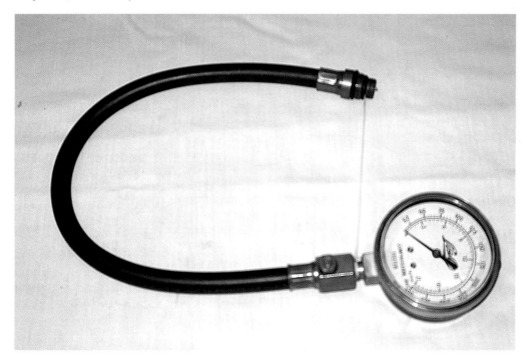

If you don't want to opt for the leakdown tester, you should at least have a compression gauge.

2 short pipe nipples
1 pipe coupling
1 pipe plug
2 100-psi gauges
1 spark plug air hose (the kind used on compression gauges)

By looking at the picture, you can see how it all goes together, but there is one secret that makes it work. The secret is in the coupling between the two gauges. The coupling is plugged with solder and then a small hole is drilled through the solder plug. The size of the hole is critical to make the leakdown tester work properly.

HERE'S HOW I MADE IT

First, I thoroughly cleaned the inside of the coupling with a wire brush (the kind you use for plumbing work) and washed the coupling with brake cleaner. The inside of the coupling must be clean, or the solder will not adhere to it.

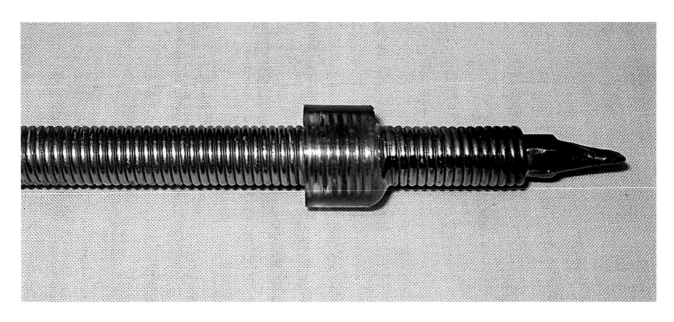

This inexpensive homemade Keihin idle mixture tool will help you avoid being burned by hot exhaust pipe crossovers.

I screwed a pipe plug into one end of the coupling, secured the base of the pipe plug in a vise with the open end of the coupling facing up, and applied some soldering flux to the inside of the coupling. I used a handheld propane torch to heat up the coupling and then melted about a 3/8-inch layer of solder over the plug in the bottom of the coupling. (Note: I placed some anti-seize compound on the pipe plug so it would not be soldered in place.)

When it cooled, I removed the pipe plug and drilled a 0.031-inch hole through the center of the solder plug using a 68 drill bit. The hole through the plug must be this size only for the leakdown tester to work correctly.

Finally, I just assembled the pieces like they are in the picture. I recommend using a good pipe thread sealant, like Leak-Lock. It comes in a blue tube and is available from plumbing stores. I use it on all oil line fittings, fuel fittings, air fittings, and just about anything I don't want to leak. Once it sets up, it's pretty tough stuff.

KEIHIN CARBURETOR IDLE MIXTURE TOOL

Have you ever tried to adjust the idle mixture screw on a stock Keihin carburetor on a bike that has an exhaust crossover pipe under the carburetor? The setup used on the Evo Sportsters painfully comes to mind.

I have tried several ways to do this with little success. As previously stated, sometimes a specialty tool is used to make a job safer. After being burned one too many times, I came up with this simple and inexpensive adjustment tool.

All you need is a small flat-blade power-drill screwdriver bit and an old-fashioned screen door spring about 1 foot long.

This simple tool does the work of two hands when soldering wires.

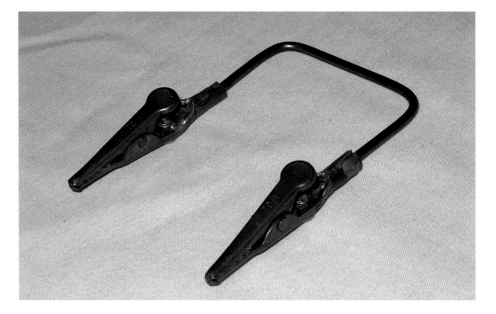

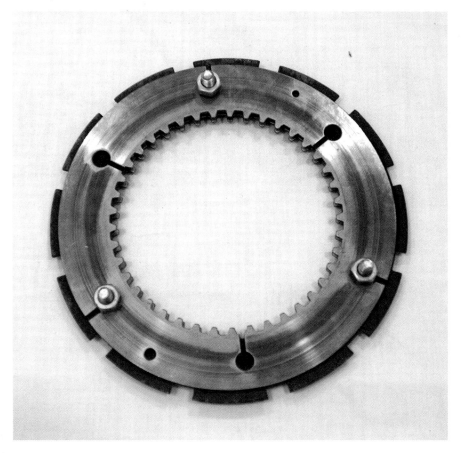

This is a homemade clutch locking tool.

Slide the bit into one end of the spring and solder it into place. You can slide the tool in from under and behind the crossover pipe and up into the jet, then safely adjust the jet while staying a safe distance from that hot exhaust pipe.

It's good idea to take a felt-tipped pen and draw a short line down the side of the spring to use as a reference mark, so you can count the number of turns as you adjust the carburetor.

SOLDERING TOOL

If you're mechanically inclined, sooner or later you are going to have to solder wires.

Soldering wires is fairly straightforward and easy: Clean the parts to be soldered; add a little flux, a little solder, a little heat; and you're good to go.

The problem with soldering wires is that you need two hands to hold the wires, and another hand to hold the solder gun or iron. Therein lies the problem. God only gave (most of us) two hands.

About 10 years ago I was soldering something and, as usual, I was one hand short. Since being ticked off is often the mother of invention, I put down the solder gun and started digging around for something to give me some extra "hands."

I ended up with what you see. It's a simple little thing, made from two alligator clips and a piece of bent metal rod. You just slide the alligator clips over each end of the rod and solder them in place. I have about 2 inches between the bends.

Now whenever I reach for the soldering gun, I also reach for this simple tool.

CLUTCH LOCKING TOOL

To remove or install the clutch shell and transmission sprocket on older Sportsters, you'll need a specialty tool to lock the two together. You can buy one or make your own.

This tool was made using three old throwaway clutch parts I rescued from my trashcan.

Simply take an old fiber friction plate and sandwich it between two old steel driven plates. Line up the three plates—make sure the insides of these plates are lined up!—and drill a couple of holes through them and bolt them together. As the required parts to assemble this came from the trashcan, the cost to make this tool is next to nothing.

PRIMARY LOCKING TOOL

As long we're in the primary case area, let's look at more homemade tools we can use.

If you have access to some scrap metal, this is another tool you can make for almost nothing. My version of this tool is not a work of art, but it works just great. This ugly tool is used to lock the mainshaft to the clutch shell and is required when you need to remove or install the entire clutch assembly.

Two of the pointed ends engage the main-shaft sprocket teeth; the other two pointed ends engage the teeth on the clutch shell. To make this tool, I used two pieces of 1/4-inch flat bar, two sections of 3/4-inch pipe, two 3/8-inch all-thread or bolts, and two 3/8-inch nuts.

To make this tool easier to use, it is important to cut the spacers a little shorter than they need to be. This puts a little slop in the tool so you can line it up with the sprocket teeth. If it's bolted together tightly, it's a bear to line up.

First, measure the distance between the mainshaft nut teeth and the clutch shell teeth, where you want the locking tool to go. Then cut two pieces of flat bar to those lengths and grind the ends of both flat bars to a rounded point.

Next, hold the two pieces of flat bar between the teeth, and measure the distance between the inside of the two pieces of flat bar. Cut two pieces of pipe to that length.

Drill two holes in each piece of flat bar a little bigger than your 3/8-inch bolts. Now, take your two bolts and bolt the whole mess together. Leave the nuts a little loose, so the tool has a little play in it, and it'll be easier to install between the sprockets teeth.

CLUTCH SPRING COMPRESSION TOOL

During the winters in Alaska, some people find they have lots of spare time on their hands. There's an old saying that goes,

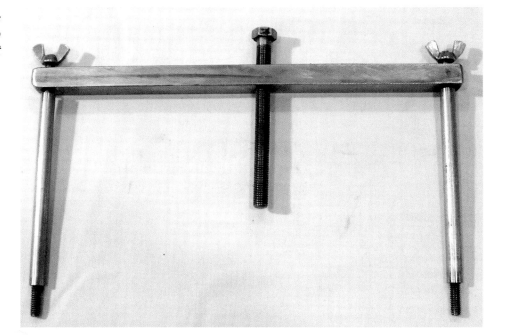

This tool is used to compress the clutch spring on 1970s to early 1980s Sportster wet clutches.

This tool is used to lock the main shaft nut and the clutch shell together for assembly or disassembly.

This tool is used to remove and install the transmission mainshaft nut, so you can remove or install the entire clutch assembly.

"Idle hands are the devil's workshop."

So, to give my idle hands something to do, I take them out to the workshop, and that's where this tool came from.

This tool is a copy of a specialty tool used to compress early Sportster wet clutches. I will not explain how I made this one, because I got carried away making it. The entire tool, except for the jacking screw, was made of stainless steel, and the pins were turned down on a lathe, and so on.

You can make a similar tool a lot more easily without getting this carried away. First, notice that the jacking screw in the middle of this tool is slightly off center; this is required because of the bolt pattern on the case base.

To make a simpler version of this tool you'll need the following:

A piece of bar stock about 11 inches long

Two 1/4x20-inch bolts about 2 inches long

A piece of 3/8-inch all-thread and a 3/8-inch nut

First, cut a piece of bar stock to the required length. Next, find two bolt holes on the case and mark on the bar where they are. Now drill those two spots with a 1/4-inch drill bit so the two 1/4-inch bolts will fit through them.

Next, mark the bar where the center of the clutch is, and drill it out with a 3/8-inch drill bit. That's it, you're done.

Simply slide the all-thread into the center hole; the 3/8-inch nut goes under the bar stock. Screw the two 1/4-inch bolts into the clutch housing. To compress the clutch spring, hold the end of bar stock with a pair of pliers or vise-grips, and turn the nut under the bar stock.

TRANSMISSION MAINSHAFT TOOL

There's nothing special about this particular homemade tool. I just want to show you that there's more than one way to skin a cat.

I didn't have a socket big or tall enough to remove the transmission's mainshaft nut in my tool arsenal, so it was off to the pawnshop.

The pawnshop only had one beat-up old socket the right size, but it was for a 3/4-inch drive socket wrench, and the socket was a little shorter than I wanted. So I paid $2 for the socket and headed home. Although I didn't have a 3/4-inch torque wrench, I could have bought a 3/4- to 1/2-inch adapter, but that would have involved spending money. And it wouldn't have been a homemade tool.

Since I had lots of old junk 1/2-inch drive sockets, I just welded one of them to the top of the big socket, so it would fit on my 1/2-inch torque wrench. Now the socket was the right height and another homemade tool was born.

COMPENSATING SPROCKET NUT WRENCH

When we think of a nut, we think of something that has six sides. Compensating nuts on old Sportsters look like flat disks with two holes in them. This homemade tool is a copy of the factory specialty tool.

To make it, I scrounged up a length of 1/4-inch flat bar and two 5/16-inch grade-8 bolts.

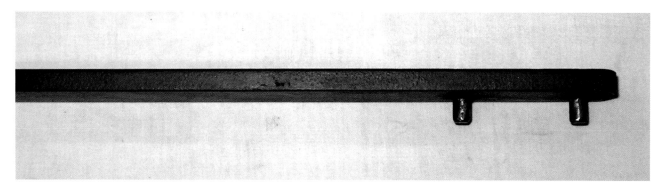

Sprocket removing tool for old-style Sportster motor sprocket compensating nut.

I measured the distance between the holes in the compensating sprocket nut, and then drilled two holes in the flat bar to match. I took a hacksaw and cut the threads and head off of the two grade-8 bolts. I inserted the two pins, which I just made from the grade-8 bolts, into the flat bar and welded them into place. That's all there was to it, and another specialty tool was born. This tool is big and heavy enough to do double duty as a crow bar.

PRIMARY COVER PLUG TOOLS

The clutch adjuster, which lives under the primary chain case on 1970s and early 1980s Sportsters, is covered with a plug. This plug has a large flat "X" groove that's about 1/4 inch wide.

The primary chain case covers on earlier K- and XLH-model Sportsters (from the 1950s and 1960s) had a similar plug that could be removed to check the primary chain's

Here you can see the oval-style plug (top) on this early Sportster primary cover.

These tools are used to remove and install the access plugs on early Sportster primary chain case covers.

adjustment and to add oil. The bottom of the groove in this plug was not flat, but curved.

Because of the groove's large size, many things fit in it. Unfortunately, these things often do not fit perfectly in the grooves. What inadvertently happens is that the plug gets all chewed up from screwdrivers and who knows what else getting jammed in it over the years.

These simple tools will fit perfectly into the plugs, and will prevent them from being damaged. They're made from using an old socket and a piece of 1/4-inch flat bar. The flat bar has been welded to the socket. The clutch adjuster plug tool for the later models is the easier of the two to make because it's flat.

The earlier models' primary chain case plug takes a little more work. The easiest way to make it is to draw an curve on your flat bar that resembles the curve at the bottom of the groove in the plug, and use a bench grinder to shape it.

By now you should be able to see where I'm going with this.

The last six tools were specialty tools just for working in or on the primary chain case, and we haven't even started on the motor or transmission.

The point I'm trying to make is that if you use your imagination and a little ingenuity, many of these fancy specialty tools are not too big of a deal to create.

I have explained how some of these specialty tools can be inexpensively assembled using scrap material on the cheap.

The service manual will show you what many of the tools look like and how they're used.

All you have to do is scrounge up some scrap material. Let's look at a few more items that will make working on your bike a little easier. Many can be purchased at your local hardware store.

OTHER USEFUL TOOLS

Many things can be useful when you're working on your bike, and here are few that will make your life easier.

If you're like me, you'll often encounter cases of fat fingers and little parts. I'm always dropping little things into hard-to-reach places.

Two wonderful tools that save the day when that happens are mechanical fingers and a magnet on a wand.

Mechanical fingers are really cool, and every mechanic should have a set. You simply squeeze the end of the grip and a set of four claws open up on the other end; release the knob and it grabs the part. You can now remove the part from its hiding place.

Another tool that does almost the same job is the magnet on a wand. The only problem with the magnet wand is it will only pick up things that contain iron. It won't pick up non-ferrous materials (aluminum, brass, stainless steel, plastic, etc.).

The only thing worse than dropping a part into an inaccessible place is dropping it into a place where you can't see it. The mirror on a wand comes in handy here.

ALLEN AND TORX SOCKETS

Harley now uses a considerable amount of Allen and Torx fasteners on its bikes. These fasteners, like all fasteners, need to be torqued properly.

The only way you're going to be able to torque them is with a set of Allen and Torx socket bits. If you drop enough hints and are really good, maybe Santa will get them for you.

Earlier I said you should only buy quality tools, because cheap tools are just that.

A while back, I went shopping for a new set of Torx bits. I

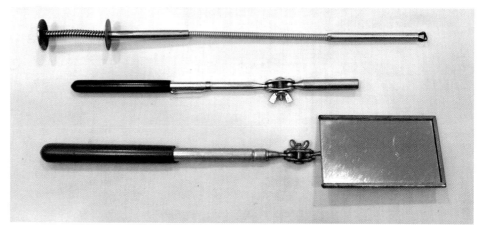

These tools are very handy to have nearby: (top to bottom) mechanical fingers, magneto wand, and mirror on a wand.

Allen and Torx sockets: Sooner or later you're going to have to buy some.

stopped by Sears to check out my favorite tool line, Craftsman. There was a nice little set, but the price tag was in the $50 range. I had the set in my hand, but put it back on the shelf. Maybe I'll buy it next time.

The wife wanted to pick up some treasures at K-Mart, so that was our next stop. The next thing I knew, I was wandering down the tool aisle. That often happens when I go shopping with the wife. I just say, "I'll be over in the tool department, honey. Get me when you're ready to go."

Anyway, there I was, looking at all these wonderful things made cheaply in Taiwan and China, when I spotted the set of Torx bits you see in the picture. It was priced at less than $12 for the whole set and it even came with a storage bar. What can I say? I knew better, but I bought them, anyway. That was over five years ago. I sure wish one of these cheap things would break, so I could buy that Craftsman set.

UNIVERSAL JOINT SOCKET FIX
When working with socket wrenches, you will occasionally find you need to use a universal joint to get to some hard-to-reach fastener.

The downside of the universal joint is trying to get the socket on the fastener with the joint attached. The socket always flops down from its own weight, and it can be a real pain to get the socket on the fastener.

My simple fix can make the universal joint a lot more user friendly. Simply take your socket to the hardware store and find a spring that will fit snugly over the universal joint. When attached, the spring will hold the joint in place to aid you in getting the socket on the fastener, but it will still allow the joint to move as designed when you turn the wrench. Maybe I should have patented this idea. I was at a tool store recently, and there it was—a universal joint socket with a spring around it. Anyway, you don't have to spend dollars to buy this tool, just spend pennies and buy a spring.

REAR-WHEEL ALIGNMENT TOOL
This tool is used to verify that your rear wheel is aligned with your frame, so you should use it to check your rear-wheel alignment when you adjust your rear belt. This one is simple to make. All you need is a piece of brazing rod, or

This rear-wheel alignment tool is one of the easiest tools to make.

even a coat hanger. Simply bend one end and put a point on the short end. Slip a small O-ring over the rod to use as a reference marker.

This is a very easy tool to use. Just find a like reference point on both sides of the bike somewhere on a horizontal plane from the rear axle. Place the pointed end of the tool on the reference point, and slide the O-ring to the center of your axle. Then compare that to the other side of the bike. The wheel is aligned to the frame when the O-ring is centered to both sides of the axle. In the case of newer Harleys with swingarms, Harley has already put a reference hole in the swingarm for you to use.

INTAKE MANIFOLD TOOL

If you have worked on the new Evo-style manifolds, you know two things by now:

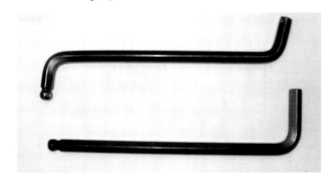

The Yost intake manifold tool (top) and a standard 1/4-inch ball-end Allen wrench (bottom).

1. The Allen bolts that hold the manifold on to the cylinder heads are easy to see.

2. Trying to get a tool on these bolts to tighten or loosen them is a nightmare.

Yost knows that, too, so it came up with a handy tool you can actually use on these Allen bolts. This is one of the "why didn't I think of that?" kind of tools. But what happens if no one sells the tool where you live, or if you're just too cheap to buy one?

You could always make one. The ball-end Allen wrench looks similar to the Yost tool, so if you were to heat the Allen wrench up with a torch until it turns red, and then bend it a little here and bend it a little there, you'd have the same sort of thing.

SYRINGES

When working on motorcycles, all kinds of items are useful. One such item is the syringe. Yes, these are the same things the doctor puts a needle onto before they stick you in the butt.

These have many uses around the shop. I like to use them to lay down perfect beads of silicone sealant on gaskets.

With a needle attached, you can get in and lubricate small parts like throttle cables, clutch cables, and brake cables without making a mess. Yes, I still have a Harley that has cable-actuated brakes!

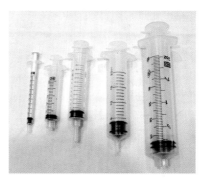

If you can get your hands on them, syringes are excellent tools for many purposes.

You can also apply a drop of Loctite onto a tiny part without making a mess.

Bleeding brakes can sometimes be a real pain, but not if you use a large syringe. Drain the master cylinder, and fill a large syringe with brake fluid. Then, open the bleeder on the caliper, attach a hose between the syringe and the brake bleeder, and squeeze the syringe. When the master cylinder is almost full, tighten down the bleeder and you're done. Be sure not to let the syringe run dry in the middle of this operation, or you'll have to start all over.

Try checking out the 1959–1969 Sportster manual instructions on filling the front forks with fork oil. It involves disassembling the top of the forks, then hanging funnels and hoses and stuff. If you use a large syringe with a large gauge needle attached, you simply insert the needle into one of the two vent holes and inject the fork oil. You're done in 60 seconds without making a mess, and you don't have to take the forks apart.

Syringes come in different sizes. I have them from the little 1-cc to the big 2-ounce ones.

Now for the bad news: In this drug-paranoid country we live in, try getting your hands on some. I work with scientists, and most of these fellows are pretty smart and know how useful syringes can be. Because of this, I have an unlimited source for this very useful tool.

They are out there and can be purchased from scientific supply places, but you're going to have to look for them.

INDEXING WASHERS

Years ago, I wasted some money and ordered a set of spark plug indexing washers. Don't make the same mistake.

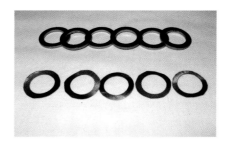

If you can't buy good spark plug index washers, you'll have to make your own. Top are store bought; the ones on the bottom are homemade.

The things I received were totally worthless. Why? In my opinion, they were too thick! Since the ones that are sold are junk, you'll just have to make your own.

Get yourself some brass shim stock in the following sizes: 0.005 inch, 0.007 inch, and 0.012 inch; or 0.005 inch, 0.010 inch and 0.015 inch. When I make mine, I use a hole-cutter to cut the center hole to 12 or 14 millimeters, depending on the application. Then, I cut the outside with a common pair of scissors. This stuff is real thin and easy to work with.

With this assortment of washers, you can properly index your spark plugs and still have them sticking into your combustion chambers.

SPARK PLUG CLEANER

After using a spark plug cleaner, remove all the blasting media from inside the spark plug! After I blast them, I rinse them out with brake cleaner and compressed air. Don't forget to apply a little anti-seize compound to the plug threads.

TWIN CAM OIL FILTER WRENCH

New Twin Cams are popping up all over my small town. So, this has recently become a common question: "How do I get that damn oil filter off?"

Just look at the pictures, and now you know. On earlier model Harleys, you could get any one of a number of tools on the oil filter.

The new Twin Cams have the crank position sensor mounted in a location that prevents other types of filter wrenches from working.

This type will fit. This style of oil filter wrench comes in several sizes, but it's not a one-size-fits-all tool. Measure the diameter of the filter or just take an oil filter with you when you go to the auto store. Note: When I went to purchase the tool pictured, the size listed on the package was metric, not based on the Society of Automotive Engineers (SAE) measurement standard. Of course, I had measured the filter in inches. Here

are the formulas to get the metric/SAE equivalents: inches x 2.54 = centimeters; inches x 25.4 = millimeters; centimeters x 0.3937 = inches; millimeters x 0.03937 = inches.

CLOSING THE TOOLBOX . . . A THOUGHT

When I was a young lad, I spent a lot of time with my grandpa. His name was Jim, but everyone called him Bill. Anyway, I liked being around him, because he was always working on something. My grandpa was an old-school do-it-yourselfer. If something needed to be done or fixed, he wouldn't reach for the phone. He'd reach for his tools and get the job done.

His example of independence and self-reliance motivated me to follow in his footsteps and do things myself.

My grandpa also tried to pass along words of wisdom to guide my young life. Unfortunately, because I was too young to understand their importance, many of his words of wisdom were lost. But I do still remember a few of them. I'll close out the tool section with one of his sayings. Now that I'm older and wiser, I understand its importance, and as always, Grandpa was right.

"A man is only as good as his tools.
If he doesn't take care of his tools,
he's not taking care of himself."

Remember: Planning makes perfect and perfect planning will not only make you happy, but it can also make you a winner!
The more you know,
The faster you go!

This is the tool you need for those stubborn Twin Cam oil filters.

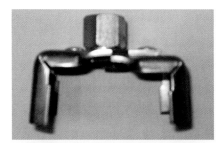

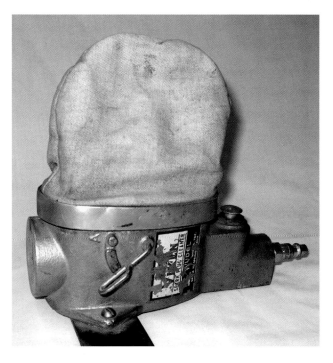

A small spark plug cleaner, like this one, will pay for itself over the years.

APPENDIX A
MAGNETO PARTS BREAKDOWN

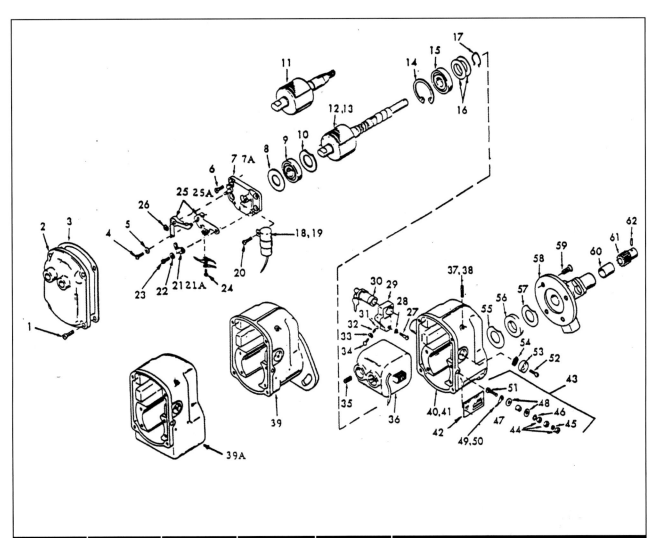

	FM Z2-2C 63B	FM Z2-2C 63A	FM Z2-2C 10A	FM Z2-C2 63A	
Rotation	CCW	CCW	CCW	CCW	Specification and engine manufacturing
	X				FMZ2-2B63C Harley-Davidson 29503-56R
		X			FMX2-2C63A Harley-Davidson 29501-62
			X		FMZ2-2C10A Harley-Davidson
				X	FMZ2-2C63C Joe Hunt

Reference number	Part number	Number of parts used				Description
1	10S12D	4	4	4	4	End cap screw 10-24x3/4
2	BY2430	1	1	1	1	End cap
3	H2498	1	1	1	1	End cap gasket
4	6S6U	1	1	1	1	Support screw 6-32x3/8
5	D2458	1	1	1	1	Support screw washer 6
6	8S6G	4	4	4	4	Support screw 8-32x3/8
7	LX4631	1	1	1	1	Bearing support
8	E2493	1	1	1	1	Outer grease retainer washer
9	D5949A	1	1	1	1	Cam end bearing
10	A2492C	1	1	1	1	Inner grease retaining washer
11	QT2480	1	0	0	0	Rotor
12	FP2480	0	1	1	0	Rotor
13	YT2480	0	0	0	1	Rotor
14	B1498B	1	1	1	1	Bearing snap ring
15	C5949	1	1	1	1	Drive and bearing
16	—	—	—	—	—	Fairbanks Morse does not list this part
17	B1498D	1	1	1	1	Shaft snap ring
18	SXT2433	1	0	0	0	Condenser
19	AXMR2433	0	1	1	1	Condenser
20	8S5NA	1	1	1	1	Condenser screw 8-32x5/16
21	H2788	1	1	1	1	Cam wick
22	B5969	1	1	1	1	Support screw washer
23	8S6U	1	1	1	1	Support screw 8-32x3/8
24	6S6Z	1	1	1	1	Terminal screw 6-32x3/8
25	B2437A	1	1	1	1	Point set
26	C1498G	1	1	1	1	Fulcrum pin snap ring
27	8S10N	0	1	1	0	Block screw 8-32x5/8
28	8LW6	0	1	1	0	Screw lock washer
29	E1355	0	1	1	0	Insulating block
30	B2468	0	1	1	0	Ground lock and key assembly
31	A2491	0	1	1	0	Ground lock spring ball
32	C3970	0	1	1	0	Ground lock spring
33	10LW2	0	1	1	0	Screw lock washer
34	10S8N	0	1	1	0	Terminal wire screw 10-24x1/2
35	B3967	2	2	2	2	Coil lead spring
36	Q2477C	1	1	1	1	Coil
37	25SS14A	2	2	2	0	Coil setscrew 1/4-20x1-1/8
38	31SS14A	0	0	0	2	Coil setscrew 5/16-24x7/8
39	RW2425	1	0	0	0	Housing
40	EU2425	0	1	1	0	Housing
41	FW2425	0	0	0	1	Housing
42	A195A	1	1	1	1	Nameplate
43	B2514B	1	1	1	1	Ground switch complete
44	8N1	3	3	3	3	Nut
45	8LW5	1	1	1	1	Screw lock washer
46	8LW6	1	1	1	1	Screw lock washer 1208
47	K2457A	1	1	1	1	Switch bushing
48	C6018	2	2	2	2	Insulating washer
49	J2499A	1	0	0	1	Terminal wire

Reference number	Part number	Number of parts used				Description
50	M2499A	0	1	1	0	Terminal wire
51	8S14N	1	1	1	1	Switch screw 8-32x7/8
52	6S4U	2	1	1	0	Cover screw 6-32x1/4
53	B6030A	2	1	1	2	Vent cover
54	C6032B	2	1	1	2	Vent screen
55	A2492C	1	1	1	1	Inner seal washer
56	G3861	1	1	1	1	Shaft seal
57	A2492A	1	1	1	1	Outer seal washer
58	L2671	0	1	1	0	Drive housing
59	25S9G	0	4	4	0	Housing screw 1/4-20x9/16
60	C5950D	0	1	1	0	Drive housing bearing
61	P142	0	1	1	0	Drive housing gear
62	E5931D	0	1	1	0	Drive housing gear pin

Colt Industries

INSTRUCTIONS
REMOVING LOCK
FMZ2-2C63A 10 005 230
MAGNETOS

ENGINE ACCESSORIES OPERATION • BELOIT, WISCONSIN 53511

REMOVING IGNITION LOCK
FMZ2-2C63A-10 005 230 MAGNETOS

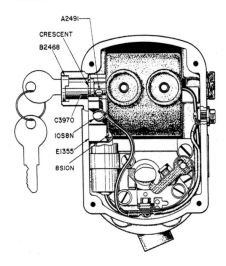

A2491
CRESCENT
B2468
C3970
IOS8N
E1355
8SION

To remove the ground lock and key assembly from the FMZ2-2C63A magneto -- proceed as follows:

With the end cap removed, turn the key plug B2468 to the left until it stops, then turn it 150° to the right, just short of a half turn. In this position, the brass crescent, between the housing and the bakelite switch block E1355, can be seen. With a thin screwdriver or a flat piece of steel, 1/16 inch thick or less, depress the crescent and remove the plug by pulling on the key.

Remove the 10S8N, #10-24x1/2 wire assembly screw from the switch block E1355. Use care not to lose the ground lock ball A2491 and the ground lock spring C3970. Remove the insulating block to housing screw 8S10N, #8-32x5/8 and lift out the insulating block E1355.

The coil can then be disassembled in the usual manner. Refer to Parts List Z4-1.

FILE SECTION—TYPE FM-Z
PRINTED IN U.S.A.

Instructions Z3-2 Rev.1
Supersedes Issue of Oct. 1965
May, 1973

201

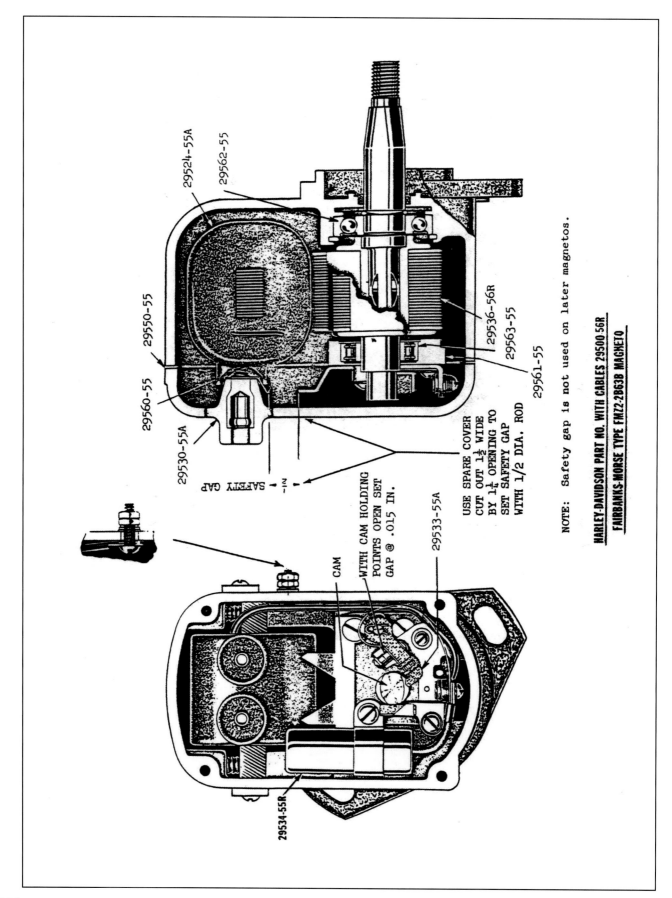

29524-55A

29562-55

29550-55

29560-55

29530-55A

SAFETY GAP $\frac{1}{2}$"

29536-56R

29563-55

29561-55

USE SPARE COVER
CUT OUT 1½ WIDE
BY 1¼ OPENING TO
SET SAFETY GAP
WITH 1/2 DIA. ROD

NOTE: Safety gap is not used on later magnetos.

HARLEY-DAVIDSON PART NO. WITH CABLES 29500-56R
FAIRBANKS-MORSE TYPE FM Z2-2B63B MAGNETO

CAM

WITH CAM HOLDING
POINTS OPEN SET
GAP @ .015 IN.

29533-55A

29534-55R

1995 Seward, Alaska. The author Bill Rook, left. Bill Davidson, of the Motor Company, right. I had brought Bill Davidson, his future wife Calie, and Joe Dowd, the former West Coast director of HOG down to my research ship for a tour.

The pictured bike is my little 1959 XLCH hot rod that I've owned for over 25 years. Many years ago, the lower end on this motor was custom-built for me by professional drag racer Guy Leaming. The cases had been opened to accept over-bored 1000-cc cylinders running forged TRW pistons. The heads were milled, ported, and dual-plugged by Zipper's Performance. They run Baisley pro-street XLR valves and Sifton valve springs with titanium collars.

Air/fuel mixing is handled by an S&S L-series gas carb with a matched intake manifold breathing through an S&S Super B air cleaner with a K&N air filter. Cams and pushrods are from Andrews, and the cams run on Torrington needle bearings on both sides. The oil pump has been bored and polished for increased volume. The clutch is a Barnett Kevlar unit and is run dry with heavy-duty springs. A re-worked Fairbanks Morse magneto with manual advance handles the ignition, and it features dual plugs operating in single-fire-only mode. One ride on this bike will let you know why I call it "my little hot rod," and you'll know where the legend of the old magneto-equipped XLCH Sportsters originated. Note: If done incorrectly, starting one of these old Sportsters can be hazardous to your health, as in a broken leg or a shattered kneecap!

VENDOR PERFORMANCE DIRECTORY

Accel Ignition (accel-ignition.com)
Mr Gasket Company
10601 Memphis Ave. #12
Cleveland, OH 44144
216-688-8300 ext.500

Aerocharger Turbo Systems
8 Apollo Dr.
Batavia, NY 14020
716-345-0055

Andrews Products (Andrews-products.com)
431 Kingston Ct.
Mount Prospect, IL 60056
847-759-0190

Baisley Hi Performance (baisley.com)
5511 N. Interstate Ave.
Portland, OR 97217
503-289-1251

Baker Drivetrain (bakerdrivetrain.com)
9804 E. Saginaw
Haslett, MI 48840
877-640-2004

Barnett Clutches (barnettclutches.com)
2238 Palma Dr.
Ventura, CA 93003
805-642-9435

Branch Flowmetrics (branchflowmetrics.com)
Branch & O'Keefe Co.
1940 Freeman Ave.
Signal Hill, CA 90755
562-579-2850

BUB Exhaust (bub.com)
180 Spring Hill Dr.
Grass Valley, CA 95945
530-477-7490

Carl's Speed Shop (carlsspeedshop.com)
390 North Beach St.
Daytona Beach, FL 32114
386-258-3777

Cometic Gaskets (cometic.com)
8090 Auburn Rd.
Concord, OH 44077
800-752-9850

Custom Chrome (www.customchrome.com)
(Offering Revtech products)
16100 Jacqueline Ct.
Morgan Hill, CA 95037
408-778-0500

Edelbrock (edelbrock.com)
2700 California St.
Torrance, CA 90503
310-781-2222

Harley-Davidson Motor Company, Inc.
 (harley-davidson.com)
3700 W. Juneau Ave.
Milwaukee, WI 53208
414-342-4680

Head Quarters (head-quarters.com)
3665 Dove Rd.
Port Huron, MI 48060
519-892-6992

James Gaskets (jamesgaskets.com)
37 Enterprise Way
Dayton, NV 89403
775-246-2220

Jim's USA (jimsusa.com)
555 Dawson Dr.
Camarillo, CA 93012
805-482-6913

Joe Hunt (huntmagnetos.com)
11333 Sunco Dr., #100
Rancho Cordova, CA 95742
916-635-5387

K & N Engineering (knfilters.com)
1455 Citrus St.
Riverside, CA 92502
800-858-3333

Khrome Werks (khromewerks.com)
PO Box 355
New Prague, MN 56071-0355
952-758-9523

Mikuni American Corporation (mikuni.com)
8910 Mikuni Ave.
Northridge, CA 91324
818-885-1242

Morris Magnetos, Inc. (morrismagneto.com)
103 Washington St.
Morristown, NJ 07960
973-540-9171

Neway Manufacturing, Inc. (newaymfg.com)
1013 N. Shiawassee St.
Corunna, MI 48817
800-248-3889

NOS (Nitrous Oxide Systems, a division of Holley
Performance Products)
(nosnitrous.com or holley.com)
2970 Airway Ave.
Costa Mesa, CA 92626
270-781-9741

Nostalgia Cycle
1568 Commerce Lane
Westminster, CA 95742
714- 891-6263

Pingel Enterprise (pingelonline.com)
2072 11th Ave.
Adams, WI 53910
608-339-7999

R B Racing (rbracing-rsr.com)
1502 W. 134th St.
Gardena, CA 90249
310-515-5720

R. C. Components (rccomponents.com)
373 Mitch McConnell Way
Bowling Green, KY 42101
888-721-6495

S & S Cycles, Inc. (sscycle.com)
235 Causeway Blvd.
LaCrosse, WI 54603
608-627-1497

STD Heads (stddevelopment.com)
10055 Canoga Ave.
Chatsworth, CA 91313
818-998-8226

Screamin' Eagle Performance Parts
Available through Harley-Davidson or Tedd Cycle

Taylor Wires (taylorvertex.com)
301 Highgrove Rd.
Grandview, MO 64030
816-765-5011

Thunderheader (thunderheader.net)
Richmond, CA
510-234-7547

TWM Induction (twminduction.com)
325D Rutherford St.
Goleta, CA 93117
805-967-9478

V-Twin Mfg. (vtwinmfg.com)
Tedd Cycle, Inc.
PO Box 473
Vails Gate, NY 12584
845-565-2806

White Bros. Exhaust [JIM: this site did not come up]
24845 Corbit Place
Yorba Linda, CA 92887
714-692-3404

Wiseco (wiseco.com)
7201 Industrial Park Blvd.
Mentor, OH 44060
800-321-1364

Yost Performance Products (yostperformance.com)
380 8th St NE
PO Box 186
Milaca, MN 56353
320-983-5410

Zippers Performance (zippersperformance.com)
6655-A Amberton Dr.
Elkridge, MD 21075
410-579-2828

INDEX

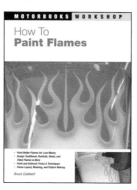

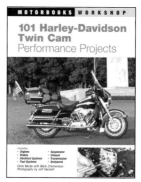